W9-CSU-812

THE 20 ESSENTIAL

Qualities *of*

an Authentic

CHRISTIAN

THE 20 ESSENTIAL

Qualities *of* *an* Authentic

CHRISTIAN

WARREN W. WIERSBE

THOMAS NELSON PUBLISHERS
Nashville

Copyright © 1996 by Warren W. Wiersbe

All rights reserved. Written permission must be secured from the publisher to use or reproduce any part of this book, except for brief quotations in critical reviews or articles.

Published in Nashville, Tennessee, by Thomas Nelson, Inc., Publishers.

The Bible version used in this publication is the NEW KING JAMES VERSION. Copyright © 1979, 1980, 1982, 1990, Thomas Nelson, Inc., Publishers.

Scripture quotations noted KJV are from the King James Version of the Holy Bible.

Scripture quotations marked NIV are taken from the HOLY BIBLE, NEW INTERNATIONAL VERSION®. Copyright © 1973, 1978, 1984 by International Bible Society. Used by permission of Zondervan Publishing House. All rights reserved.

Verses marked TLB are taken from *The Living Bible*, copyright © 1971 by Tyndale House Publishers, Wheaton, IL. Used by permission.

Scripture quotations noted NASB are from the New American Standard Bible, © 1960, 1962, 1963, 1968, 1971, 1972, 1973, 1975, 1977 by The Lockman Foundation. Used by permission.

Scripture quotations noted PHILLIPS are from J. B. Phillips: THE NEW TESTAMENT IN MODERN ENGLISH, Revised Edition. © J. B. Phillips 1958, 1960, 1972. Used by permission of Macmillan Publishing Co., Inc.

Scripture quotations noted JB are from THE JERUSALEM BIBLE, copyright © 1966 by Darton, Longman & Todd Ltd. and Doubleday & Company, Inc. Used by permission.

Scripture quotations noted ASV are from the American Standard Version of the Holy Bible.

Every effort has been made to contact the owners or owners' agents of copyrighted material for permission to use their material. If copyrighted material has been included without the correct copyright notice or without permission, due to error or failure to locate owners/agents or otherwise, we apologize for the error or omission and ask that the owner or owner's agent contact Thomas Nelson Inc. and supply appropriate information. Correct information will be included in any reprints.

Library of Congress Cataloging in Publication Data

Wiersbe, Warren W.

20 Essential Qualities of an Authentic Christian
Originally published as Being a child of God: your guide for the adventure / Warren Wiersbe. p. cm.

Includes bibliographical references.

ISBN 0-7852-4597-9

1. Christian life. 1. Title.
BV4501.2.W5173 1995
248.4—dc20

Printed in the United States of America.

1 2 3 4 5 6 - 05 04 03 02 01

CONTENTS

PREFACE

To all of God's children:

This book is about what it means to be a child of God and how to mature spiritually. It's about living the Christian life successfully to the glory of the Father and the building of His church.

Living the Christian life isn't easy, but the principles that govern Christian living are simple. In writing this book, I've majored on principles, not rules or methods.

As you read, please don't skip over the Scriptures that are quoted just because you're familiar with some of them; and keep your Bible handy so you can refer to it. If you feel the urge to lay this book down and read your Bible, by all means do so. What God says to you personally from His Word is far more important than what I say about God's Word.

I've put technical discussions of doctrinal matters in the Notes, and you can refer to them at your convenience. But don't let the Notes detour you from the main highway of the text.

Being a child of God is the greatest privilege in life, and becoming more like Christ is the greatest challenge for any believer. May we all bring joy to the Father's heart as we are day by day "conformed to the image of His Son" (Rom. 8:29).

Warren W. Wiersbe

Part 1

THE WONDER OF ETERNAL LIFE

I have come that they may have life and that they may have it more abundantly.
John 10:10

Chapter 1

BIRTH: HOW IT ALL BEGINS

Except for people who inhabit the fantasy world of fairy tales and science fiction, the only way to get into the human family is to be born. Everybody you meet has a birthday every year because birth is the method God has ordained for transmitting human life from one generation to the next.

What's true of the physical is also true of the spiritual: the only way to possess God's life and enter God's family is through birth. Jesus said, "You must be born again" (John 3:7).[1]

As we begin this adventure of better understanding what it means to be a child of God, let's explore the meaning of this familiar yet profound metaphor of spiritual birth.

OUR PARENTS

Like physical birth, spiritual birth involves two parents, and these two parents are the Spirit of God and the Word of God.

Jesus said, "Unless one is born of water and the Spirit, he cannot enter the kingdom of God" (John 3:5).[2] When you believe the gospel, repent of your sins, and trust Jesus Christ, you are immediately born into God's family and receive everlasting life: "He who believes in the Son has everlasting life" (John 3:36). First John adds that "this is the testimony: that God has given us eternal life, and this life is in His Son. He who has the Son has life; he who does not have the Son of God does

3

not have life" (5:11–12). The Holy Spirit of God imparts life because He is "the Spirit of life in Christ Jesus" (Rom. 8:2).

The second spiritual parent is the Word of God: "Having been born again, not of corruptible seed but incorruptible, through the word of God which lives and abides forever" (1 Peter 1:23); "Of His own will He brought us forth by the word of truth" (James 1:18). The Spirit of God uses the Word of God to impart the life of God to the believing sinner who turns to Jesus Christ for salvation.

Jesus promised that "he who hears My word and believes in Him who sent Me has everlasting life, and shall not come into judgment, but has passed from death into life" (John 5:24). The Word of God can *impart* life because it has life. It is "the word of God which lives and abides forever" (1 Peter 1:23), and "the word of God is living and powerful" (Heb. 4:12). Putting your faith in the Word of God is like plugging in to a dynamo. Through the ministry of the Holy Spirit, God's Word releases the power that resurrects you from spiritual death and places you in the family of God.

No matter what we may profess about our "religion," if we don't possess the life of God within, we have never been born of God. When I was a young teenager, most of the people in the church I attended thought I was a Christian. I had been confirmed in the church, I was faithful in my attendance, and I lived a respectable life; but I didn't have God's life within my heart. It wasn't until shortly before my sixteenth birthday that I responded to the gospel and became a child of God, and then I could honestly say, "I'm spiritually alive!"

OUR LIVES

Birth involves two parents, and *these parents impart life*. Being a Christian doesn't mean simply agreeing intellectually with Christian doctrine or participating enthusiastically in Christian activities. Being a Christian means possessing the life of Christ within, being able to boldly say, "Christ lives in me" (Gal. 2:20).

The Scottish science professor and evangelist Henry Drummond used to illustrate this truth by reminding his university students that they had to distinguish five kingdoms in this world. The lowest of them, the mineral kingdom, possesses no life at all. The vegetable kingdom, the animal kingdom, and the human kingdom all have life; and the highest kingdom of all—God's kingdom—is the source of all life. The point Drummond made was that no lower kingdom can push its way into the next higher kingdom, but each kingdom can reach down and pull the other kingdoms up.

Minerals can't transform themselves into plants, but plants can reach into the mineral kingdom and transform mineral into vegetable. Animals eat the plants and transform vegetable into animal, and humans eat animal flesh and transform it into human flesh. In salvation, God reaches down into the human kingdom and lifts believing sinners into His divine kingdom.

This is what Jesus did when He came to earth and died on the cross: "No one has ascended to heaven but He who came down from heaven, that is, the Son of Man who is in heaven" (John 3:13); "In this the love of God was manifested toward us, that God has sent His only begotten Son into the world, that we might live through Him" (1 John 4:9).

Too many people have the notion that they have to "pull themselves up" into God's family through devout religious practices and good works before they can enter the kingdom of God; but this idea is wrong. The truth is that "not by works of righteousness which we have done, but according to His mercy He saved us" (Titus 3:5). Sinners can no more work their way into God's family than robots can work their way into the human family.

Thirty-six times in the Gospel of John, the apostle writes about life, because life is a major theme of his book. John's purpose in writing was "that you may believe that Jesus is the Christ, the Son of God, and that believing you may have life in His name" (John 20:31). When you trust Jesus Christ, you are no longer in darkness because He is the light of life (John 8:12). You are no longer hungry and thirsty within because Jesus satisfies you with the water of life (John 4:13–14) and nourishes you with the bread of life (John 6:48–51). In fact, He *is* the life (John 14:6).

OUR NATURE

Birth involves two parents who impart life to us, and *this life-giving birth determines our nature*. Those who have been born again are "partakers of the divine nature, having escaped the corruption that is in the world through lust" (2 Peter 1:4).[3] We were born the first time of "corruptible seed," because humans eventually die and our bodies turn to dust. But Christians are people who have been born again of incorruptible seed (1 Peter 1:23); they possess the nature of God and will be the children of God forever.

My wife and I have four children, each of whom has a genetic structure that came from us. If you met them, you would agree that they belong to the *familia Wiersbe*. Our two sons-in-law and two daughters-in-law are also in the Wiersbe family, but they do not have the same family nature as their mates. The daughters-in-law took the Wiersbe name, but they don't have the Wiersbe nature. (They may be relieved at this.) The two sons-in-law call us "Mom" and "Dad," but we didn't give them birth. If the eight people lined up, you'd probably have no difficulty separating our natural children from our in-laws simply because, for good or ill, the natural children have the Wiersbe nature.

A friend of ours owns a golden retriever that must think she is a cat. Whenever you pet her, she lies down and comes as close to purring as is possible for a dog. But her "purring" doesn't fool us: she was born a dog and has the nature of a dog. Cats act like cats because they have a cat's nature; dogs act like dogs because they have a dog's nature; and Christians act like Christians because they have God's divine nature within.

Let me be more specific about what it means to have a divine nature within.

To begin with, *nature determines appetite*. Although they watch the birds hungrily, the neighbors' cats never invade our bird feeders; but the squirrels do. Why? Because it's the nature of squirrels to eat nuts and seeds. Foxes track down rabbits, bears fish for salmon, lions chase antelopes, and giraffes eat the spiny leaves of the acacia trees that grow on the African plains. (I've watched them do it, and it amazes me that the thorns don't kill them.) Now, if I profess to be a child of God, with God's divine nature within me, wouldn't you expect me to have an appetite for the things of God?

Nature not only determines appetite, but *it also determines environment*. It's the nature of fish to live in the water and the nature of birds to fly in the air. The goats in Estes Park, Colorado, prefer the mountain heights, while squids and anemones prefer the ocean depths. Pigs enjoy mud while sheep prefer green pastures. Unsaved people live "according to the course of this world" (Eph. 2:2) and enjoy it, but God's children seek to keep themselves "unspotted from the world" (James 1:27). Lost people love "darkness rather than light" (John 3:19), but God's children choose to "walk in the light" (1 John 1:7) because "God is light" (1 John 1:5).

Nature determines our associations. Zebras don't pal around with lions nor robins with cats. Lions congregate in prides with other lions, sheep in flocks, cattle in herds, and Christians in the fellowship of other Christians. This doesn't mean we isolate ourselves from the lost world, because Christians have important ministries in this world as "the salt of the earth" and "the light of the world" (Matt. 5:13–16). But it's the nature of the people of God to meet together for fellowship and mutual encouragement. We read of the early church: "Now all who believed were together" (Acts 2:44).

Nature determines danger. Water is no danger to fish, but it can drown people. A garbage dump poses few threats to rats, but it might infect a child and make him sick. Disease germs that can prostrate a husky quarterback create no problems for your pet gerbil. Because Christians possess the divine nature within, they are subject to dangers and enemies against which they must fight.

When I was a young believer, somebody gave me a copy of the well-known tract "Others May, You Cannot"; and reading it helped me considerably. Its message is simple: don't govern your choices by what others do, but seek God's will for your life and conduct. What's safe for others may be harmful for you, so stay alert; and don't use the conduct of others as an excuse for sin.

We could go on in this study of what it means to possess the divine nature, but let me add just one more insight: *nature determines abilities.* Because I was born with human nature, I can't imitate the whale and live underwater without air for long periods of time, nor can I run seventy miles an hour like the cheetah. I don't have the telescopic vision of the eagle or the radar of the bat or the inner compass of the homing pigeon.

But since I have God's nature within, all that He is and all that He can do are available to me. Passages throughout the Bible reinforce this concept: "I can do all things through Christ who strengthens me" (Phil 4:13); "His divine power has given to us all things that pertain to life and godliness" (2 Peter 1:3). This doesn't make us junior gods, of course, because only God is God. But it does make us, the children of God, equipped to face life with its challenges and make a success out of it to the glory of God.

OUR TRAVAIL

Birth involves travail. Our older daughter is an obstetrical nurse and occasionally is called to deliver a baby at home. But whether it's at home or in the elegant birthing room of the most modern hospital, the birth of a baby involves pain and travail for the mother. For us to be born into the family of God, Jesus Christ had to suffer and die on the cross: "He shall see of the travail of his soul, and shall be satisfied" (Isa. 53:11 KJV).

But there is also travail on the part of the people of God as they pray for lost sinners to be saved: "For as soon as Zion travailed, she brought forth her children" (Isa. 66:8 KJV). Commenting on that verse, the British preacher Charles Haddon Spurgeon said, "The church must either bring forth children unto God, or die of consumption; she has no alternative but that. A church must either be fruitful or rot, and of all things a rotting church is the most offensive."[4]

He didn't tell me about this until years later, but during the months I attended confirmation class, our pastor knew I wasn't really born again. Each week after the class had gone, he would prostrate himself on the floor of his study and pray for me with tears. Because he travailed, I was eventually converted to Christ and called to ministry.

OUR FUTURE

Birth involves a future. You're not likely to find a police officer in the OB ward of the hospital, waiting to arrest a newborn baby, because babies have no responsible past (Rom. 9:11). All a baby has is a future! Our loving heavenly Father has "begotten us again to a living hope through the resurrection of Jesus Christ from the dead" (1 Peter 1:3). We have a living hope because we have a living Savior!

Christians are people who live in the future tense. Our sins have been forgiven, so our past no longer haunts us; and God says of us, "Their sins and their lawless deeds I will remember no more" (Heb. 10:17). No matter how difficult the day or how depressing the news, the children of God have a bright future as we walk with Christ, obey His will, and wait for His coming. We have this promise: "For I know the thoughts that I think toward you, says the LORD, thoughts of peace and not of evil, to give you a future and a hope" (Jer. 29:11).

We'll discover later in this book that the blessed hope of seeing Christ and being with Him in heaven forever has great power to give us victory over sin. For the Christian, heaven isn't simply a *destination*; it's a *motivation*.

OUR FINAL BIRTH

One last thought for now on the subject of spiritual birth: *birth is final*. It would certainly be weird if all babies were born with parts missing and the parents had to return to the hospital periodically to have the baby's body completed. But the tiny baby is born with everything she needs to grow up and become an adult. I can still recall seeing our first child shortly after he was born. He seemed so small and fragile—but you should see him today! Built into that little body was everything he needed to become a mature man, beard and all. All he had to do was grow.

At conception, I received the genetic structure that determined the characteristics and abilities I've carried throughout my life. When I was attending public school, it bothered me that I didn't have the athletic ability and the manual skills that other students had; and I wondered why God was punishing me. But then I discovered that God had given me other skills, the ones He wanted me to develop and use years later in His service. Once I had graduated from high school, it didn't really matter to me or anybody else that I wasn't good at shooting free throws or making bookends.

God's children are born into His family with all that we need to become mature Christians who can serve God and glorify Him. "You are complete in Him" (Col. 2:10) simply means that "all things that pertain to life and godliness" (2 Peter 1:3) became ours the instant we entered God's family through faith in Jesus Christ. Our spiritual birth is final, and we don't have to search for anything more to supplement our completeness in Christ. We only need to appropriate what we already have and "grow in the grace and knowledge of our Lord and Savior Jesus Christ" (2 Peter 3:18).

It was a happy day in my life when I learned this truth. As a young believer, I passionately wanted more and more of what God had for me, and there was certainly nothing wrong with these holy desires. What was wrong was the way I went about trying to satisfy these longings. Instead of allowing an experienced believer to disciple me, I read every book I could find on "the deeper life," "the victorious life," and "the fullness of the Spirit"; and I searched for that "extra something" I needed to enable me to leap from spiritual childhood to glorious maturity. What I wanted was a "quick fix" theology that would make me Mr. Successful Saint overnight.

Well, fortunately, I didn't find it. There are such theologies, and you can believe them if you want to; but you'll find as I did that they just don't work. Just as a baby is born complete and has to grow, so the believer is born complete in Christ and must mature in Him; and maturing takes time.

We Christians are all different in our spiritual gifts and personal abilities, interests, and personalities; but we know that God's goal for each of us is the same: "to be conformed to the image of His Son" (Rom. 8:29). In every aspect of character and conduct, the Father wants us to become like Jesus Christ. That's what the new birth is all about. Birth is only the beginning, the crisis; conforming to His image is the process; being like Christ is the goal.

When I was a lad, Mr. Stickler, our Sunday school superintendent, often opened the general assembly by asking us to sing one of two songs I from the old *Covenant Hymnal*: either #190, "More About Jesus Would I Know," or #241, "I Would Be Like Jesus." I haven't heard or sung either song in a long time, but now I better understand why he chose them: they summarized what Sunday school was all about. We were there to learn more about Jesus so we would become more like Jesus, "conformed to the image of His Son."

But before we can devote ourselves to the process of becoming more like Christ, we must be sure that we truly are the children of God. We must heed this admonition: "Examine yourselves as to whether you are in the faith. Test yourselves" (2 Cor. 13:5). That means we must honestly search our hearts before God to see if we bear the birthmarks of true believers.

That will be our next study.

Chapter 2

ASSURANCE: HOW TO KNOW YOU ARE A CHILD OF GOD

I picked up the morning newspaper, and the headline shouted at me:

POLICE BEWARE OF SCAMS!

Usually the international news captures the front page of our paper, but it didn't that day. The editors felt that the con artists who were bilking retired people were far more dangerous to our city than the tanks and guns in Europe or the insurgents in Africa, and the editors were probably right.

Whether you're buying a used car, donating to charity, or making a financial investment, you don't want to be deceived. But there's one thing worse than *being* deceived by a con artist, and that's being your own con artist and *deceiving yourself*. Deception that steals your money is costly, but deception that condemns your soul is fatal.

When it comes to personal salvation from sin, don't settle for anything less than full assurance, not false assurance. The Pharisees thought they were the children of God, but John the Baptist called them "a brood of vipers" (Matt. 3:7); and Jesus said they were the children of the devil (John 8:44). No wonder our Lord issued this solemn warning:

Not everyone who says to Me, "Lord, Lord," shall enter the kingdom of heaven, but he who does the will of My Father in heaven. Many will say to Me in that day, "Lord, Lord, have we not prophesied in Your name, cast out demons in Your name, and done many wonders in Your name?" And then I will declare to them, "I never knew you; depart from Me, you who practice lawlessness!" (Matt. 7:21–23).

What a shock to get to the end of your life and discover that you've been practicing lawlessness instead of righteousness! What a rude awakening to face Jesus and discover that, instead of being welcomed into heaven, you're cast away from His presence! This is the tragedy of self-deception.

However, you can know for sure that you are a child of God. That's one reason why the apostle John wrote his first epistle: "These things I have written to you who believe in the name of the Son of God, that you may know that you have eternal life" (1 John 5:13). Seven times in his letter, John used the phrase "born of God"; and when you summarize these statements, they describe the birthmarks of the true child of God.

PRACTICING RIGHTEOUSNESS

When you are "born of God," *you don't practice sin:* "No one who is born of God will continue to sin, because God's seed remains in him; he cannot go on sinning, because he has been born of God" (1 John 3:9 NIV).[1]

Certainly, Christians have the ability to sin, but the point John makes is that Christians don't have the habitual desire to sin. God has planted His divine nature ("God's seed") within us, and we've acquired new ambitions and new appetites. I like the way it's stated in 2 Corinthians: "Old things have passed away; behold, all things have become new" (5:17). Christians aren't sinless, and we won't be until we see Christ; but we do sin less . . . and less . . . and less.

Christians are tempted, but it isn't a sin to be tempted (Jesus was tempted and He was sinless). The fact that we don't consistently yield to temptation or deliberately try to get into situations where we tempt ourselves indicates that God has changed our hearts.

Sometimes a person is converted to Christ who has been the slave of a bad habit, and immediately that habit is gone. I recall counseling a church member who had secretly been getting drunk every Friday night, sleeping it off on Saturday, and then faithfully coming to church on Sunday. It was obvious that, though he was a church member, he had never trusted Christ; but when he did, his thirst for alcohol vanished, and he became a faithful Christian.

But for some reason, not all new Christians enjoy that kind of immediate deliverance, and they find themselves struggling to overcome old enemies. They keep asking themselves, "Am I really born again?" But the fact that they don't want to cling to their old way of life is an indication that new desires have been planted in their hearts. According to John, for professed Christians to love sin—and habitually make every effort to enjoy sin—is proof that they aren't really born of God. We expect unsaved people to live "according to the course of this world . . . fulfilling the desires of the flesh" (Eph. 2:2–3), but true children of God don't live that way.

What 1 John 3:9 states negatively, 1 John 2:29 states positively: "If you know that He is righteous, you know that everyone who practices righteousness is born of Him." After you experience the new birth, you discover that you have a new desire to obey God and do what's right, and this new desire reveals itself in the little things of life as well as the big things. You find yourself becoming more and more sensitive to the sins that are in good standing, like pride, gossip, self-will, and criticism; and you ask the Lord to help you overcome them. Not practicing sin (the negative) and practicing righteousness (the positive) are obvious birthmarks of the believer.

LOVING OTHERS

When you are "born of God," *your life is motivated by love*:

Beloved, let us love one another, for love is of God; and everyone who loves is born of God and knows God (1 John 4:7).

Everyone who believes that Jesus is the Christ is born of God, and everyone who loves the father loves his child as well (1 John 5:1 NIV).

Since "God is love" (1 John 4:8, 16) and those who are born of God have God's nature within, it's reasonable to expect that the children will act like the Father and manifest love. Remember, what we *desire* and what we *do* depend largely on the nature that we possess. Humanly speaking, it's my nature to enjoy bookstores, not hardware stores, and symphony concerts, not horse races. It's the Christian's desire to experience and express the love of God in a basically selfish and competitive world.

One of the first evidences that I had been born again was a desire to be with God's people. As I experienced "the love of God [being] poured out" in my heart (Rom. 5:5), I began attending the Sunday evening service and the midweek service, and I sincerely enjoyed them. Before long, the powers that be in our church encouraged me to give my testimony at the street meetings the young people conducted; and then, when I was ready for it, I started to help in Sunday school and vacation Bible school. When you're one of the Lord's sheep, you want to be with the flock.

At least twelve times in the New Testament, God commands us to love one another; and later in this book, we'll flesh out those commands and discover how practical they really are. Just keep in mind that Christian love means treating other people the way God treats you. It means allowing His new nature within to motivate us in every relationship of life.

OVERCOMING THE WORLD

When you are "born of God," *you overcome the world*: "For whatever is born of God overcomes the world. And this is the victory that has overcome the world—our faith" (1 John 5:4).

"The world" that John wrote about isn't the world of people or the world of creation, both of which God declared were good (Gen. 1:31). "The world" is the invisible system in human society that hates God and opposes Jesus Christ and His people. It's society without God, the "Egypt" of the Old Testament and the "Babylon" of the Book of Revelation. In his excellent commentary on 1 Peter, Peter H. Davids defines the *world* as "human culture in its independence of and hostility toward God."[2]

When the television anchorman says, "And now the news from the world of sports," he is referring not to a special continent or planet where athletes live but to the whole system of things that makes up sports. "The world of finance" includes the people, philosophies, ambitions, and organizations that make up what goes on in the money markets of the nations. Here's what John says:

> Do not love the world or the things in the world. If anyone loves the world, the love of the Father is not in him. For all that is in the world—the lust of the flesh, the lust of the eyes, and the pride of life—is not of the Father but is of the world. And the world is passing away, and the lust of it; but he who does the will of God abides forever (1 John 2:15–17).

Distilled to its essence, this warning tells us *what the world is*: anything in our lives that keeps us from enjoying the Father's love and doing the Father's will. From the human point of view, it might even be a "good thing"; but if it keeps us from enjoying God and obeying God, it's from the world and it's wrong. We'll deal more with this truth later.

This warning also tells us *how the world tries to influence us*. It puts pressure against three critical areas in life: the body ("lust of the flesh"), the mind ("lust of the eyes"), and the will ("pride of life"). The world system around us pressures us constantly to gratify our desires and act the way the world acts, to abandon God's truth and think the way the world thinks, and to satisfy our egos and promote ourselves the way the world promotes itself.

When I was a young believer, I thought that worldly Christians were only the people who used tobacco and alcohol, attended movies, played baseball (or watched baseball) on Sundays, and went to school dances; and I prided myself that I was guilty of none of those transgressions. (Of course, I couldn't play baseball successfully on Sunday or any other day!) But as I matured in the faith, I quickly discovered that my pride was just as worldly as any of the aforementioned activities, and that my imagination was occasionally the scene of fantasies that were far from spiritual. I also found out that even a good thing like my love for reading might consume valuable time that I should have invested in Bible study, prayer, and ministry.

When I was born the first time, I was born a loser; but when I was born again, I was born an overcomer. The crowd that belongs to the world walks by sight and thinks it's enjoying life and succeeding, but Christians walk by faith and overcome the world. We know that "this world is fading away, and these evil, forbidden things will go with it, but whoever keeps doing the will of God will live forever" (1 John 2:17 TLB).

So, if you have trusted Jesus Christ and have tasted "the powers of the age to come" (Heb. 6:5), you'll not be too enthusiastic about what's offered you in "this present evil age" from which Christ has delivered you (Gal. 1:4). You'll see that this is a dark world where you need to be a light, a decaying world where you must minister as salt, a dead world where you must share the Word of life. This world is the only heaven your unsaved friends will ever know unless you tell them about the place Jesus is preparing for His own.

WITHSTANDING THE DEVIL

When you are "born of God," *you overcome the devil*: "We know that whoever is born of God does not sin; but he who has been born of God keeps himself, and the wicked one does not touch him" (1 John 5:18).

Before we trusted Christ, we "walked . . . according to the prince of the power of the air, the spirit who now works in the sons of disobedience" (Eph. 2:2). Satan had us in bondage, and the worst part of that bondage was the fact that we thought we were free! But when we believed on Christ, God "delivered us from the power of darkness and conveyed us into the kingdom of the Son of His love" (Col. 1:13). The picture behind "conveyed" is that of prisoners of war being moved to another location. We were once Satan's prisoners; Christ fought the battle and delivered us from Satan's dominion; and now we're citizens of heaven, enjoying the freedom we have in Christ.

When John wrote that the child of God "keeps himself," he wasn't suggesting that Christians keep themselves saved, because that's the work of the Spirit of God who has sealed us (Eph. 1:13–14) and the Son of God who intercedes for us in heaven (Rom. 8:31–39; Heb. 7:25). We don't keep ourselves *saved*, but we do keep ourselves *safe*. Some people, places, and activities make it easier for the devil to tempt us; and now that we've been delivered from the kingdom of Satan, we have no desire to deliberately get back into his clutches. When we pray, "Do not lead us into temptation" (Matt. 6:13), we're asking the Father to help us so we won't *tempt ourselves* by disobeying, or *tempt God* by willfully getting into a situation out of which only He can deliver us. Martin Luther said, "I can't keep the sparrows from flying around my head, but I can keep them from making a nest in my hair."

Not only are we careful where we walk, but we're also careful what we wear. We are told to "put on the whole armor of God, that [we] may be able to stand against the wiles of the devil" (Eph. 6:11). The armor described in Ephesians 6:10-20 isn't a luxury for the spiritual elite; it's a necessity for every Christian soldier who wants to be an overcomer. Satan can come as a serpent to deceive (2 Cor. 11:3), a lion to devour (1 Peter 5:8–9), or a dragon to destroy (Rev. 12); but if we're trusting the Lord, the armor will help us successfully resist and overcome the adversary.

COMPARING BIRTHMARKS TO DEATHMARKS

By now, you've probably discerned that the four birthmarks that John names have a definite relationship to the life we lived before we were saved, the deathmarks that are described in Ephesians 2:1–3. Let me summarize it this way:

The Deathmarks of the Old Life (Eph. 2:1–3)	The Birthmarks of the New Life (1 John)
We lived for this world (v. 2).	We overcome the world (5:4).
We were energized by Satan (v. 2).	We overcome the devil (5:18).
We satisfied the flesh (v. 3).	We overcome the flesh (2:29).
We pleased ourselves (v. 3).	We overcome selfishness with love (4:7; 5:1).

The fact that we've been born into God's family doesn't mean that we've automatically defeated the world, the flesh, and the devil once and for all, or that selfishness will never rear its ugly head again. If that were the case, the New Testament wouldn't contain so many admonitions to believers to fight the good fight of faith and overcome the enemy. In the light of what I've outlined above, consider what James wrote to a group of believers in the early church:

Where do wars and fights come from among you? Do they not come from your desires for pleasure that war in your members? You lust and do not have. You murder and covet and cannot obtain. You fight and war. Yet you do not have because you do not ask. You ask and do not receive, because you ask amiss, that you may spend it on your pleasures. Adulterers and adulteresses! Do you not know that friendship with the world is enmity with God? Whoever therefore wants to be a friend of the world makes himself an enemy of God. . . . Therefore submit to God. Resist the devil and he will flee from you (James 4:1–4, 7).

In reading this paragraph, you discovered that these saints had problems with the world, the flesh, and the devil. Not only that, but they had a bad case of selfishness that was corrupting their prayer life and robbing their fellowship of blessing. No, there's no automatic once-and-for-all deliverance from these enemies; but there are resources available to defeat these enemies because you've been born again. This book is about what these spiritual resources are and how you can use them.

However, before we discuss spiritual growth and victory, we must consider another aspect of what it means to be in God's family, and that's *adoption*. Regeneration (the new birth) explains how you enter God's family, but adoption tells you how to *enjoy* God's family.

Chapter 3

ADOPTION: BEING ACCEPTED IN THE FAMILY OF GOD

After his grandmother's funeral, Gary was leafing through Grandma's well-worn Bible, and he found his name on the family register page. He expected to see his name there, but what he didn't expect to see was the word written next to his name—*ADOPTED*. Gary was bewildered, hurt, and not a little angry that nobody had ever told him. It wasn't the best way for him to find out how he got into the family.

Unless it's done for selfish reasons, adoption can be a beautiful experience for everybody involved. Sad to say, many children come into their birth families unwanted; but when children are adopted, you get the feeling that they're really wanted and that they'll be loved in a very special way.

However, you don't get into God's family by adoption. You get into God's family by regeneration. Why? Because you must be born into God's family *in order to possess God's nature*. Adopted children experience the family love; they carry the family name; they enjoy the family home and wealth; but they don't have the family nature. We've already learned how important it is for us as God's children that we are "partakers of the divine nature" (2 Peter 1:4), because we can't be conformed to the image of Christ if we don't have His life and nature within us.

The key Bible text that deals with adoption is Romans 8:14–17.[1]

For as many as are led by the Spirit of God, these are sons of God. For you did not receive the spirit of bondage again to fear, but you received the Spirit of adoption by whom we cry out, "Abba, Father." The Spirit Himself bears witness with our spirit that we are children of God, and if children, then heirs—heirs of God and joint heirs with Christ, if indeed we suffer with Him, that we may also be glorified together.

What, then, is adoption? Adoption is the act of God whereby He gives each of His children *an adult standing* in the family of God. The moment you were born into God's family through faith in Jesus Christ, God began to deal with you as with an adult, not an infant; and that adult standing will never be changed or revoked.

No matter how long we've been in God's family, the heavenly Father treats us like adults. None of God's children can make excuses for not growing more like Jesus Christ, because each one of us has the same spiritual privileges. In terms of *experience*, you may have been a child of God only a short time; but in terms of *standing*, you have the same spiritual resources and privileges as the most seasoned saint. Adoption is God's way of saying that we, His children, have everything we need to become mature Christians. These spiritual privileges are explained in Romans 8:14–17.

ASSURANCE

Lets start with the privilege of *assurance*: "The Spirit Himself bears witness with our spirit that we are children of God" (v. 16). Because of adoption, we know we are God's children.

As far as doctors can tell, no newborn baby knows that he is a baby or even that he is a human being. We have no evidence that he knows where he came from, how he got here, or what he is supposed to be and do. Quite early, infants learn that they're cared for when they make noise and signal for attention. Infants gradually discover their bodies and the things and people in their surroundings that are pleasant and unpleasant. They get acquainted with the other members of the family. Children are dependent for several years, gradually mature, and then are expected to be equipped to go out on their own and start the cycle all over.

But what the natural child learns gradually, the child of God discovers very quickly through the witness of the Holy Spirit of God. The witness of the Spirit isn't necessarily a highly emotional experience;[2] it's primarily a quiet confidence in your heart that God is your Father and you are His child.

The witness of the Spirit comes to us in many ways, but primarily, it's through the Word of God. Even before they can understand what their parents are saying, children hear their parents talk to them and assure them of their love. (Some doctors encourage the parents to talk to the child even before he or she is born.) God talks to us through His Word, and the Holy Spirit illumines that Word and teaches it to us. People who don't belong to God's family simply don't understand the Word of God and can't hear the Father's voice speaking in it.[3]

When I turned sixty-five, I had to enter into certain required negotiations with our local Social Security office; and a part of these proceedings was presenting proof that I, who had been on earth for sixty-five years, had actually been born. All I had to do was show them my birth certificate, which they copied and dropped into my official file.

The witness of the Spirit of God within us and the witness of the Word of God before us comprise our "birth certificate" as the children of God. They bear witness that we've been born again. The apostle John explains it this way:

> If we receive the witness of men, the witness of God is greater; for this is the witness of God which He has testified of His Son. He who believes in the Son of God has the witness in himself; he who does not believe God has made Him a liar, because he has not believed the testimony that God has given of His Son. And this is the testimony: that God has given us eternal life, and this life is in His Son. He who has the Son has life; he who does not have the Son of God does not have life (1 John 5:9–12).

When you're fellowshipping with God's people and worshiping the Lord, the Spirit witnesses to you, and you say to yourself, "This is where I belong! My heart responds to this!" When a brother or sister is in need, your heart reaches out with love, and your hand reaches out with help. It isn't just humanitarian sympathy; it's the love of Christ over-flowing from within. If you disobey the Lord, the Spirit of God convicts your conscience; and you find yourself broken and repentant before your Father, asking His forgiveness. When you have opportunity to share the gospel with a lost person, the Spirit gives you the power you need to present Jesus Christ. In these and other ways, the Holy Spirit bears witness that you are in the family of God.

FREEDOM

Another privilege of adoption is *freedom*: "For as many as are led by the Spirit of God, these are sons of God" (v. 14).

Before birth, a child has no freedom because he is safely nestled in his mother's womb. After birth, the baby doesn't enjoy much more freedom as people bundle him up, carry him from place to place, and keep him in a crib. Little by little, the child learns to turn over, then pull himself up, then creep and crawl, and finally toddle and walk. But even then, the child doesn't have freedom to go where he wants to go or do what he wants to do. The crib and playpen are like juvenile jails, and some parents even use a harness to keep a wandering child under control!

The verb in Romans 8:14 is literally "willingly led." It speaks of the freedom we have in Christ to know God's will and obey it. Note that Paul writes about *sons* and not *children*. The Spirit witnesses that we are God's *children*, that is, born ones; but when we willingly follow the Spirit's leading, we are behaving like *sons*, that is, mature children of God. To get them to obey, parents must either reward or punish little children, but mature sons and daughters obey because they know it's right and because they love their parents. They recognize the wisdom in abiding by this verse: "For this is the love of God, that we keep His commandments. And His commandments are not burdensome" (1 John 5:3).

If a child were to begin walking immediately after birth, the medical world would be amazed. But because of adoption, God's children have the privilege of walking with the Lord and following the leading of the Spirit of God as He teaches us the Word. Because of adoption, no child of God can successfully defend disobedience by arguing, "But,

Father, I've been saved only six months! You surely can't expect me to be obedient already!" One evidence that we're truly His children is that "[we] do not walk according to the flesh but according to the Spirit" (Rom. 8:4). If we want adult privileges, we must accept adult responsibilities.

The goal of parents is to see their children mature and free, able to handle the responsibilities of life and to contribute to the welfare of society. God's goal is for His children to use freedom responsibly for the good of others and the glory of the Lord. I'll have more to say about freedom in a later chapter.

CONFIDENCE

A third privilege we have because God has adopted us is *confidence:* "For you did not receive the spirit of bondage again to fear, but you received the Spirit of adoption by whom we cry out, 'Abba, Father'" (v. 15).

It's a good thing most of us don't remember the first few years of life, because the world of infants must be filled with a multitude of fears: fear of falling; fear of abandonment; fear of the dark; fear of loud noises; fear of pain. (Adults have these same fears, but we're able to identify them and to a large extent control our responses.) God adopts us and treats us like adults in order to take away our fears. Second Timothy reassures us, "For God has not given us a spirit of fear, but of power and of love and of a sound mind" (1:7).

It's encouraging to see how many "fear not" verses there are in the Bible, promises of God that we can claim as His adopted children.[4] If you lovingly whisper to a child, "Now, don't be afraid," the child may or may not really understand what you're saying. But when the Father speaks to His children through the Word, we're able to hear and understand what He is saying because we have an adult standing in the family.

But something else is involved: not only can the Father speak to us, but *we can speak to the Father!* "We cry out, 'Abba, Father.'" If at our local hospital a newborn baby recognized his or her father *and spoke to him,* the news would astonish the world. In spite of the bonding that takes place when mother and father welcome the child, the little one doesn't yet know what the words *mother* and *father* mean. (Alas, some children never learn what they mean.) But God's children know who our heavenly Father is, and we are able to talk to Him in prayer.

In the Aramaic language that Jesus spoke, the word *Abba* was the equivalent of the English word *Papa* or *Daddy*, a term of endearment used by little children when they spoke to their father. Along with Romans 8:15, you find this word in Mark 14:36 and Galatians 4:6. *Father* expresses our understanding of the relationship we have with the God who gave us life, while *Abba* speaks of the intimate affection we have for Him; and both affection and intelligence are necessary for true worship.[5]

Whenever I have the privilege of leading someone to faith in Christ, I ask, "Do you now know that you're truly a child of God?"

"Yes, I do," the person usually replies.

"And how do you know you're a child of God? What is the basis for your assurance?"

"Well, God promised in His Word to save me if I would call upon Him, and there's something in my heart that tells me I belong to God."

Then I say, "Why don't you thank the Lord for saving you, and tell Him you want to live for Him?"

Now, here's the interesting thing. When sinners call upon God for salvation, their prayer almost always begins with *Lord*. But invariably, when newborn believers bow to thank the Lord for salvation, the first word uttered is *Father*. Why? Because that new believer has the Holy Spirit within and can say, "Abba, Father."

INHERITANCE

Adoption brings us the privilege of *inheritance*: "And if children, then heirs—heirs of God and joint heirs with Christ" (v. 17).

No matter how rich their parents are, children can't inherit the family wealth until they reach the age stated in the will. Consider these words of Paul:

> Now I say that the heir, as long as he is a child, does not differ at all from a slave, though he is master of all, but is under guardians and stewards until the time appointed by the father. Even so we, when we were children, were in bondage under the

elements of the world. But when the fullness of the time had come, God sent forth His Son, born of a woman, born under the law, to redeem those who were under the law, that we might receive the adoption as sons. And because you are sons, God has sent forth the Spirit of His Son into your hearts, crying out, "Abba, Father!" Therefore you are no longer a slave but a son, and if a son, then an heir of God through Christ (Gal. 4:1–7).

In this long (but important) passage, Paul makes it clear that two factors are involved in receiving an inheritance: you must be a son of the testator, and you must be named as the legal heir. I think Paul had Abraham, Isaac, and Ishmael in mind when he wrote these words.[6] Abraham's firstborn son was Ishmael, a son born out of the will of God (Gen. 16); but though he was the firstborn son, Ishmael didn't receive the inheritance. Isaac did, because Isaac was the one named by God in the will (Gen. 15:1–6; 17:20–21).

So, God's children have a twofold claim to our inheritance: we have the nature of God because we've been born into His family; and we have been adopted by God, so we cannot be treated as children who are too young to receive the inheritance. Ishmael the slave son was born poor, but Isaac was born rich; and so is every child of God.

Your Bible is the "will" that tells you how rich you are in Christ. You've been blessed with "every spiritual blessing" (Eph. 1:3), which includes the riches of God's mercy (Eph. 2:4) and the riches of God's grace (Eph. 2:7). These are "unsearchable riches" (Eph. 3:8) because they are the "riches of His glory" (Eph. 3:16). God supplies all that we need "according to His riches in glory by Christ Jesus" (Phil. 4:19).

Not only are all these spiritual riches available to us today, but we will also share in a future inheritance because we are "joint heirs with Christ" (Rom. 8:17). God has appointed His Son "heir of all things" (Heb. 1:2); and since we are joint heirs with Christ, that makes us "joint heirs of all things." We have been born again "to an inheritance incorruptible and undefiled and that does not fade away" (1 Peter 1:4). Part of this glorious future inheritance will be the blessing of a redeemed body (Rom. 8:23) as well as a redeemed creation (Rom. 8:19–23).

At a summer Bible conference, I counseled with a brokenhearted woman whose brother took advantage of their father's age and illness and swindled her and her sister out of the family inheritance. It was a sad story, but there is something even sadder: when God's children live like paupers by failing to appropriate the spiritual riches we have in Christ. Nobody can change His will and steal these riches from us, but we can ignore them or neglect them and live as though we're not in the family of God.

During the days of the Great Depression in the United States, a schoolteacher noticed that one of her pupils looked ill. "When you get home, dear," said the teacher, "be sure to have something to eat. You don't look well."

With downcast eyes, the girl replied, "I can't. This is my sister's day to eat."

When it comes to drawing on the spiritual riches we have in Christ, God's children need never say, "I can't. There isn't enough to go around." We can be spiritually bankrupt only when Jesus is spiritually bankrupt, *and that will never occur!*

SUFFERING

The fifth privilege of spiritual adoption may surprise you. It's *suffering*: "If indeed we suffer with Him, that we may also be glorified together" (v. 17).

Most people will do all they can to shield children from suffering, and rightly so; but God has ordained that suffering for the name of Christ is a normal part of the Christian life. Jesus told His disciples, "In the world you will have tribulation; but be of good cheer, I have overcome the world" (John 16:33); and "We must through many tribulations enter the kingdom of God," Paul reminded the early Christians (Acts 14:22).

Suffering comes early in the Christian life *to test the reality of our faith*. The person whose heart is shallow and whose faith has no roots "endures only for a while. For when tribulation or persecution arises because of the word, immediately he stumbles" (Matt. 13:21). But suffering also *strengthens our faith*: "May the God of all grace, who called us to His eternal glory by Christ Jesus, after you have suffered a while, perfect, establish, strengthen, and settle you" (1 Peter 5:10). The only way to become a mature, established Christian is to endure suffering. There are no shortcuts.

Note that Peter agrees with Paul in connecting suffering with glory, for Paul wrote, "If indeed we suffer with Him, that we may also be glorified together" (Rom. 8:17). One of the hardest lessons Jesus' disciples had to learn was that, in the kingdom of God, there can be no glory without suffering. Peter strongly urged Jesus not to go to the cross (Matt. 16:21–28), and the two Emmaus disciples found no place in their theology for a cross (Luke 24:13–35). But Jesus asked the two men, "Ought not the Christ to have suffered these things and to enter into His glory?" (Luke 24:26).[7] No cross, no crown.

Suffering here on earth prepares God's children to be part of the glory that is yet to be revealed: "For I consider that the sufferings of this present time are not worthy to be compared with the glory which shall be revealed in us" (Rom. 8:18). Note that it says "in us" and not "to us." We will behold the glory of God in heaven (John 17:22–24), but we will also glorify God in heaven because of the suffering we've experienced on earth, "when He comes, in that Day, to be glorified in His saints" (2 Thess. 1:10).

For us, suffering for the name of Christ isn't easy or enjoyable; but when God puts His children into the furnace, He always keeps His eye on the clock and His hand on the thermostat. He knows how long and how much. He is treating us like adults and not like infants, and He knows how much we can bear. Instead of complaining, we should consider suffering for Christ a privilege: "So they departed from the presence of the council, rejoicing that they were counted worthy to suffer shame for His name" (Acts 5:41).

GOD'S CHILDREN

These, then, are some of the adult privileges of God's adopted children:

- Assurance—we know that we're God's children and that God is our Father.
- Freedom—we're able to walk and follow the leading of the Spirit of God.
- Confidence—we aren't afraid, for we can speak to the Father and He to us.

- Inheritance—we are rich in Jesus Christ and can appropriate right now all the spiritual wealth we need.
- Suffering—this proves the reality of our faith, strengthens our faith, and prepares us to glorify God when we get to heaven.

There is no reason why any child of God should complain to the Father about his or her lot in life. He is not pampering us; He is perfecting us and preparing us for the glory yet to come. He is dealing with us as with adult sons and daughters, not infants; and He makes available to us all the resources we need to be overcomers in the difficult experiences of life.

Part 2

THE GROWING CHRISTIAN

*As newborn babes, desire the pure milk
of the word, that you may grow thereby.*
1 Peter 2:2

Chapter 4

MOTIVATION: GROWING SPIRITUALLY FOR THE RIGHT REASONS

B irth is our introduction to life, and life is God's invitation to growth. The new birth isn't the end of the Christian experience; it's the beginning. Growth is the natural expression of life because where there is life, there is growth.

Christian growth is governed by some basic principles, among them:

- We grow from within.
- We grow in a balanced way.
- We grow through nutrition, exercise, and cleansing.
- We grow in an atmosphere of love.
- We grow to a predetermined image, the likeness of Jesus Christ.
- We grow to glorify God in character and conduct.

But before we consider these principles of spiritual growth in detail, we must answer the question, *Why* should we as the children of God want to grow spiritually? What motives compel us?

EXPRESS LIFE

The first answer is because *growth is the normal expression of life.* Spiritual growth is inherent in the spiritual life. If we've truly been born again, then the new life within has to express itself and transform what we are and what we do.

If you are one of God's children, then you are a partaker of the divine nature (2 Peter 1:4); and that is reason enough for growth. "For this very reason" (2 Peter 1:5)—because you possess the divine nature—you should "add to your faith virtue, to virtue knowledge, to knowledge self-control, to self-control perseverance, to perseverance godliness, to godliness brotherly kindness, and to brotherly kindness love" (2 Peter 1:5–7).

In His parable of the sower (Matt. 13:1–9, 18–23), Jesus described four kinds of soil, which represented four different hearts and their responses to the seed of the Word of God. The first heart was so hard, it couldn't receive the seed. The second heart was so shallow, the seed couldn't take root. The third heart was so crowded, there was no room for the plant to grow and produce fruit. Only the fourth heart received seed, which then took root and produced fruit. The fourth heart represents the person who is truly born again and proves it by becoming "fruitful in every good work" (Col. 1:10).

Simply hearing God's Word is no evidence of salvation. It's when we receive the Word, cultivate it, and produce fruit that we prove we've been born into God's family. And because fruit has in it the seed for more fruit, there is a constant increasing harvest to the glory of God. Jesus described it as "fruit . . . more fruit . . . much fruit" (John 15:1–8).

BRING JOY TO THE FATHER

A second motive for spiritual growth is *that we might bring joy to our Father*. Parents and grandparents delight in seeing their children and grandchildren mature, and our Father in heaven rejoices to see His children become more like His beloved Son. Paul declared, "Finally then, brethren, we urge and exhort in the Lord Jesus that you should abound more and more, just as you received from us how you ought to walk and to please God" (1 Thess. 4:1). To please God is to glorify God, and to glorify God is the highest privilege on earth.

Your Father in heaven is not passive or indifferent in His relationship toward you. He actively and lovingly desires that you be "conformed to the image of His Son" (Rom. 8:29). He rejoices at every victory you experience, He feels every burden you bear, and He watches every step of growth you achieve through His power: "The steps of a good man are ordered by the LORD, and He delights in his way" (Ps. 37:23). How marvelous that the eternal God delights in you as you learn to walk so as to please Him!

It's unfortunate when our relationship to the Father is cold and mechanical and we become like the prodigal son's elder brother. We obey the rules, we do the work, and we serve the Father; but we lack that close loving relationship with the Father that brings Him joy. (See Luke 15:25–32.) The son who left home grieved the father, but the son who stayed home grieved him also and might just as well have left home. Like the prophet Jonah, the older son did the father's will but didn't delight the father's heart (Jonah 4).

As we grow in the spiritual life, this is what our Lord wants us to enjoy:

> If anyone loves Me, he will keep My word; and My Father will love him, and We will come to him and make Our home with him (John 14:23).

> He will rejoice over you with gladness,
> He will quiet you with His love,
> He will rejoice over you with singing (Zeph. 3:17).

FULFILL GOD'S PURPOSES

We want to grow spiritually because *in growing, we can fulfill the purposes for which God saved us*: "For we are His workmanship, created in Christ Jesus for good works, which God prepared beforehand that we should walk in them" (Eph. 2:10).

The Greek word translated "workmanship" is *poiema*; it means "something made" and gives us the English word *poem*. The Christian who boasts, "I'm a self-made person!" doesn't understand this basic principle that God must work in us before He can work through us. He must prepare us for what He has prepared for us.

One of the few advantages of being a "senior saint" is the privilege I've had of looking back and seeing how God has prepared and led during these fifty plus years of Christian pilgrimage. Dr. A. T. Pierson said, "History is His story"; and he was right. God must work in us before He can work through us, and He works in us as we "grow in the grace and knowledge of our Lord and Savior Jesus Christ" (2 Peter 3:18).

Knowing that my Father in heaven is in control of circumstances brings great confidence and peace to my heart; and if I'm yielded to Him and growing, "the LORD will perfect that which concerns me" (Ps. 138:8). Maturing believers always have a place of service prepared for them, and they don't have to promote themselves or use political maneuvers to open the doors through which God wants them to walk. Their assurance is Revelation 3:8: "See, I have set before you an open door, and no one can shut it."

LIVE FOR HIM

We seek to grow spiritually *so that the grace of God will not be wasted in our lives*: "We then, as workers together with Him also plead with you not to receive the grace of God in vain" (2 Cor. 6:1).

God has paid a great price to make His grace available to us. For us to deliberately go our own way and live only to please ourselves is to receive His grace in vain. It means putting a cheap price tag on the cross of Christ and grieving the Holy Spirit who lives within us. Christ died our death for us that we might live His life for Him, and He makes His grace available to us so that we might live effectively for His glory.

When he was a fifty-two-year-old man in poor health, missionary C. T. Studd was asked by a young newspaper reporter why he would leave his wife, family, and country to go to Africa, where the doctors said he would probably die. "What?" Studd said. "Have you been talking of the sacrifice of the Lord Jesus Christ tonight? If Jesus Christ be God and died for me, then no sacrifice can be too great for me to make for Him."[1] God's grace wasn't wasted on C. T. Studd.

I asked a friend of mine what his son was going to be when he graduated from the university, and he replied, "An old man." The father was pouring out his resources on his son, but the young man was only a professional student, "dying by degrees." Education for him wasn't preparation for service; it was simply a handy escape from the responsibilities of life. What the father was giving him appeared to be in vain, for the son had no intentions of getting a job and becoming a useful citizen, let alone a grateful son.

OBEY GOD'S COMMANDS

One more thing ought to motivate us: *a desire to be obedient to the commands of God.*

The New Testament is filled with admonitions that relate directly to our spiritual growth and maturity. Jesus said, "Therefore you shall be perfect, just as your Father in heaven is perfect" (Matt. 5:48). Among Peter's last written words are, "Grow in the grace and knowledge of our Lord and Savior Jesus Christ" (2 Peter 3:18). Paul wrote many practical admonitions, such as: "Set your mind on things above, not on things on the earth" (Col. 3:2); "But you, O man of God, flee these things and pursue righteousness, godliness, faith, love, patience, gentleness" (1 Tim. 6:11); and "Therefore be imitators [followers] of God as dear children" (Eph. 5:1).

If we're satisfied with "life as usual," we can ignore these commands or explain them away. But if we want God's very best in our lives, we will seek to obey them; and then we will discover the joyful freedom that comes from fulfilling the will of God.

Now let's look at the principles of spiritual growth and seek to apply them in our daily lives.

Chapter 5

FOCUS: GROWING FROM THE INSIDE OUT

This principle is so obvious, you'd think people wouldn't overlook it, but they do. However, ignoring this principle has brought disappointment to the lives of some of God's children, and I don't want that to happen to you.

The principle is simply this: *You care for the spiritual life of the inner person just as you care for the physical life of the outer person.* Both the inner person and the outer person need food, exercise, and cleansing; and both of them must develop from within. Just as a baby is born complete, with everything he needs for a normal life, so the child of God is born complete in Christ. All the child of God has to do is grow, and this growth comes from within.

Suppose a pediatrician tells a mother that her baby is underweight. To solve the problem, the mother goes to the supermarket, buys five pounds of meat, and attaches it to the baby's body. Now when the doctor puts the baby on the scale, the weight will be just right!

You may smile at the naivete of that mother, but some Christians are just as naive when it comes to spiritual growth. Buying a new study Bible, attending another seminar, subscribing to one more magazine, and keeping the dial tuned to their favorite Christian radio station can do them good only if the spiritual nourishment they're exposed to gets into their systems. Unless we grow from within, we don't grow at all. Carrying around a lot of impressive "religious luggage" doesn't guarantee growth at all.

SPIRITUAL SENSES

The parallel between the physical life and the spiritual life is frequently found in Scripture. Peter counseled Christian wives to cultivate the beauty of "the hidden person of the heart" (1 Peter 3:4) and not just the beauty of the body; and John prayed that his friend Gaius would "prosper in all things and be in health, just as your soul prospers" (3 John 2). The spirit can be healthy or sick just as the body can be healthy or sick.[1] As we get older, we find encouragement in Paul's words, "Even though our outward man is perishing, yet the inward man is being renewed day by day" (2 Cor. 4:16).

Hebrews 5:14 cautions us to have our spiritual senses in good working order so we can "discern both good and evil." This applies to our spiritual sense of *hearing*. When Jesus cried out, "He who has ears to hear, let him hear!" (Matt. 13:9), He wasn't referring to the physical organs of hearing because everybody in the crowd (except people who were deaf) could hear what He had to say. He was referring to the ability of the inner person to hear God's Word and understand it. "He who is of God hears God's words," Jesus said to the Pharisees. "Therefore you do not hear, because you are not of God" (John 8:47). Sad to say, some of God's children are "dull of hearing" (Heb. 5:11), but His true sheep hear His voice and follow Him (John 10:27).

God's people also have a spiritual sense of *taste*: "Oh, taste and see that the LORD is good; blessed is the man who trusts in Him!" (Ps. 34:8). God's children have "tasted the heavenly gift . . . and have tasted the good word of God and the powers of the age to come" (Heb. 6:4–5). We have "tasted that the Lord is gracious" (1 Peter 2:3). When we read His Word, it's like honey to our taste (Ps. 119:103).

Unbelievers are spiritually blind (John 3:3), but God's children have spiritual sight that can discern the things of God. Paul prayed that the Christians in Ephesus might have the eyes of the heart opened to spiritual truth (Eph. 1:18), and Peter lamented the fact that immature believers were "shortsighted, even to blindness" (2 Peter 1:9). Each time I open my Bible to read and meditate, I need to pray, "Open my eyes, that I may see wondrous things from Your law" (Ps. 119:18).

SPIRITUAL HEALTH

If we were to care for the inner person, the hidden person of the heart, as we care for the outer person, and if we would pursue and cultivate spiritual health as we do physical health, then we would all be holier and happier people. God's children would be strong, and His work would prosper in this world. But we're prone to make the same mistake the Pharisees made in Jesus' day: we major on what people see—the outer person—and we neglect the inner person that only God sees. Jesus compared the Pharisees' lives to a bad job of dishwashing and a good job of whitewashing.[2] He said,

> Woe to you, scribes and Pharisees, hypocrites! For you cleanse the outside of the cup and dish, but inside they are full of extortion and self-indulgence. Blind Pharisee, first cleanse the inside of the cup and dish, that the outside of them may be clean also. Woe to you, scribes and Pharisees, hypocrites! For you are like whitewashed tombs which indeed appear beautiful outwardly, but inside are full of dead men's bones and all uncleanness. Even so you also outwardly appear righteous to men, but inside you are full of hypocrisy and lawlessness (Matt. 23:25–28).

When we're more concerned with *reputation* than we are with *character*, life starts to erode from within; and if nothing is done to stop the decay, life eventually falls apart.

The English word *hypocrite* comes from a Greek word that means "an actor in a play." In the Greek dramas, the actors wore masks to identify their roles; and when they changed roles in a play, they simply changed masks. That way the spectators knew which parts the actors were playing, and the drama didn't become confusing.

Hypocrites are people who wear masks and pretend to be something other than what they really are. For them, life isn't real; life is only a drama in which people wear masks and do their best to conceal the real self from others. But for the Christian believer, life is real and life is serious. The important thing in life isn't seeing how many people we can impress with our reputation but seeking to please the Lord by building godly character.

That's why the Christian life is lived from the inside out: "For the LORD does not see as man sees; for man looks at the outward appearance, but the LORD looks at the heart" (1 Sam. 16:7); "Keep your heart with all diligence, for out of it spring the issues of life" (Prov. 4:23).

HEART MOTIVES

A major theme of the Sermon on the Mount is the true righteousness of Christ as opposed to the false righteousness of the Pharisees. Jesus points out that sin comes from the heart (Matt. 5:21–37). I may not murder my neighbor; but if I hate him, I'm murdering him in my heart. Furthermore, deliberate lust in the heart is the moral equivalent of adultery.

Since sin has its origin in the heart, righteousness must come from the heart (Matt. 6:1–18), and we must live as those who are under the watchful eye of God. Jesus said, "Take heed that you do not do your charitable deeds before men, to be seen by them. Otherwise you have no reward from your Father in heaven" (Matt. 6:1). In our giving (Matt. 6:1–4), praying (Matt. 6:5–15), and fasting (Matt. 6:16–18), we must act only to please God and win His approval, no matter what people may think. It's important that our only motive be to please the Father in heaven, who alone sees the hidden intents of the heart; "and your Father who sees in secret will Himself reward you openly" (Matt. 6:4, 6, 18).

Faith is living without scheming. Once I start to scheme my way into or out of a situation, I know I'm not living from within. Instead of diligently guarding my heart, I'm deceitfully hiding what's really in my heart and trying to impress others with my reputation for godliness. In attempting to build up my reputation with the people around me, I'm tearing down my character within me; *and it isn't worth it.*

Character is the basic building block of the Christian life. No matter what else we may possess—talent, ability, money, fame, authority—if we don't have character, we don't have anything. The American patriot Thomas Paine wrote, "Reputation is what men and women think of us. Character is what God and the angels know of us." Evangelist Dwight L. Moody defined *character* as "what you are in the dark."

In recent years, the world has been shocked and the church has been shamed by the public exposure of religious leaders guilty of living double lives. Of course, every profession has its hypocrites. Lawyers, doctors, bankers, professional athletes, and politicians have been indicted for violating their code of ethics; but the world expects something better from the church, and rightly so.

What was the first step these religious leaders took toward sin and disgrace? *They started to wear masks.* They neglected "the hidden person of the heart" and started majoring on reputation, not character. Gradually, what little character they had eroded within, and they began to convince themselves that they could get away with it. Like the evil man described in Psalm 10, they said to themselves,

> God has forgotten;
> He hides His face;
> He will never see (v. 11).

Phillips Brooks said that the purpose of life was the building of character through truth, and I concur. (I like to add "to the glory of God," and I think Brooks would agree.) But when you abandon truth, you can't build character. "Behold, You desire truth in the inward parts," prayed penitent King David, "and in the hidden part You will make me to know wisdom" (Ps. 51:6).

IMMORTAL LIES

Mark Twain wrote that there was evidence to prove "that a truth is not hard to kill and that a lie told well is immortal." If he is right, then what are some of these "immortal lies" that, when believed, destroy character and wreck lives?

God doesn't really mean what He says. This is the oldest lie in human history; it goes all the way back to the Garden of Eden when the serpent tempted Eve (Gen. 3:1–5). I recall pleading with a man to abandon his sinful course and return to his wife and family. I showed him verse after verse verse from the Bible, only to hear him say repeatedly, "That's *your* interpretation." The verses I read to him really needed no interpretation; but when you're looking for an excuse to sin, "That's your interpretation" is as good an excuse as any.

I can get away with it. We live in a world that doesn't want to believe in either truth or consequences. Many people believe they can lie, cheat, steal, and even murder and not be called to account for their deeds, either in this life or in the life to come. "Be sure your sin will find you out" (Num. 32:23) applies to somebody else, *if* it applies at all. God is merciful and long-suffering, and sometimes He does delay executing a just sentence to give people time to repent; but this delay may encourage people to sin even more! "Because the sentence against an evil work is not executed speedily, therefore the heart of the sons of men is fully set in them to do evil" (Eccl. 8:11).

I'll do it only once. That was the approach Satan attempted with the Son of God: "All these things I will give You if You will fall down and worship me" (Matt. 4:9). But how often must we disobey God in order to become sinners and reap what we've sown? Like eating pistachio nuts or potato chips, enjoying the pleasures of sin just once is hard.

Sow a thought and you reap an action.
Sow an action and you reap a habit.
Sow a habit and you reap a character.
Sow a character and you reap a destiny.

Everybody's doing it. Even if everybody were sinning and we could prove it, which we can't, that wouldn't make the sins of others acceptable to God or our sins approved by God. The Bible clearly states, "You shall not follow a crowd to do evil" (Ex. 23:2).

I can make up for it somehow. Sin hurts the one who commits it, and it also hurts the people connected to the one who commits it—family, friends, neighbors. No amount of remuneration can compensate for the damage done. The idea that the consequences of deliberate sin can be wiped out by gifts and the memory forgotten was born in hell.

When I was a lad, I went uptown with my parents one Friday, and I recall our walking past two men on the sidewalk who were arguing. As young as I was, I knew what was going on: one of the men wanted to go into a nearby tavern, and the other one was telling him not to do it. "Think of your family!" the second man was saying. "Think of what it does to them!" And the first man kept saying, "I'll make it up to them somehow."

That childhood scene is etched on my mind, and I'm glad it is. It reminds me that we never sin alone. In one way or another, we involve others.

Nobody will know about it. But God will know about it and so will you, and your character will know about it and feel the deadly assault. We forget our decisions, but our decisions never forget us. "Thou shalt not get caught" may be the eleventh commandment; but whether or not anybody else knows what we've done, we still pay for our sins. The gradual erosion of character is one of the tragedies of a life of secret sin; and like a tree that's rotting at the core, that life will topple over one day.

UNIFIED AND SIMPLIFIED LIFE

When you live to please God and to keep the inner person healthy, you discover that life gradually becomes *unified*. Instead of running here and there, trying to do everything and please everybody, you calmly face the challenges of each day without feeling pulled apart. You find it's much easier to make decisions because life is centered on one thing: seeking first "the kingdom of God and His righteousness" (Matt. 6:33).

At the same time, life becomes *simplified*, something that's essential in this busy, complex world. Activities that once were very important are seen to be trivial; and we find we don't really need possessions we simply had to have. Thoreau said that a person is rich in proportion to the number of things he can afford to do without, and Jesus told Martha that "one thing is needed" (Luke 10:42). When you cultivate the inner person and live to glorify Christ, your values change, and your priorities change with them.

Without becoming stoic, you discover that circumstances don't upset you as much as they used to and that what people say or do doesn't worry you as it did before. You experience what Paul wrote in Philippians 4:11: "I have learned in whatever state I am, to be content." The Greek word translated "content" means "contained, self-sufficient, adequate." Inner-directed believers are self-sufficient because they are Christ sufficient. Their source of strength comes from the unchanging

Christ within them, not from the changing resources of the world and people around them.

People who depend on circumstances and other people for the strength they need to keep going will be constantly frustrated and worried, like a pilot flying a plane whose fuel tank is empty and there is no place to land for refueling. But people who depend on Jesus Christ to energize and motivate the inner person have all the adequacy they need for every circumstance of life.

Here's a good verse to memorize and practice: "And God is able to make all grace abound toward you, that you, always having all sufficiency in all things, may have an abundance for every good work" (2 Cor. 9:8).

Chapter 6

BALANCE: MAINTAINING THE RIGHT PERSPECTIVES

I was experiencing recurring back and neck pains. One day a friend asked, "Have you ever thought that the problem might be with your bones? Maybe your posture's out of whack."

With my doctor's approval, I visited a specialist; and sure enough, I needed a riser in my left shoe to compensate for something awry on my left side. Thanks to the riser and a simple exercise, the pains soon vanished; and I thanked my friend for his advice.

"Well," he said with a chuckle, "when you live in Kentucky and walk around these mountains, it's easy to get out of balance."

The human body is an amazing machine, genetically structured to grow in a balanced way. Hippocrates, the father of medicine, believed that "nature was the healer of disease" and that something within the human organism sought to reestablish and maintain equilibrium. Borrowing from that concept, the famed psychiatrist Karl Menninger defined *health* as "the vital balance," which isn't a bad definition of the healthy Christian life. Healthy Christian living is the maintaining of a "vital balance" through union with Jesus Christ.

THE PERFECTLY BALANCED LIFE

If the goal of the Christian life is "to be conformed to the image of His Son" (Rom. 8:29), then balance is important because Jesus was balanced as He lived and ministered on earth. There was nothing eccentric or erratic about Him.[1] His character was perfectly balanced, and His character and conduct harmonized.

As a child, His growth was balanced: "Jesus increased in wisdom and stature, and in favor with God and men" (Luke 2:52). Physically, mentally, socially, and spiritually, Jesus was perfectly balanced so that the Father was able to say to Him, "You are My beloved Son; in You I am well pleased" (Luke 3:22).

When you study our Lord's life and ministry, you see the deeds and hear the words of One who was always in control. He was both tough-minded and tenderhearted, fearlessly confronting His enemies on the one hand and graciously forgiving penitent sinners on the other. He patiently taught those who hungered for truth, but He refused to get caught in the theological prisons of the proud religious leaders who tried to trap Him.

If opposition arose, Jesus could face it courageously or quietly move with His disciples to another village; but when the time came for Him to die, "He steadfastly set His face to go to Jerusalem" (Luke 9:51). In the Garden of Gethsemane, He prayed that the cup might pass from Him; and yet He willingly drank that cup and suffered for the sins of the world. He could be as bold as a lion or as meek as a lamb, the King of kings or the Servant of servants; and His entire life was like the tunic He wore, "woven from the top in one piece" (John 19:23). No rips, no ragged edges, no seams.

We might be tempted to defend our lack of balance by arguing, "But after all, He was the sinless Son of God. You would expect Him to be perfectly balanced." The excuse won't do, however, because Jesus lived on earth just as you and I must live: by faith in the Father's Word and the Holy Spirit's power.

Jesus was tempted by Satan to use His divine powers for His own benefit, and He refused to yield. The only miracles He ever performed for Himself were providing the money to pay His temple tax (Matt. 17:24–27) and raising Himself from the dead (John 10:17–18), and Peter was included in the first miracle and the whole world in the second. While ministering here on earth, Jesus lived by faith, in the power of the Spirit, just as you and I must live.

THE SELF AND OTHERS

What, then, is a balanced Christian life? In what areas of life must this balance be maintained?[2]

To begin with, there must be a balance between *solitude* and *service*, time spent alone with God and time spent ministering in a needy world. Two phrases in the epistle to the Hebrews state this well: "within the veil" (6:19 KJV) and "without the camp" (13:13 KJV). "Within the veil" refers to the high priest's visit into the Holy of Holies of the tabernacle on the annual Day of Atonement (Lev. 16:1–19). "Without [outside] the camp" refers to the sin offering, sacrificed on the Day of Atonement and taken outside the camp (Lev. 16:27). It's a picture of how Jesus, our sin offering, suffered "outside the gate" of Jerusalem and died for us (Heb. 13:12; John 19:17–20).

Jesus began each day in solitary prayer, going "within the veil" to meet with His Father. Mark described one example: "Now in the morning, having risen a long while before daylight, He went out and departed to a solitary place; and there He prayed" (1:35). This was the source of His power and wisdom as He did the Father's will on earth:

The Lord GOD has given Me
The tongue of the learned,
That I should know how to speak
A word in season to him who is weary.
He awakens Me morning by morning,
He awakens My ear
To hear as the learned (Isa. 50:4).

But Jesus didn't remain in the cloistered place of prayer. He left it and went out to be with the people, to teach and to heal them and to preach the good news of salvation.

I will confess that the whisper of the cloister is much stronger to me than is the cry of the crowd. When I was serving in pastoral ministry, the thing I enjoyed most was being in my study, turning the pages of my books, studying the Word of God, meditating on divine truth, and preparing messages. I was happy for rainy days that gave me a good excuse to stay indoors. (Now I realize that rainy days were the best days to visit people. They were more likely to be at home.) But week after week, I made myself leave the cloister and go out among the people to serve them. I wanted to be like Jesus, who always had time for people, and like Paul, whose ministry was "publicly and from house to house" (Acts 20:20). I sought to be balanced.

The Christian life must also balance *receiving* and *giving*. The mind grows by taking in, but the heart grows by giving out; and the two activities must be balanced. Jesus urged, "Freely you have received, freely give" (Matt. 10:8). We can't give to others what we don't have; and what we have, we can get only from God. John the Baptist was clear on this point: "A man can receive nothing unless it has been given to him from heaven" (John 3:27). Ministry simply means sharing with others what God gives to us.[3] The Christian who takes no time to receive will have nothing to give.

There must also be a balance between *ourselves* and *others*. Although we don't want to be guilty of "saving our lives" so that we lose them (John 12:24–26), we can't afford to destroy our lives foolishly by losing our balance. Jesus took time to eat and sleep and to care for His personal needs. He accepted invitations to meals; He took time for little children and probably played with them; He attended the Jewish feasts and worshiped in the synagogues. These activities weren't an end in themselves; they were a means to the end of ministering to others.

The familiar cliche "I'd rather burn out than rust out" sounds spiritual, but rusting out and burning out aren't the only possibilities. Paul tells us to "work out [our] own salvation with fear and trembling" (Phil. 2:12). Caring for ourselves isn't necessarily selfish, although it can be overdone. But being careless about ourselves could mean we're asking for trouble. The key word is *balance*. Vance Havner used to remind us that if we don't come apart and rest, we might come apart!

As you read the Gospel of John, you discover that Jesus lived on a divine timetable that climaxed with the hour of His suffering and death.[4] When His disciples warned Him that it wasn't safe to go to Judea, He quietly replied, "Are there not twelve hours in the day?" (John 11:9). He was reminding them that His enemies couldn't touch Him until the right hour had struck on God's clock. However, Jesus never took needless chances with His enemies; He even departed to another place in order to avoid unnecessary conflict (John 4:1–3; 7:1).

HEART AND MIND

Perhaps the most difficult challenge in Christian living is maintaining the balance between the *heart* and the *mind*, loving God and learning about God.[5] We tend to go to one of two extremes: either we study the Bible a great deal and major on knowledge, or we focus on worship and seek to have an intimate relationship with God that keeps us on a spiritual high. Human nature being what it is, we develop a big head and a cold heart or a warm heart and a stagnant mind.

Of course, what God has joined together, we must not put asunder. When asked to name the greatest commandment in the law, Jesus replied, "You shall love the LORD your God with all your heart, with all your soul, and with all your mind" (Matt. 22:37). Paul prayed for his friends in Philippi that their "love may abound still more and more in knowledge and all discernment" (Phil. 1:9), which tells us that Christian love is neither blind nor ignorant. Certainly, the more we know about God, the more we should love Him; and loving Him more gives us more opportunity to come to know Him better.

One of the classic texts on the so-called mind/heart conflict is John 14:21–24. Jesus explained to His disciples:

> He who has My commandments and keeps them, it is he who loves Me. And he who loves Me will be loved by My Father, and I will love him and manifest Myself to him. . . . If anyone loves Me, he will keep My word; and My Father will love him, and We will come to him and make Our home with him. He who does not love Me does not keep My words; and the word which you hear is not Mine but the Father's who sent Me.

Before we can obey God, we must know His Word, which means exercising our intelligence. The knowledge of God is the highest knowledge possible, but it must always lead to obedience; and that's where the will comes in. But obedience without love is drudgery, perhaps even slavery, so we must do the will of God from our hearts

(Eph.6:6). Thus, the whole of the inner person—mind, emotions, will—is involved, and the reward is a fuller experience of God's love as the Father and Son make their home in our hearts in a deeper and more satisfying way.

Truth and love—the mind and the heart—aren't enemies; they're friends. "Speaking the truth in love" (Eph. 4:15) is one of the ways we grow in the Christian life. Peter admonishes us to "grow in the grace and knowledge of our Lord and Savior Jesus Christ" (2 Peter 3:18), which reminds us that if our learning and loving are both centered in Christ, they will be balanced.

However, it's possible for us to grow in knowledge and not grow in grace. This explains why there are people in our churches who will argue the fine points of Scripture at the drop of a cross-reference but who know little about loving lost souls or ministering to the saints. Acquiring a store of Bible knowledge that is never really put into practice can make a person proud, and pride often leads to a hard heart and a critical spirit. Paul put it this way: "Knowledge puffs up, but love edifies [builds up]" (1 Cor. 8:1).

However, the loving saints who know little about Scripture can also create problems. If a doctrinal matter comes up in the church, their tendency is to say, "Now, those things really aren't important, so let's not split hairs. What's really important is that we love each other and promise not to disagree." Paul and Barnabas didn't take that approach with the legalists who tried to compromise the gospel (Acts 15), nor did Paul take that stance when he confronted Peter for his inconsistency (Gal. 2:11–21). Yes, we should love each other, especially when we disagree, but "the wisdom that is from above is first pure, then peaceable" (James 3:17). Purity comes first. We must love the purity of God's truth as well as the unity of God's people.

Emotions that aren't examined and controlled by the Word of God can produce zeal without knowledge (Rom. 10:2), and that might turn us into troublesome fanatics. However, if the mind is filled with Bible truth but the heart isn't ignited by love for Christ, we could become cold academic Christians who are better at arguing about the Bible than obeying it. Bishop Hendley Moule once said that he'd much rather tone down a fanatic than try to resurrect a corpse, and I agree with him; but there is no reason why anybody should go to either extreme.

An inordinate love for knowledge that isn't balanced by devotion to Christ and service to others can be a source of trouble in the Christian life. Seeing the dangers involved in prying into God's hidden knowledge, Charles Spurgeon prayed, "My Lord, I leave the infinite to you. I pray that you will keep me away from a love for the tree of knowledge and give me a great love for the tree of life."[6] Spurgeon wasn't anti-intellectual; after all, he started a college, wrote scores of books, and collected a large library and used it profitably. But he realized that knowledge can lead to pride, and pride is the womb out of which every other sin can be born.

The whole of God's truth must possess the whole of the inner person. The mind learns the truth, the heart loves the truth, and the will obeys and lives the truth; and they work together to keep our lives balanced.

FELLOWSHIP WITH GOD IN THE WORD

Satan doesn't tremble when he sees Christians studying the Bible if he knows they're pursuing some personal hobby and not practicing a balanced Christian life. The British moralist Samuel Johnson once said of an acquaintance, "That fellow seems to me to possess but one idea, and that is a wrong one." Possessing and being possessed by one wrong idea is the luxury of the person who pursues religious hobbies.

Avoid theological hobbies; they don't edify, they keep your religious revolver charged, and they generate unprofitable strife in the family of God. This doesn't mean that you shouldn't have convictions and be able to defend them, but it does mean that you respect the fact that other Christians have convictions, that heated arguments don't promote holiness, and that it's possible you might be riding a hobbyhorse instead of defending the faith. All truth is God's truth, and all truth intersects. The key is balance.

During a local church Bible conference, a young man approached me and furtively began to ask about a doctrine that has been a focal point of dissension among some saints for centuries. I soon detected that he held to an extreme position and that he didn't seek truth but wanted to declare war. I carefully answered his question so as not to add fuel to the smoldering fire within him, but to no avail. He began to debate and raise his voice, a crowd gathered, and nothing I said would quiet him down. Finally, I had to excuse myself because the pastor had other people waiting to see me; and the young theologian went away angry, never to return to the conference.

What I suspected about the young man was later verified by the pastor, who said, "Oh, he's got a collection of books and tapes, and the more he studies, the more it inflates his ego. If you accept his theology, you belong to the spiritual elite. If you don't, you're a dummy. He's got such a big head, he's going to topple over one of these days."

Doctrinal Bible study is a good and necessary thing in the church, but we must beware lest pride and contention creep in and we start building walls that divide us instead of bridges that bring us together. Good and godly people don't always agree on some theological matters, and we must learn from one another; but we must also be careful not to make a doctrinal hobby the supreme test of spirituality and fellowship.[7] After all, God can and does bless people we disagree with.

If our fellowship with God in His Word doesn't gradually make us more like Christ, then something is wrong because that's what Bible study and meditation are all about. When we gaze into the mirror of the Word and see the glory of Christ, we are "being transformed into the same image from glory to glory, just as by the Spirit of the Lord" (2 Cor. 3:18). If we're becoming more like Christ, then we're becoming more and more balanced.

Chapter 7

NUTRITION: FEEDING ON GOD'S WORD

Physical life is sustained by a regular supply of air, water, and food. We've already seen that there is a parallel between the physical life and the spiritual life. Therefore, if we're going to grow and be strong in the inner person, we need air, water, and food.

The Gospel of John, which is the gospel of eternal life (20:31), illustrates this parallel. The Holy Spirit is the wind of God, the breath of life (3:5–8).[1] After the Resurrection, Jesus breathed on His disciples and said, "Receive the Holy Spirit" (20:22). When you believe on Jesus Christ, it's like breathing fresh air, taking a drink of living water (4:7–14), and feeding on living bread that always satisfies (6:26–40). In Christ, we have all that we need for life and growth.

The spiritual nourishment of the child of God is the Word of God, and you must discover for yourself what your Bible will do for you if only you will let it.

FOLLOWING A BIBLICAL DIET

The inner person has an appetite that must be satisfied. If it isn't satisfied by truth and reality, it will feed on lies and illusion; but it must be fed. Most people in our world today are trying to survive on a diet that neither imparts life nor sustains life. It can't bring lasting satisfaction, either: "Why do you spend money for what is not bread, and your wages for what does not satisfy?" (Isa. 55:2). The lost don't know that through faith in Jesus Christ, they can have the spiritual bread that gives life and the living water that satisfies permanently, and it's our job to tell them. Perhaps they're living on substitutes because nobody has told them that something better is available.

However, some of God's children, who ought to know better, are living on a nutritional level that's not much higher than that of their unsaved neighbors. Like the prodigal son, some of God's children are eking out an existence on husks when they could be feasting at the Father's table; but unlike the prodigal, they don't realize how starved they are.

> "Behold, the days are coming," says the Lord GOD,
> "That I will send a famine on the land,
> Not a famine of bread,
> Nor a thirst for water,
> But of hearing the words of the LORD" (Amos 8:11).

When the Jewish people were hungry during their wilderness journey, six days a week God dropped manna into their camp to feed them, the very bread of God from heaven. The people had only to step outside their tents, stoop, gather as much manna as they needed, and eat it; and the manna sustained them during their journey. If they waited too long to gather it, the manna melted, and their opportunity to eat "angels' food" (Ps. 78:25) was gone for the day. (See Ex. 16.)

According to John 6, the manna pictures Jesus Christ, the Bread of Life. The similarities are clear: both came from heaven; both were graciously given by God; both were given to meet a great need; both had to be received personally; and to reject God's gift meant death. However, in His sermon, Jesus pointed out two important contrasts: the Old Testament manna only *sustained human life* while Jesus Christ *imparts divine life;* and the manna was given to the Jewish nation only, but the Father sent His Son to give life to the world. That includes you and me.

Jesus Christ is the spiritual nourishment of His people, and we receive that nourishment through His Word. He said, "It is the Spirit who gives life; the flesh profits nothing. The words that I speak to you are spirit, and they are life" (John 6:63).[2] Jesus Christ is the Word become flesh (John 1:14), so when we meditate on Scripture and take its truths into our hearts, we are feeding on Jesus Christ, the Bread of Life.[3]

God's people today would do well to follow the example of the faithful Jews in the Old Testament who got up early in the morning and gathered the manna before the sun rose to melt it. We must gather our spiritual food early so it can nourish and sustain us throughout the day.

Your Bible provides exactly the diet you need to become a mature, balanced Christian. God's Word is *bread*: "Man shall not live by bread alone, but by every word that proceeds from the mouth of God" (Matt. 4:4; cf. Deut. 8:3). The Word is *milk*: "As newborn babes, desire the pure milk of the word, that you may grow thereby" (1 Peter 2:2). It is also *solid food*: "I fed you with milk and not with solid food" (1 Cor. 3:2).[4] God's Word is like *honey*: "How sweet are Your words to my taste, sweeter than honey to my mouth!" (Ps. 119:103).[5] What a menu!

Perhaps these four images of God's Word suggest stages in our spiritual growth. As newborn Christians, we receive and swallow the milk given to us by others, food that they have predigested and prepared. It doesn't take much effort on our part to be nursed, but who wants to remain at that stage? As we grow older, we learn to appreciate and appropriate the bread, and we can even feed ourselves. With further growth, we learn to "chew on" the solid food (meat). Pediatricians warn us that honey isn't good for babies; but it doesn't take long for children to discover the sweet things available in the cupboard! However, we aren't really ready for the sweetness until we can take the bitterness with it. Remember, life has to be balanced.

"EATING" GOD'S WORD

Whenever he felt ill, Emperor Menelik II of Ethiopia (1844-1913) would rip a page out of the Bible, chew it up, and swallow it. Apparently, this great ruler felt that if eating the Word of God was good enough for Ezekiel and John, it was good enough for him. But even if he did get well, the mighty emperor was making two mistakes: we don't "eat" God's Word literally, chewing it up page by page; and we don't "use" the Bible only in emergencies just to make us feel good. The Word of God is our daily nourishment, no matter how we feel, but "eating" it is the spiritual experience of the inner person.

"I have treasured the words of His mouth more than my necessary food," said suffering Job (23:12). And the prophet Jeremiah told the Lord,

> Your words were found, and I ate them,
> And Your word was to me the joy and rejoicing of my heart;
> For I am called by Your name (15:16).

Of course, you can't eat anything unless you have life. An appetite for food is one evidence that you're alive. When Jesus raised Jairus's little girl from the dead, He commanded them to give her something to eat (Luke 8:55); and Lazarus, whom Jesus raised from the dead, sat at the table with Jesus and enjoyed a banquet (John 12:2). Dead people can't eat.

Because God's children have spiritual life, we have an appetite for spiritual nourishment. We've "tasted the good word of God" (Heb. 6:5); and having tasted, we want more. Unconverted people don't want to read God's Word and enjoy it because they're spiritually dead and have no appetite for spiritual things.

When I became a Christian, I discovered that I had an insatiable desire to read and study the Bible. One day I found a *Scofield Reference Bible* in the religion section of our local public library, and I took it home to learn how to use it. (I don't know how long it had been on the shelf, but I think I was the first person to check it out.) I asked my parents to give me Bible study books for Christmas, and they bought me a concordance, a one-volume commentary, and a Bible dictionary. Uncle Simon, who was a retired pastor, gave me some excellent books from his library; and that small collection of "tools" helped me get started in a lifetime of studying the Bible.

One of the first evidences of sickness is often a loss of appetite, and this is true in the spiritual life. When we have no desire for God's Word, it could mean that something has gotten into our system that shouldn't be there. If we're feeding on what the world has to offer—"the lust [appetite] of the flesh, the lust [appetite] of the eyes, and the pride of life" (1 John 2:16)—then our desire for and enjoyment of spiritual things will become weak. The cultivating of an appetite for spiritual food is essential to a healthy Christian life. Anything that robs us of our desire for spiritual food is wrong and must be avoided.

At the same time, we must not feed the "old appetite." The old nature ("the flesh") that controlled our former preconversion life certainly has an appetite that yearns to be fed; and if we cater to this appetite, we'll only make it stronger. Paul urges, "Rather, clothe yourselves with the Lord Jesus Christ, and do not think about how to gratify the desires of the sinful nature" (Rom. 13:14 NIV). The world points to something sensual and says, "Feast your eyes on that!" But the Holy Spirit says, "Let us fix our eyes on Jesus, the author and perfecter of our faith" (Heb. 12:2 NIV). The Book of Proverbs advises, "Let your eyes look straight ahead, and your eyelids look right before you" (4:25).

During an annual physical checkup several years ago, my doctor discovered that I was marginally diabetic. He advised me to lose weight or else spend the rest of my life suffering the consequences. Having been raised in a Swedish family that enjoys pastries and other sweets, I had to make some radical changes.

"Let me give you a simple system for eating that really works," said my doctor. "Just learn to dislike the things that are bad for you, *and never give them that second look. Don't even enjoy them in your imagination.*"

I took his advice, and it worked. Now when I walk through an airport, I'm not even tempted by the candy vendors and the pastry shops. In fact, the smell of chocolate makes me a bit nauseous.

The first human sin was committed because of a wrong look that led to a wrong desire: "So when the woman saw that the tree was good for food, that it was pleasant to the eyes, and a tree desirable to make one wise, she took of its fruit and ate" (Gen. 3:6). Abraham's nephew Lot "lifted his eyes and saw all the plain of Jordan, that it was . . . like the land of Egypt" (Gen. 13:10). Lot moved into Sodom and lost everything he had when God's judgment fell. King David's eyes wandered to his neighbor's wife, and the result was a series of sins whose consequences plagued David's life for years to come (2 Sam. 11—12).

Charles Wesley knew something about the importance of a spiritual appetite when he wrote:

I want a principle within of watchful godly fear,
A sensibility of sin, a pain to feel it near.
Help me the first approach to feel of pride or wrong desire;
To catch the wandering of my will, and quench the kindling fire.

We don't often sing that song in our worship services today, but we still need its message.

DISCOVERING JESUS

Before we think about how to feed on the Word of God, we need to understand why the Scriptures were written in the first place. Of course, their overriding aim is *to reveal the Lord Jesus Christ:* "And beginning at Moses and all the Prophets, He [Jesus] expounded to them in all the Scriptures the things concerning Himself" (Luke 24:27). From beginning to end, the Bible is a book about Jesus.

The religious leaders in Jesus' day studied the minute details of the Old Testament, thinking that their diligent studies of the law would make them acceptable to God; but they completely missed seeing the Savior in their own Scriptures. "You search the Scriptures," Jesus told them, "for in them you think you have eternal life; and these are they which testify of Me" (John 5:39).

Unless we see Christ in His Word, we can never feed on Him and become more like Him. It's the work of the Holy Spirit to teach us the Scriptures (personally and through Spirit-filled teachers) and to show us the Savior:

But when the Helper[6] comes, whom I shall send to you from the Father, the Spirit of truth who proceeds from the Father, He will testify of Me (John 15:26).

However, when He, the Spirit of truth, has come, He will guide you into all truth; for He will not speak on His own authority, but whatever He hears He will speak; and He will tell you things to come. He will glorify Me, for He will take of what is Mine and declare it to you (John 16:13–14).

I've met people who read and study the Bible only so they can impress others with their knowledge of Bible facts, and I feel sorry for them. Their Christian faith is primarily cerebral, and they miss the wonderful heart satisfaction that believers experience when they feed on Christ in the Word and become more like Him. Cerebral saints are like starving people at breakfast who study the panels of the cereal boxes, learn all the facts about nutrition, and go away from the table hungry and weak. Yes, it's important to know Bible facts, but it's also important to be "taught by Him, as the truth is in Jesus" (Eph. 4:21).

Because they reveal Christ, the Scriptures make us "wise for salvation" (2 Tim. 3:15), but they also *equip us for life and service:* "All Scripture is given by inspiration of God,[7] and is profitable for doctrine, for reproof, for correction, for instruction in righteousness, that the man of God may be complete, thoroughly equipped for every good work" (2 Tim. 3:16–17). Seeing Jesus in the Word and feeding on Him ought to give us busy hands ("every good work") as well as burning hearts (Luke 24:32).

Paul wrote that the Scriptures, rightly used, can equip us for life and service because God's Word "is profitable for doctrine, for reproof, for correction, for instruction in righteousness" (2 Tim. 3:16). Each purpose is important:

- Doctrine—what's right
- Reproof—what's not right
- Correction—how to get right
- Instruction—how to stay right

Suppose I must drive from Lincoln, Nebraska, to Denver, Colorado, to speak at a conference. Being notorious for getting lost when I travel, I first sit down with a road atlas and plot my course, my navigator wife assisting me. That correct course is like *doctrine:* it tells me *what's right* and will guide me to my destination.

But suppose, as we drive along, my wife is napping, not navigating; and I foolishly take the wrong exit. (I've been known to do that even when she's been awake!) Her sensitive navigational alarm clock tells her to wake up immediately. "You shouldn't have turned there," she says. That's *reproof*. She told me I was *not right*. So, I pull off the detour, turn the car around, and get back on the main road. That's *correction, getting right*. Then my wife puts the marked map on the seat beside me and says, "Follow this and you won't go wrong." That's *instruction, staying right*.

It isn't enough to let the Holy Spirit teach us the basic truths of Scripture; we must also let Him reprove us when we've erred, correct us and get us back on the right path, and then show us how to stay on that path once we've been restored. We don't like reproof, but it's an important part of learning and maturing: "He who keeps instruction is in the way of life, but he who refuses correction goes astray" (Prov. 10:17). How we respond to reproof reveals whether we're wise or foolish, humble or proud: "Whoever loves instruction loves knowledge, but he who hates correction is stupid" (Prov. 12:1).

Note that this sequence begins with the positive—doctrine, what's right. Perhaps it's best summed up, "This is the way, walk in it" (Isa. 30:21). Whenever the Bible is negative, it's so that we can get back to the positive. Imagine how confusing and frustrating travel would be if the street and highway signs were all negative: "This road does not go to Denver," or "This street does not go to downtown." I need to know where the road is going! Christians who focus only on the negative— "Thou shalt not!"—usually end up unbalanced in their attitudes and actions and have a pessimistic view of the Christian life. They forget that whenever God says, "No!" it's because He wants to say, "Yes!"

DISCIPLINING THE DEVOTIONAL LIFE

Nourishing the inner person, like feeding the outer person, must be an activity that involves discipline, system, and balance. Unbalanced menus and erratic eating schedules can often lead to physical weakness and sickness, and an undisciplined devotional life usually results in chronic spiritual fatigue. For those who want to "be strong in the Lord and in the power of His might" (Eph. 6:10), religious fast food is unacceptable. We must "take time to be holy," and that means taking time to receive and digest the milk, bread, meat, and honey of the Word.

I use the term *devotional life* to describe what others may call the quiet time or the morning watch or the prayer time. Whatever we call it, it's that daily time alone with the Lord when we worship Him, read His Word and meditate on it, and seek His face in confession, prayer, and intercession. Our purpose isn't simply to fulfill an obligation ("I've taken care of that; now the rest of the day is mine!") but to deepen our relationship with the Lord and grow in our satisfaction with His will. When God's children are unhappy with God's will, we become fair game for the kind of satanic attacks that can lead to misery and even tragedy.

Our time alone with the Lord each day is basic to our spiritual health; and as I mentioned earlier, a nourishing devotional life involves discipline, system, and balance.

Let's begin with *discipline*. Most people don't find it difficult to plan and enjoy three meals a day—and perhaps a few snacks in between—but they have a problem when it comes to setting aside time each day to fellowship with the Lord. What ought to be their highest delight becomes their greatest burden and a source of guilt. They determine to have a disciplined devotional life and perhaps make a good beginning; but then they start to falter, and soon the whole enterprise falls apart. Their accumulated disappointments convince them that it isn't worth it to try again, so they just keep muddling their way through the Christian walk when they could be marching in victory.

I may be wrong, but my guess is that most devotional dropouts make two common mistakes: they aim too high, and they start with too much self-determination. Having heard about famous men and women of God who devoted many hours each day to prayer and meditation, they determine to imitate them, which is like asking a Cub Scout to lead a fifty-mile hike. There is a basic principle in the Christian life, explained in Romans 7, that when we determine *not* to do something bad, we do it; and when we determine *to do* something good, we don't do it. This happens whenever we depend on our own strength and determination instead of yielding to the Holy Spirit who alone can fulfill God's righteousness in our lives (Rom. 8:1–4).

Perhaps the best way to get started in a satisfying devotional life is to set aside fifteen minutes *when you are at your best* and make it a commitment that you hold sacred between you and the Lord every day. You know when you are at your best, and you want to give that prime time to the Lord. I happen to be a morning person, so that's when I have my personal devotions. I like to start the day early, reading His Word and sharing my concerns, because it's one time during the day when I'm not likely to be interrupted. However, not all people function effectively early in the day; they find that late afternoon or early evening is their best time for meditation and prayer. The decision is yours; just be sure you give God your best time and not the ragged remnants of the day.[8]

Having set aside the time, ask the Lord to help you a day at a time, and anticipate with excitement this appointment with God. Don't see yourself as a soldier or slave showing up reluctantly to get orders. Your devotional time is more like two good friends meeting each other and enjoying each other's fellowship, as when Abraham talked with the Lord (Gen. 18:16–33) and Mary sat at Jesus' feet and heard His words (Luke 10:38–42).

As it deepens, this fellowship becomes like that of a husband and a wife enjoying the loving communion that's described in the Song of Solomon, that most intimate and mystical of Bible books. Jesus promised that "he who loves Me will be loved by My Father, and I will love him and manifest Myself to him" (John 14:21).[9] If your quiet time is simply a routine religious appointment that you keep each day, it will eventually become a boring ritual; but if your meeting with the Lord is an honest expression of your love for Him, then it will deepen and grow; and you will eagerly anticipate meeting Him in His Word day by day. In due time, that original fifteen minutes will expand to thirty minutes and more, not because you're trying to set new records, but because you're enjoying the communion so much you want to spend more time with your Lord.

SETTING UP A SYSTEM

So much for discipline. Now let's consider *system*.[10]

David wrote, "In the morning I will direct it [my prayer] to You, and I will look up" (Ps. 5:3). The word translated "direct" means "to set in order." In the Old Testament, it's used to describe organizing soldiers for battle (Gen. 14:8), arranging a sacrifice on the altar (Lev. 1:8), setting a meal before a guest (Ps. 23:5), and even presenting a legal brief in court (Job 13:18). Each of these activities pictures doing something in an orderly fashion.

David is suggesting in Psalm 5:3 that we approach our devotional life in an orderly way so that our devotions aren't spontaneous and unrehearsed like an amateur hour at a summer camp. Paul counsels, "Let all things be done decently and in order" (1 Cor. 14:40). The general has a battle plan, the host and hostess carefully plan the meal and set the table, and the lawyer prepares the brief in a logical fashion. If they wish, the general, the host and hostess, and the lawyer can spontaneously make last-minute changes; but those changes won't destroy the original purposes they had in mind.

Better to have a plan and change it than to have no plan at all. A plan gives us the structure we need to keep us from falling prey to our feelings and religious impulses and then going on detours. Few things are as deceptive as our changing feelings, even our "religious" feelings; and if we base our devotional practices only on how we feel, we'll never make much progress in the Christian life. In fact, those days when we don't feel like spending time with the Lord may be the very days we need Him the most!

Your devotional time should include worship and praise, Bible reading and meditation, and confession and prayer. If you're going to start with a fifteen-minute period, then the first few minutes should be devoted to worship, coming into the presence of the Lord just to adore Him and praise Him. Perhaps you have sins to confess before your worship will be acceptable to Him: "If I regard iniquity in my heart, the Lord will not hear" (Ps. 66:18). The word translated "regard" means "to look upon with approval." I can never fellowship with God if I approve what He condemns. David stated, "Behold, You desire truth in the inward parts" (Ps. 51:6).

Having come into His presence and worshiped Him, you next want to read a portion of the Word and think about it, applying what it says to your life. Don't play religious roulette and just open the Bible at any place, because that's no way to read the world's greatest Book, or any book, for that matter. And if you're just getting started in your devotional life, don't try to read straight through the Bible in one year. Genesis is fascinating; but when you get to the middle of Exodus and into Leviticus, the laws and details about the tabernacle and the sacrifices might discourage you.

For someone just getting started, I recommend that you start in Psalm 1 and Matthew 1. Read a psalm first, and use it as an expression of worship. (If the psalm is long, just read a meaningful paragraph and finish it the next day.) Then read a portion of a chapter in Matthew, and give the Spirit time to speak to your heart. Keep reading systematically day after day, and one day you'll discover that you've read the entire book of Psalms and you're well on your way to completing the whole New Testament. You'll also discover that you're devoting more than fifteen minutes a day to your devotional time.

With more time, and a greater appetite for the Lord and His Word, you can move into a more mature reading schedule. Some believers like to start in Genesis 1, Psalm 1, and Matthew 1, and read three chapters (or portions of long chapters) each day, systematically meditating their way through Scripture. When they've completed reading the whole Bible, some believers like to change translations, just so they don't get so familiar with the language that they fail to hear the voice of God speaking to them.

The key Hebrew word translated "meditate" means "to mutter, to murmur, to talk to oneself." We meditate on Scripture when we talk to ourselves about what God is saying to us. God commanded Joshua to keep the Word in his mouth (Josh. 1:8), suggesting that he repeated it to himself and talked about it. Meditation involves understanding the Word with your mind, receiving it in your heart, and submitting your will to its authority so that you obey it. Meditation is to the soul what digestion is to the body: what you take in becomes a part of you.

ACHIEVING BALANCE

Our third key concept for the devotional life is *balance*.

The Bible is a balanced book containing many different kinds of writing—history, biography, poetry, songs, letters, proverbs, parables, prophecies, laws, and precepts—and a balanced diet of biblical truth leads to a balanced Christian life. Granted, some passages in the Bible are easier to read, understand, and apply than others, but all Scripture is necessary for balanced spiritual nutrition.

The danger, of course, is that we do with the Bible what we do with our physical diet: we major on the things that we enjoy the most and are the easiest to prepare. But this approach robs us of the spiritual nour-ishment we can gain from the food that we neglect. Both Moses (Deut. 8:3) and Jesus (Matt. 4:4) remind us that we must live "by *every* word that proceeds from the mouth of God" (italics mine). I meet Christians whose devotional diet consists only of the four Gospels and the Psalms, or the Psalms and the Prison Epistles; and they never have the joy of walking with Moses and seeing the glory of God or listening to Isaiah and Jeremiah and hearing the comforting words of God. An unbalanced diet can lead only to an unbalanced Christian life.

As you begin your devotional life, you don't want to take on too heavy a reading load, lest you get discouraged and quit. But as your devotional experience matures and you discipline yourself to spend more time with God, you can expand the spiritual menu and read the whole Bible and benefit from it. I don't suggest you turn your Bible read-ing into a contest and try to read through the Bible in a given period of time or even read a given number of verses a day.[11] I can still hear my mother saying to me and my siblings at the table, "Don't gulp down your food!" (Of course, we were anxious to eat dessert and then go out and play before it became dark.) That motherly counsel applies to me as I read God's Word.

The Bible is a balanced book. It contains law and grace, precept and promise, instruction and example, encouragement and warning, expla-nation and mystery; and all of it is inspired and profitable. We must not ignore anything the Spirit of God has written because He wrote it for our learning and encouragement: "For whatever things were written before were written for our learning, that we through the patience and comfort of the Scriptures might have hope" (Rom. 15:4); "Now all these things happened to them [Israel in the Old Testament] as exam-ples, and they were written for our admonition" (1 Cor. 10:11).

Your Father longs to meet with you each day, and the Holy Spirit enjoys teaching you the Word and revealing Christ to you. As time goes on, they will help you develop the kind of satisfying devotional life that leads to spiritual strength, insight, and maturity. Just be sure that you balance the essential ingredients—meditation, worship and praise, con-fession and intercession—and that your reading schedule enables you to read through the whole Bible, no matter how long it takes. When your devotional time is over each day, you want to be happy with God's will and ready to go into the hostile world and do the will of God. It isn't enough just to have good feelings when you're alone with God. You must also do good works when you're in the busy marketplace.[12]

Some days, your devotional time will be especially exciting and enriching; but on other days, it may be somewhat routine and perhaps even boring. Admit this to yourself and to the Lord, and do your reading and meditating anyway. We've all eaten many a routine meal that wasn't a gastronomical adventure, but the food nourished us just the same; and the same principle applies to the devotional life. Of course, prolonged periods of spiritual dullness may indicate a special problem or need that must be faced, and I suggest you chat with an advanced believer and get his or her spiritual guidance.

Finally, what about the use of devotional books? Having written several of them myself,[13] I do feel they have an important ministry, but never as substitutes for your Bible. If I use a devotional book, it's always after I've done my meditating and praying, not before. Use a devotional book that has some substance to it, one that helps you better understand God's Word for yourself. Reading a Bible verse, a story, and a poem, plus a "thought for the day," is like gulping down fast food and not taking time for a balanced meal. Eating fast food is better than starving; but if it takes away your appetite for satisfying meals that give you what you need, it's doing you more harm than good. You don't want to live on substitutes.

Chapter 8

EXERCISE: TRAINING THROUGH WORSHIP

Nourishment without exercise will make a person overweight, sluggish, and fair game for a variety of physical problems. What's true of the body is also true of the inner person: unless we devote our' selves to spiritual exercise, the nourishment we take will probably do us more harm than good. Too many saints are overfed and underexercised, and that's why Paul tied food and exercise together when he wrote these words to Timothy:

> If you instruct the brethren in these things, you will be a good minister of Jesus Christ, nourished in the words of faith and of the good doctrine which you have carefully followed. But reject profane and old wives' fables, and exercise yourself toward godliness. For bodily exercise profits a little, but godliness is profitable for all things, having promise of the life that now is and of that which is to come (1 Tim. 4:6–8).

EXERCISING SELF-CONTROL

The word *exercise*, like the word *discipline*, irritates some people, particularly those who prefer to saunter their way through life indulging in pleasure rather than investing in character. "Whenever I think about exercising," said a contemporary wit, "I just sit down and rest until the feeling goes away." The fact that one day he may sit down and never stand up again probably never enters his mind.

Whether it's playing a musical instrument, mastering a computer program, or learning a foreign language, any worthwhile endeavor demands discipline and exercise. Aristotle called self-control "the hardest victory," and he was probably right. Until we learn how to exercise self-control, we aren't likely to learn anything else that's important to a successful life. We must exercise discipline even to sit still and read a book or listen to somebody teach.

During the years when our two daughters were learning to play the piano, I had to get accustomed to hearing them practice their scales. Granted, scales aren't as beautiful as "The Moonlight Sonata" or "To a Wild Rose"; but practicing the scales is the first step toward playing beautiful music. Learning the basics isn't easy, but it's essential.

When Paul told Timothy to "exercise [himself] toward godliness," the apostle used a metaphor that was especially meaningful to the people of that day, for athletics was an important part of life in the Greco-Roman world. Just about every city had its gymnasium where the boys learned to exercise, wrestle, box, and run; and every local athlete aspired to compete in the Olympics and bring glory to his city.

Athletic references in the New Testament epistles include statements about running the race (1 Cor. 9:24–26; Phil. 3:12–14; Heb. 12:1–2), boxing (1 Cor. 9:26–27), and obeying the rules of the game (2 Tim. 2:5). Our English word *athletic* comes from a Greek word that means "to strive, to contend in the games";[1] and our word *gymnasium* is from a word that means "to train the body." Paul used it when he admonished Timothy to "exercise [himself] toward godliness"; and you find the word also in Hebrews 5:14 and 12:11. "A sound mind in a sound body" was the Greek ideal of perfection. "A healthy soul in a healthy, dedicated body" is a great ideal for Christian maturity. "Beloved," John wrote to his friend Gaius, "I pray that you may prosper in all things and be in health, just as your soul prospers" (3 John 2).[2]

There was a time in church history when believers delighted to discuss the spiritual disciplines of the Christian life, but today, anything that smacks of discipline is branded as "legalistic" and alien to the New Testament emphasis on grace.[3] Contemporary Christians don't have time for spiritual disciplines such as worship, fasting, prayer, meditation, self-examination, and confession. We're too busy running to meetings and looking for guaranteed shortcuts to maturity.

This neglect of personal discipline is evidenced by the titles I see in Christian bookstores, like *Thirty Days to a Victorious Christian Life* or *Prayer Made Easy*.[4] Spiritual classics like *Pilgrim's Progress* or *The Imitation of Christ* collect dust on the bookstore shelves because they present a picture of the Christian life that isn't popular with an easygoing spectator generation of believers, people who want to enjoy the happy dividends but don't want to make the costly investments.

Some of today's Christians remind me of the millions of fans who crowd the sports arenas and stadiums week after week, cheering their favorite teams to victory. After each game, these fans shout, "We won! We won!" when in reality the athletes did both the playing and the winning. All the fans did was pay for a ticket, fill a seat, and make a lot of noise. The spectators, not the players, are the ones who really need the exercise; but they settle for shouting, "We won!" and claiming the credit that belongs only to the disciplined athletes.

It doesn't take much effort to be a successful spectator; but we must remember that spectators don't experience the joy that comes with being disciplined, working with teammates, and giving their best; nor do spectators win any awards. Too many evangelical church services are attended by enthusiastic people who buy their tickets (the offering), watch the game (the service), and cheer when there is victory (people responding). They know little or nothing about exercising the disciplines that transform spectators into winning athletes who glorify God.

If you want to be a child of God who does more than watch and cheer, you'll have to learn the disciplines of the Christian life. You'll have to become a disciple. Disciples are believers who practice discipline. They understand spiritual exercise.

DEDICATING OURSELVES

Our most important spiritual exercise, and perhaps the most difficult to learn, is worship. Everything we are and everything we do in the Christian life flows out of worship. Jesus said, "Without Me you can do nothing" (John 15:5).[5]

What is worship? To someone brought up in the Quaker tradition, worship might mean waiting quietly before the Lord and listening for His word in the silence; to a charismatic believer, worship might imply a more enthusiastic expression of praise and adoration. I think that the definition of worship by William Temple covers the essential elements involved in personal and corporate worship:

> For worship is the submission of all our nature to God. It is the quickening of conscience by His holiness; the nourishment of mind with His truth; the purifying of imagination by His beauty; the opening of the heart to His love; the surrender of will to His purpose—and all of this gathered up in adoration, the most selfless emotion of which our nature is capable and therefore the chief remedy for that self-centeredness which is our original sin and the source of all actual sin.[6]

Believers who have no time for worship, or whose worship lacks discipline, have their priorities confused. After all, if God is the greatest and most important Being in the universe, then worshiping Him has to be the greatest and most important activity of men and women made in the image of God and saved by the grace of God. So, read that paragraph again, slowly and meditatively, and let it sink in. Understanding this definition and applying it could transform your worship experience and thus transform your life.

The Old Testament Jewish priests brought the dead bodies and the shed blood of animals to the Lord; but as New Testament priests of God (1 Peter 2:5, 9), we bring Him *living* sacrifices, starting with our bodies. Paul wrote, "I beseech you therefore, brethren, by the mercies of God, that you present your bodies a living sacrifice, holy, acceptable to God, which is your reasonable service [spiritual act of worship, NIV]" (Rom. 12:1).

When you give your body to the Lord, you give Him all the elements mentioned in Temple's definition of worship because the word *body* includes the whole person—the conscience, mind, imagination, heart, will, and all the faculties, talents, and gifts inhabiting that holy temple. Just as the Old Testament priest placed a whole burnt offering on the altar each morning, so we must present ourselves completely to the Lord, to live for His glory that day. The animal on the Jewish altar didn't die voluntarily, but ours must be a voluntary act of worship that comes from the heart.

The tense of the verb *present* indicates a once-and-for-all step of faith as we present ourselves to the Lord in a solemn act of dedication. But I like to renew that dedication at the beginning of each day. It's like the bride and groom at the marriage altar: they give themselves to each other once and for all, but they belong to each other for the rest of their lives. The wedding dedication only introduces them to the marriage devotion, which should get richer as the years pass. Any married couple that tries to live on the memories of a beautiful wedding, without cultivating a deepening relationship of love, doesn't understand what marriage is all about.

A professional photographer told me about a wedding he covered at a fashionable suburban church. As he waited outside the door of the church for the happy couple to emerge, he noticed a car parked across the street with the motor running and a young man sitting at the wheel. When the couple emerged, the bride took one look at the car and its driver, dropped her bouquet, ran across the street, got into the car, and away she and the young man went. The father of the bride chased them down and discovered the young man was a former suitor who had told his daughter, "I can have you any time I please."

The young woman's husband had the marriage annulled. After all, what husband wants a wife who presents herself to him at the marriage altar and then takes her body and gives it to another man?

PRAISING AND MEDITATING

Worship involves not only *presentation* but also *adoration* as we offer our spiritual sacrifices of praise and thanksgiving to God: "Therefore by Him let us continually offer the sacrifice of praise to God, that is, the fruit of our lips, giving thanks to His name" (Heb. 13:15). Whether we praise Him by using one of the psalms, a text from the hymnal, something spontaneous from the heart, or perhaps all three,[7] we ought to focus our full attention on Him and Him alone. David expressed his praise this way: "Bless the LORD, O my soul; and all that is within me, bless His holy name!" (Ps. 103:1).

Worship also includes *meditation,* reading the Word of God, thinking about it, praying over it, asking the Spirit to show us Christ and teach us the truth and then help us apply the truth to our own lives. This is what Temple calls "the nourishment of mind with His truth." All that we need to know about God will be given to us in the Scriptures; and the better we know Him, the more we will love Him.

King David lived in a lovely royal palace, yet his heart's desire was to:

> dwell in the house of the LORD
> All the days of [his] life,
> To behold the beauty of the LORD,
> And to inquire in His temple (Ps. 27:4).

We will never abhor the ugliness of sin until we learn to appreciate the beauty of holiness: "Oh, worship the LORD in the beauty of holiness!" (1 Chron. 16:29; Pss. 29:2; 96:9). The brittle piety of the Pharisees wasn't beautiful, but everything about Jesus Christ is beautiful and ought to claim our attention and adoration. We should be able to join the psalmist in saying, "You are fairer than the sons of men; grace is poured upon Your lips" (Ps. 45:2).

When we invest time worshiping Christ and beholding Him in the Word, the Spirit of God goes to work in the inner person to make us more like Jesus. Paul compared this to looking in a mirror (the Word) and seeing, not ourselves, but the glory of Christ! He wrote, "But we all, with unveiled face, beholding as in a mirror the glory of the Lord, are being transformed into the same image from glory to glory, just as by the Spirit of the Lord" (2 Cor. 3:18).

The word translated "transformed" is translated "transfigured" in Matthew 17:2 where it describes the glory of Christ radiating from within. As you worship the Lord, you can have your own "mount of transfiguration" and experience the transforming power of His glory.[8] Moses reflected the glory of God from his face (Ex. 34), and the three apostles only beheld the glory of God (Matt. 17); but we can actually share His glory as it radiates from within. Like Stephen, we can have a shining face, even when on trial for our lives (Acts 6:15).

EXERCISE

PRAYING

Worship must include *prayer*.

Jesus didn't give His followers a philosophy of prayer or even a theology of prayer.[9] Instead, He gave them an example of prayer as they watched His own prayer life; He told them encouraging parables about prayer; and He taught them a model prayer to guide them in their praying. What we call the Lord's Prayer is the inspired pattern for us to follow as we pray.[10]

> Our Father in heaven,
> Hallowed be Your name.
> Your kingdom come.
> Your will be done
> On earth as it is in heaven.
> Give us this day our daily bread.
> And forgive us our debts,
> As we forgive our debtors.
> And do not lead us into temptation,
> But deliver us from the evil one (Matt. 6:9–13).

The first thing that strikes you about this prayer is that it uses *only plural pronouns* when referring to God's people. It's not "My Father" but *"Our* Father"; it's not "Give *me*" but "Give *us*." This prayer is a family prayer that involves all the people of God. In fact, a dual relationship is expressed with "Our Father": a relationship *with other believers* ("Our"), and a relationship *with God* ("Father").

As a child of God, I can pray in solitude, but I can never pray alone. I must consider other believers as well. I must keep before me all the family of God and not pray for anything for myself that would in any way harm one of God's children. The blessings that come to me in answer to prayer must also bring blessing to the rest of God's family. James said that one reason God's children were at war with each other was because their praying was selfish (James 4:1–3). They were praying "My Father" instead of *"Our* Father."

So, praying must focus first of all on relationships with the Father and with His children. If there is anything between me and the Father or one of His children, it could become a barrier to answered prayer. Jesus said, "For if you forgive men their trespasses, your heavenly Father will also forgive you. But if you do not forgive men their trespasses, neither will your Father forgive your trespasses" (Matt. 6:14–15). And Peter reminds Christian husbands and wives that a wrong relationship in the home can hinder their prayer life (1 Peter 3:7).

Prayer involves relationships, and it also involves *responsibilities*: the glory of God's name ("Hallowed be Your name"), the success of God's kingdom ("Your kingdom come"), and the fulfilling of God's will ("Your will be done"). Before we even pray about our own concerns, we must focus on the concerns of God. I dare not ask anything of the Father that would dishonor His name, hinder the coming of His kingdom,[11] or obstruct the fulfilling of His will on earth.

Why are God's concerns put ahead of my personal needs and requests? First of all, because they're far more important than any needs I may have. Second, they are put first so that I can evaluate my prayers and see if they are truly a part of what God is doing in this world. "If God granted me this request," I must ask myself, "would it glorify His name, hasten Christ's coming, and accomplish God's will on earth?" If not, I have no right to pray for it. John assures us, "Now this is the confidence that we have in Him, that if we ask anything according to His will, He hears us. And if we know that He hears us, whatever we ask, we know that we have the petitions that we have asked of Him" (1 John 5:14–15). As Robert Law said, "The purpose of prayer is not to get man's will done in heaven but to get God's will done on earth."

If my relationships are right with God and God's family, and if I sincerely accept the responsibilities that go along with being a praying Christian, then I'm ready to come to the Father with my *requests*. These include daily bread, forgiveness, and protection from the evil one.

Daily bread includes every need I have in *the present* ("this day"), whether it's food to eat, clothes to wear, money to pay my bills, or the strength to get through a difficult day. Forgiveness looks to *the past* and deals with whatever God has on my record that needs to be wiped clean (1 John 1:9).[12] Deliverance relates to whatever *future* decisions I make that might lead me too close to Satan's snares and make me vulnerable to his attacks.[13] So, these three requests cover the past, the present, and the future, and each of our prayer needs can be put into one of these categories.

INTERCEDING

Worship means prayer, and prayer includes *intercession*. We have the privilege of praying not only for ourselves but also for others. Remember, the Lord's Prayer has plural pronouns referring to God's people, which means it's a prayer for the members of God's great family around the world. What right do I have to ask God to feed me if other believers are starving and I'm not concerned to help them?

> But whoever has this world's goods, and sees his brother in need, and shuts up his heart from him, how does the love of God abide in him? (1 John 3:17).

> If a brother or sister is naked and destitute of daily food, and one of you says to them, "Depart in peace, be warmed and filled," but you do not give them the things which are needed for the body, what does it profit? (James 2:15–16).

First we pray, and then we do what God enables us to do to help answer our prayers.

To *intercede* means to "come between," in this case, to come between God the Provider and people in need. Intercession is seen in Abraham praying for Lot and the lost people of Sodom (Gen. 18), Moses beseeching God to spare sinning Israel (Ex. 32), Elijah requesting rain from heaven (1 Kings 18:20–46), David pleading with God to end the devastating plague (2 Sam. 24), and Nehemiah, Ezra, and Daniel asking God to forgive Israel and heal the land (Neh. 1; Ezra 9; Dan. 9). And don't forget that our Lord Jesus Christ is today in heaven interceding for His people, and any activity that engages His interest ought to be followed by His people on earth. The intercessor stands "between the dead and the living" (Num. 16:48) and seeks God's help for the helpless.

If I'm to be a genuine intercessor, I must have a heart of concern that wants to know what others' needs are so I can pray about them because self-centered people don't think about bearing other people's burdens. On Sunday morning, August 11, 1861, Charles Spurgeon said to his people at the Metropolitan Tabernacle in London:

> Brethren, I commend intercessory prayer, because it opens man's soul, gives a healthy play to his sympathies, constrains him to feel that he is not everybody, and that this wide world and this great universe were not after all made that he might be its petty lord, that everything might bend to his will, and all creatures crouch at his feet.[14]

As we pray for others, our praying not only helps them, but it helps us!

For whom do we intercede? Certainly for our family, friends, neighbors, and other loved ones, but also for our enemies and those who may oppose us (Matt. 5:43–48). We're admonished to pray for people in places of civil authority (1 Tim. 2:1–2), a commandment that I fear isn't obeyed as it should be in many American churches. While ministering in Great Britain, Northern Ireland, and Canada, I've heard pastoral prayers that mentioned the queen and the royal family, the prime minister, and even the president of the United States! I pray daily for our president, governor, and mayor and for all in authority because that's my Christian duty.

We should pray for the people of God and the servants of God. "Praying always with all prayer and supplication in the Spirit . . . for all the saints—and for me," was Paul's request of the Ephesian believers (Eph. 6:18–19). I don't know "all the saints" in this big world or the names of all the Christian servants; but God does, and He wants me to intercede for them.[15]

In my itinerant ministry, I've asked many pastors, "Do you ever pray publicly for any other church in town?" The response to my query is usually a shocked expression and a short exclamation, "No!" When I ask them why, they mumble something about how many churches there are in their city and the fact that some of them aren't too evangelical and spiritual. My wife and I happen to belong to a fellowship with pastors who each Lord's Day pray for another pastor and church in our city, and this practice has led to real blessing. If nothing else, it has sent out the signal that our congregation doesn't promote a spirit of competition or pride, and that we want to help answer Christ's prayer for unity among His people (John 17:20–23).

Jesus instructed us to pray for laborers for the harvest fields of the world (Matt. 9:38), and Paul encouraged us to pray for the lost people who need to be harvested (Rom. 9:1–5; 10:1). Let's not try to avoid the responsibility of reaching the lost by hiding behind some distortion of the doctrine of divine election.[16] The same God who ordains the end—the salvation of lost sinners—also ordains the means to the end—the praying and witnessing of God's people. In fact, the doctrine of divine election is one of the greatest encouragements to evangelism. "Do not be afraid, but speak, and do not keep silent," Jesus said to Paul when things were tough in Corinth. "For I am with you, and no one will attack you to hurt you; for I have many people in this city" (Acts 18:9–10).[17]

If you read your Bible and follow the example of the intercessors found there, you'll have no problem knowing what to pray about. Your problem will probably be making sufficient time to pray about so many pressing needs. Notice I didn't say "finding the time" because true intercessors make time to pray. It's a priority.

My own practice, which you can adopt, adapt, or reject, is to have a prayer list for each day of the week, plus a list that I use every day. This gives me two lists for each day, plus special prayer calendars that come from various ministries. I find I can pray about all these specific people and needs without having to hurry through my prayer and end up crying in desperation, "Lord, help all these people—and bless the missionaries!"

Whatever plan best works for you, follow it; and you'll find that intercessory prayer will enrich your life.

FASTING

In the Sermon on the Mount, after Jesus completed His instructions about prayer, He gave a brief word about fasting:

Moreover, when you fast, do not be like the hypocrites, with a sad countenance. For they disfigure their faces that they may appear to men to be fasting. Assuredly, I say to you, they have their reward. But you, when you fast, anoint your head and wash your face, so that you do not appear to men to be fasting, but to your Father who is in the secret place; and your Father who sees in secret will reward you openly (Matt. 6:16–18).

The Mosaic law required Israel to fast only once a year on the annual Day of Atonement;[18] but the Pharisees had instituted a tradition of fasting each Monday and Thursday, and they let people know they were doing it (Luke 18:12). They thought their fasting would gain them merit with the Lord, but they forgot the basic truth that the act of going without food needed to be accompanied by a brokenness of heart and a confession of sin (Joel 2:12–13; Isa. 58:3–11; Zech. 7).

Fasting isn't something we do either to impress people or to earn something from God. True fasting grows out of an inner concern, a burden so great that we set aside the normal activities of life[19] and concentrate wholly on the spiritual purpose at hand, which could include praying for others in great need (Deut. 9:9, 18; Ps. 35:13–14), resisting Satan (Matt. 4:1–2), seeking God's will (Acts 13:1–3; 14:23), or imploring God's special help at a time of crisis (1 Sam. 7:6; 2 Sam. 12:1–23; Ezra 8:21, 23; Neh. 1:4–11; 9:1–2; Est. 4:3).

Jesus made it clear that fasting must be voluntary and come from the heart; it must be sincere; and unless others are fasting together with us, it must be a private exercise between the believer and God. If we gain the applause of others, we lose the blessing of God, and it isn't worth it.

One reason true fasting is effective is that there's a subtle but dynamic relationship between the physical and the spiritual. When the body is disciplined, as during fasting, the Holy Spirit has the freedom to clarify the mind and purify the intentions and make our praying and meditating much more powerful. The spirit/body relationship is a mysterious one, and perhaps nobody can explain all that it involves; but the Holy Spirit knows our hearts and our desires, and He can use times of fasting and prayer to sanctify our lives and glorify the Lord.

Finally, we should recognize that some Christians have a difficult time fasting. For whatever physical or emotional reason, they become weak and irritable; and the discipline does them more harm than good. God knows their hearts, and that's all that counts. We must be careful not to pass judgment.

TAKING WORSHIP BREAKS

As God's children, we worship privately each day, at whatever time God finds us at our best; and we worship with His children each Lord's Day and whenever God's people meet for worship and witness. Husbands and wives, as well as parents and children, cultivate a time for reading the Word and praying together. As children get older and schedules change, parents must stay alert to maintain a meaningful family altar that will encourage, educate, and enrich the family.

But we must not get the idea that worship is something we turn on and off like a CD player. Worship isn't *a part* of our lives; it's *the heart* of our lives. Just as spouses find life motivated and controlled by their love for each other, and parents by their love for their children, so Christians are motivated and controlled by their love for God. We should never say, "Well, my worship time is ended, so now I can do what I please!" any more than a husband at work would say, "Well, I'm not at home now, so I can forget my wedding ring and live like a single man."

This leads me to one final suggestion: during each day, take worship breaks and lift your mind and heart to God in spontaneous acts of adoration and thanksgiving. Whoever wrote Psalm 119 had the same idea, for he said, "Seven times a day I praise You, because of Your righteous judgments" (v. 164). While standing in the checkout line at the supermarket, waiting at the barbershop or beauty salon, or traveling home after a hard day at work, take time to worship God and turn your feelings, your work, and your responsibilities over to Him. Love Him and let Him love you.

Brother Lawrence made it his practice to take worship breaks as he served in the kitchen, cleaning dirty pots and pans. "A little lifting of the heart suffices," he wrote. "A little remembrance of God, one act of inward worship, are prayers which, however short, are nevertheless acceptable to God."[20] It's like your spouse or your child spontaneously dropping his or her work or play and just giving you a hug and a kiss, for no special reason except love for you. God delights to receive the love of His children and to share His love with them.

One of the best examples of this is Nehemiah, the Jewish government official who restored the gates and walls of Jerusalem. The Book of Nehemiah opens with Nehemiah's longer prayer of confession and intercession; but throughout the book, he sends up to God spontaneous expressions of prayer and devotion in the midst of his busy schedule.[21] The strength of his brief prayers was certainly his longer times of prayer, all of which aren't recorded in his book. If we don't spend leisurely time with the Lord, our spontaneous prayers may not have much power. Just as coffee breaks shouldn't become substitutes for regular meals, so worship breaks can't take the place of our daily quiet time with the Lord.

There are only three spiritual temperatures in the Christian life: our hearts are cold (Matt. 24:12) or lukewarm (Rev. 3:14–16) or burning (Luke 24:32). Worship is both the thermometer and the thermostat of the Christian life. If my heart is cold or lukewarm, it will show up in the way I worship God; my worship will be routine, and I'll be in a hurry to get through my Bible reading and praying and be on my way. If my heart is warm toward God, there won't be time enough to meditate on His Word and tell Him all that's on my heart.

If I want to raise my spiritual temperature, the place to start is with my worship. "Therefore I remind you to stir up the gift of God which is in you," Paul advised Timothy (2 Tim. 1:6). The word translated "stir up" is composed of three Greek words: again, life, and fire. Together they mean, "Get the fire burning again and keep it in full flame!" This image reminds us of the morning duties of the Jewish priest as he removed the cold ashes from the altar, added fuel to get the fire burning again, and then placed the burnt offering on the altar as an act of total dedication to God.

What a wonderful way to begin each day!

Chapter 9

CLEANSING: DEALING HONESTLY WITH SIN

I n February 1958, my wife and I and our two small children moved from Indiana to Wheaton, Illinois, into a modest new house that was completely surrounded by snow—and mud. The snow lasted until early April and the mud until we had opportunity to plant seed and grow a lawn. However, our son David, not yet three years old, thought that the combination of snow and mud was quite challenging, and he was determined to enjoy it.

You know what happened. While playing in the snow, David got acquainted with the mud; and before long, he was a juvenile Abominable Snowman, complete with mud accessories. He came to the door for help; and as I looked at him in pity, I was reminded of a spiritual lesson: it's one thing to be *accepted* but quite something else to be *acceptable*.

ACCEPTABLE TO THE LORD

In Scripture, sin is pictured in a variety of ways: darkness (1 John 1:5–10), disease (Isa. 1:5–6), distance (Luke 15:13; Eph. 2:11–13), death (John 5:24; Eph. 2:1), debt (Luke 7:40–43), desolation and destruction (Isa. 1:7–9; Lam. 1), and especially defilement (Ps. 51).[1] What dirt is to the body, sin is to the soul; and apart from God's cleansing, we can't enjoy the spiritual health and growth that come when we have a clean heart. Children who aren't kept clean eventually get sick, and some of them die.

The key words here are *accepted* and *acceptable*. Being accepted in Christ is justification; being acceptable is sanctification. Justification means being declared righteous in Christ, while sanctification means being made righteous in Christ. When you trusted Christ as your Savior, you were declared righteous and were "accepted in the Beloved" (Eph. 1:6). This is your spiritual position in Christ, and it will never change. But those who are *accepted* should have a deep desire to want to live in such a way that they are "finding out what is *acceptable* to the Lord" (Eph. 5:10, italics mine). Our practice on earth should be worthy of our position in heaven because that's what pleases the Father the most.

So, when we've sinned and we come to the door for help, the Father *accepts* us because we belong to His family; but He also wants us to be *acceptable*. Therefore, He deals with us to bring us to the place of confession and cleansing. John expressed this concern: "My little children, these things I write to you, so that you may not sin. And if anyone sins, we have an Advocate with the Father, Jesus Christ the righteous" (1 John 2:1).[2]

Perhaps the easiest way to examine this matter is to note three biblical statements that refer to personal cleansing: "wash me" (Ps. 51:2, 7), "wash yourselves" (Isa. 1:16), and "wash one another" (John 13:14). The first is the prayer of a penitent believer; the second and third statements are commandments from the Lord.

THE COSTS OF SIN[3]

If the tragic story of David's adultery and treachery is unfamiliar to you, you can read it in 2 Samuel 11—12. "David did what was right in the eyes of the LORD," says the royal historian, "and had not turned aside from anything that He commanded him all the days of his life, except in the matter of Uriah the Hittite" (1 Kings 15:5). What an expensive exception that "matter" turned out to be!

We don't have to do what David did to learn the lessons that David learned. When you read the account (2 Sam. 11—19; Pss. 32; 51), you discover that the first lesson David learned was *the high cost of committing sin*. Next to our salvation in Christ, sin is the most expensive thing in the world.

There are always painful consequences to sin, not only from the act itself[4] but also from the heavy hand of God's chastening. Ordinarily strong of body, David became like an old man. "When I kept silent, my bones grew old through my groaning all the day long," he wrote. "For day and night Your hand was heavy upon me; my vitality was turned into the drought of summer" (Ps. 32:3–4). If David had confessed his sins, God would have forgiven him and ended the painful discipline; but instead, David "kept silent" and tried to cover up what he had done.

Psalm 51 reveals that David's entire being was affected by his unconfessed sins. Something happened to his eyes ("my sin is always before me," v. 3), his ears ("Make me hear joy and gladness," v. 8), his joy ("Restore to me the joy of Your salvation," v. 12), his mouth ("O Lord, open my lips, and my mouth shall show forth Your praise," v. 15), and his fellowship with God ("Do not cast me away from Your presence, and do not take Your Holy Spirit from me," v. 11).[5] David's inner person was defiled ("Wash me thoroughly from my iniquity, and cleanse me from my sin," v. 2) because his heart was unclean ("Create in me a clean heart, O God," v. 10).

The second lesson David learned was *the high cost of confessing sin.* A wealthy king, David could have brought as many sacrifices as God demanded, but he knew the blood of bulls and goats could not take away his sins (Heb. 10:4). "For You do not desire sacrifice," he prayed, "or else I would give it; You do not delight in burnt offering" (Ps. 51:16). Confession of sin to God is a costly thing because it demands an honest and a broken heart:

Behold, You desire truth in the inward parts,
And in the hidden part You will make me to know wisdom. . . .
The sacrifices of God are a broken spirit,
A broken and a contrite heart—
These, O God, You will not despise (Ps. 51:6, 17).

The American psychologist William James wrote, "For him who confesses, shams are over and realities have begun." We can lie to each other about what we've done, and even lie to ourselves; but we can't successfully lie to God.

People who have never comprehended the ugliness of sin or the holiness of God pray shallow and flippant prayers that are more like alibis than confessions. There was nothing beautiful or manly about David's adultery, his murder of Uriah, or his refusal to confess what he had done. David sinned against a flood of light and against a holy and generous God who had showered wonderful gifts upon him all his life, and "to whom much has been committed, of him they will ask the more" (Luke 12:48).

The Bible commands us to take drastic measures when we deal with sin. We must lay the ax to the root of the tree (Matt. 3:10); pluck out the lustful eye and cut off the wandering hand (Matt. 5:27–30);[6] thoroughly wash the dirty vessels and clean out the filthy tomb (Matt. 23:25–27); and take off the putrid and polluted grave clothes and put on clean clothes (Col. 3:5–11). No alibis or halfway measures here! Of course, the ultimate and final measure in God's dealing with sin is the cross. "When we repent," Spurgeon said, "we must have one eye on sin and another on the cross."[7]

We have this assurance: "If we confess our sins, He is faithful and just to forgive us our sins and to cleanse us from all unrighteousness" (1 John 1:9). The word translated "confess" means "to say the same thing," that is, to say the same thing about our sin that God says about it. We don't see sin the way a holy God sees it, but we can agree with what He says about it, "that You may be found just when You speak, and blameless when You judge" (Ps. 51:4). In other words, we judge that sin as God judges it and then turn from it.

One evidence that we have truly confessed and judged a sin is that we're ashamed of it, we loathe it whenever we remember it, and we don't want to repeat it. If we enjoy recalling our sins and reliving the experiences in the imagination, then it's obvious that we haven't really judged our sins and repented of them. Twice Abraham lied about his wife (Gen. 12; 20), which indicates that he really hadn't judged his sin when he confessed it the first time. Confession isn't just a matter of words on the lips, like little children obediently saying, "I'm sorry," to somebody they've hurt. Real confession is a matter of the heart, what David called "a broken and a contrite heart" (Ps. 51:17).

I received a letter from a radio listener who felt that Joseph was too hard on his brothers and should have forgiven them the first time he saw them (Gen. 42—45). Apart from the vital fact that God's Word had to be fulfilled and *all* the brothers bow before Joseph (Gen. 37:1–11), the way he handled the matter was wise and loving. Joseph yearned to be reconciled to his family, and he even wept over the matter (Gen. 42:24; 43:30; 45:2). But he knew that the only sure foundation for reconciliation is forgiveness; and true forgiveness involves conviction, repentance, and confession.[8]

Just as Joseph put his brothers through difficult circumstances to bring them to the end of themselves, so our Father lovingly disciplines us to bring us to the place of honesty and confession. Discipline is a positive thing:

> My son, do not despise the chastening of the LORD,
> Nor be discouraged when you are rebuked by Him;
> For whom the LORD loves He chastens,
> And scourges every son whom He receives (Heb. 12:5–6; Prov.
>   3:11–12).

For perhaps a year, David suffered under the disciplining hand of God; and finally, he repented, confessed his sins, and was forgiven (2 Sam. 12:13).

David learned the high costs of committing sin and of confessing sin. He had one more lesson to learn: *the high cost of cleansing sin.* The blood of sacrifices could never wash the stains away (Ps. 51:16), but there was cleansing because of the mercy of God. That's why David prayed,

> Have mercy upon me, O God,
> According to Your lovingkindness;
> According to the multitude of Your tender mercies,
> Blot out my transgressions.
> Wash me thoroughly from my iniquity,
> And cleanse me from my sin (Ps. 51:1–2).[9]

But God's mercy is by no means cheap. Forgiveness is a costly thing; the price of our forgiveness was the suffering and death of Jesus Christ on the cross. I'm moved when I hear about somebody donating a kidney to a family member because it's a noble and sacrificial deed that might shorten his or her own life. Then I remember that Jesus Christ didn't simply donate something for me; He gave Himself completely and bore my sins on His body on the cross (1 Peter 1:18–19; 2:24). Forgiveness isn't cheap, but it is free.

David's prayer "Purge me with hyssop" (Ps. 51:7) suggests that he understood the meaning of blood atonement. Hyssop was the shrub that the Jews used on Passover in Egypt to apply the lamb's blood to the doorposts (Ex. 12:22–24). It's as though David prayed, "Lord, I need the cleansing blood applied to my heart!" Jesus is the Lamb of God whose blood takes away the sin of the world (John 1:29).

First John 1:9 tells us that God is "faithful and just" to forgive those who confess their sins. He is *faithful* in that He keeps His promises, and He is *just* in that He will not hold against us sins for which Jesus died and which we have confessed to Him. Charles Wesley expressed this truth beautifully:

Depth of mercy, can there be
Mercy still reserved for me?
Can my God His wrath forbear—
Me, the chief of sinners, spare?

I have long withstood His grace,
Long provoked Him to His face,
Would not hearken to His calls,
Grieved Him by a thousand falls.

Now incline me to repent;
Let me now my sins lament;
Now my foul revolt deplore,
Weep, believe, and sin no more.

There for me the Saviour stands,

Holding forth His wounded hands;
God is love, I know, I feel,
Jesus weeps and loves me still.

SELF-EXAMINATION

But what do we do *after* we've confessed our sins and God has forgiven us and restored us to His fellowship? This is where the second
statement comes in: "Wash yourselves, make yourselves clean" (Isa.
1:16). "Wash me" is our prayer to God; "wash yourselves" is His command to us. Obviously, we can't wash away our own sins, but we can
cleanse our lives of the things that make it easy for us to sin. Remember,
if we judge our sins, we won't want to repeat them; and that means we
will take whatever steps are necessary to get rid of them.

I heard about a pious hypocrite in a church who loved to pray long
public prayers, each of which he closed with, "And, Lord, take the cobwebs out of my life!" One of the godly elders of the church became
weary of hearing this empty ritual week after week. One evening, after
the man had concluded his long routine prayer and had mentioned the
cobwebs, the elder stood up and prayed, "And, Lord, while You're at it,
kill the spider!"

It was the spider Paul had in mind when he wrote, "Therefore, having these promises, beloved, let us cleanse ourselves from all filthiness
of the flesh and spirit, perfecting holiness in the fear of God" (2 Cor.
7:1). *Kill the spider!*

God commands us to cleanse ourselves of *two kinds of sin:* "filthiness
of the flesh and spirit." The prodigal son was guilty of sins of the flesh
(Luke 15:13, 30), but his elder brother was guilty of sins of the spirit
(Luke 15:25–32). Both are wrong, but it's worth noting that Jesus forgave adulteresses and prostitutes but spoke sternly to the proud, self-
righteous Pharisees.

What were the sins of the elder brother? He wouldn't forgive his
younger brother; he wouldn't attend the feast; he was angry with his
father; he was proud of his faithful hard work and boasted about it; and
he openly exposed his brother's wicked conduct. He had no love for his
father or his brother, but he had a great deal of love for himself.

When he committed adultery, David yielded to a sin of the flesh;

but when he covered up his sin and hardened his heart, he yielded to sins of the spirit. Adultery is a grievous sin, but it was the sin of pride thatturned Lucifer the angel into Satan the adversary (Isa. 14:12–15). Like the Pharisee praying in the temple, we may pride ourselves that we're better than other people and go home from the prayer meeting in worse shape than when we came (Luke 18:9–14).

Not only are there two kinds of sin that we must deal with, but there are *two responsibilities* that we must fulfill: "Let us cleanse ourselves . . . perfecting holiness." One is negative; the other is positive. It isn't enough merely to root out sin; we must also plant seeds that will produce "fruit to holiness" (Rom. 6:22). Actually, this entire book is about the subject of growing in holiness and becoming more like Jesus Christ.

Finally, Paul gives us *two motives* for obeying these commands: the promises of God and the fear of God. We've already noted that the love of God and the fear of God belong in the heart of every believer, for though He is our "Abba, Father," He is also our Master and Lord who will one day judge our works. The writer to the Hebrews declared, "Therefore, since we are receiving a kingdom which cannot be shaken, let us have grace, by which we may serve God acceptably with reverence and godly fear. For our God is a consuming fire" (12:28–29).

How do we go about cleansing ourselves in the sight of God? It begins with honest self-examination:

> Search me, O God, and know my heart;
> Try me, and know my anxieties;
> And see if there is any wicked way in me,
> And lead me in the way everlasting (Ps. 139:23–24).

As we read the Bible and apply it to our hearts, the Spirit of God can show us what we need to acknowledge and confess to the Lord. God's Word is a light that exposes the dark secrets (Eph. 5:8–13), a knife that cuts deep into our hearts and reveals our motives (Heb. 4:12), and a mirror that shows us as we really are (James 1:22–25).

Do my library, magazine rack, video collection, and music collection need to be scrutinized and some of these things removed permanently? Why did I even buy these questionable items? Perhaps there is a hidden appetite in my life that needs to be exposed and excised. The most insidious sins in our lives are the ones that we think are harmless but that Satan can use to gain control of areas that should belong to the Lord.

One word of caution: don't spend so much time examining yourself that you end up performing countless spiritual autopsies and becoming so introspective you become discouraged and lose touch with reality. Remember what Spurgeon said: "When we repent, we must have one eye on sin and another on the cross." Then he went on to say, "But even better is to fix both eyes on Christ and see our transgressions only in the light of His love."[10]

Satan is the accuser of God's people (Zech. 3; Rev. 12:10), and he can use our times of self-examination to accuse us and make us want to quit. We remember our sins and failures, as well as our prayers of dedication when we told God we would do better; and the reminder of these things discourages us. Keep in mind that there is a great difference between the Holy Spirit's conviction and Satan's accusation. When the Spirit convicts us, He uses the Word of God as a mirror and as medicine; He shows us Christ and His merits; and He brings encouragement to our hearts. But when Satan accuses us, he bludgeons us with the Bible; he offers no hope; he distracts us from the merits of Christ and His cross; and he leaves us defeated and discouraged.

People who focus only on themselves and listen to the devil's accusations instead of the Spirit's encouragements are prone to think they aren't saved at all and that they've committed an unpardonable sin. I've counseled with people who were in this deplorable state, some of whom were even contemplating suicide; and it took a great deal of prayer and application of the Word for the Spirit to bring them to a place of assurance and freedom. The tragedy is, they shouldn't have gotten into that condition to begin with! As God's children, we must stay alert lest we fall into the snares of the evil one.

WASHED ONCE AND FOR ALL

"Wash me," "wash yourselves," and "wash one another."

Jesus showed us and taught us that we should "wash one another's feet" (John 13:1–17). When Jesus washed His disciples' feet, He gave them an example of humility, a lesson they badly needed (and so do we) because even in the Upper Room they argued about which of them was the greatest.

But along with this lesson on humility, the Lord taught His disciples about purity: "If I do not wash you, you have no part [communion] with Me. . . . He who is bathed [all over] needs only to wash his feet, but is completely clean" (John 13:8, 10). The disciples understood the illustration, for they knew how their own feet got dirty as they walked from place to place, and how refreshing it was to have their feet washed before reclining at the table. However, none of them had offered to wash anybody's feet that evening, so Jesus did it for them. He graciously took the place of a servant.

When you trusted Christ and were born into God's family, you were "washed all over." "Do you not know that the unrighteous will not inherit the kingdom of God?" asked Paul. "Do not be deceived. Neither fornicators, nor idolaters, nor adulterers, nor homosexuals, nor sodomites, nor thieves, nor covetous, nor drunkards, nor revilers, nor extortioners will inherit the kingdom of God." That doesn't leave many people going to heaven! But then Paul added, "And such were some of you. But you were washed, but you were sanctified, but you were justified in the name of the Lord Jesus and by the Spirit of our God" (1 Cor. 6:9–11).

This once-and-for-all complete washing doesn't have to be repeated;[11] all we need to do is keep our feet clean, which means practice 1 John 1:9 and confess our sins. As we walk through this life, and even as we serve the Lord,[12] we become defiled, and this affects our relationship with the Lord and with other believers. If we walk in the light, we recognize the defilement, and we can come to the Lord for cleansing.

But Jesus told His disciples not only to come to Him for cleansing, but also to follow His example and "wash one another's feet" (John 13:14). This suggests that believers have a responsibility and privilege to help keep one another clean.[13]

How do we help others stay clean? For one thing, we seek to be the best examples possible so that people will not follow us on the wrong path and get their feet soiled. It also means we don't deliberately tempt people to do what's wrong. In our speech, we avoid anything that will soil somebody else's mind and heart. Here is a good guideline: "Let your speech always be with grace, seasoned with salt" (Col. 4:6). We must never say, "Now, take this with a grain of salt." It's our responsibility to put the salt into what we say or write so that the words will be pure. In Ephesians 4:25–32, Paul names a number of sins of speech that defile believers and, through careless believers, can defile others. Like the Pharisees in Jesus' day, some Christians are "toxic" and make other people dirty (Matt. 23:25–28).

A second aspect to this cleansing needs to be addressed. Not only are we to wash one another's feet, but we're also to wash the wounds that we've caused in the lives of others. That's what the keeper of the prison did to Paul and Silas after he trusted Christ: "And he took them the same hour of the night and washed their stripes" (Acts 16:33).

We may not wound other people physically with whips, but we can wound them emotionally by what we say and do. The tongue can be like a sword and our words like poisoned arrows:

There is one who speaks like the piercings of a sword,
But the tongue of the wise promotes health (Prov. 12:18).

Like a club or a sword or a sharp arrow
    is the man who gives false testimony against his neighbor
        (Prov. 25:18 NIV).

Never underestimate the awesome power of human speech!

If wounds aren't washed, they become infected; and infection creates pain, fever, and the danger of death. I heard about a church that was struggling and finally called in one of the denominational leaders to help. In his first meeting with the church board, the leader asked quietly, "Does this church owe any previous pastor an apology for the way you treated him.?" There was silence, and then one of the officers put his face in his hands and began to weep. Yes, there were wounds that needed to be washed; and the church washed them, and then the Lord began to bless.

Jesus said that washing somebody's wounds was more important than bringing a sacrifice to the altar (Matt. 5:23–24), and He told us exactly how to do it (Matt. 18:15–20). It isn't easy to say, "I'm sorry," to somebody we've hurt, but those two words have healed many a wounded heart and mended many a broken relationship.

A man said to John Wesley, "I never forgive!"

Wesley replied, "Then I hope, sir, that you never sin."

We do well to remember these words: "And be kind to one another, tenderhearted, forgiving one another, even as God in Christ forgave you" (Eph. 4:32).

Chapter 10

LOVE: UNITING IN GOD'S FAMILY

A century ago, a most revealing experiment was performed in a New York City foundling hospital. In one of the wards, over a period of weeks, all the children were ministered to in the usual way, but some of the children *were not deliberately shown love*. The nurses cared for them, but they didn't talk or sing to them, hold them lovingly in their arms, or show them any special affection. The children received care, but it wasn't TLC—tender loving care.

The result? The "unloved" children became more difficult to take care of, and they had more problems and illnesses than the other children in the ward. The doctors concluded that the love given to the children was an important part of their lives and growth, and nothing else could take its place. If children are to grow up healthy and happy, they must experience love.

The eminent anthropologist Margaret Mead said, "No matter how many communes anybody invents, the family always creeps back." Why? Because it's in the family that we experience nurturing love. That's one reason why God has put His church into the world. The church is His special family to help His children grow because Christians grow in an atmosphere of love.

Augustine said, "He cannot have God for his father who refuses to have the Church for his mother." I don't interpret that to mean that God dispenses His grace through the church or that initiation into a local church is the same as membership in the family of God. It isn't.

Multitudes of people who belong to churches have never experienced salvation through faith in Jesus Christ.

What Augustine says to me in that statement is this: anybody who claims to be a member of God's family will prove it by loving God's people and fellowshipping with them as part of a local congregation. Christians are sheep and sheep flock together. They are members of the same spiritual body and therefore belong to one another and need one another. Christians don't mature in isolation.

So, don't ever lose the wonder of being a part of God's church in this world. If you become critical of the church and lose that wonder, your spiritual growth will be arrested because we grow in an atmosphere of love.

THE CALLED OF JESUS CHRIST

Of all the many names and images of God's people found in the Bible, a favorite of mine is the one Paul used when he wrote to the Romans. He referred to believers as "the called of Jesus Christ" (Rom. 1:6).

What does it mean to be "the called of Jesus Christ"? To begin with, it means that God's people have been *called out*, which defines our relationship to the world system around us. The Greek word for "church" is *ekklesia*, which comes from the verb meaning "to call out." It gives us our English word *ecclesiastic*. God's people are called out of this world system to belong exclusively to God. Jesus said, "They are not of the world, just as I am not of the world" (John 17:14). Like Jesus, we aren't isolated from the world, for we have a ministry to perform as lights in this dark world. But we do keep ourselves separated from the world (2 Cor. 6:14–18) and "unspotted from the world" (James 1:27); and we're careful to avoid "the corruption that is in the world through lust" (2 Peter 1:4).

God's people are called out, but we are also *called together;* and this defines our relationship with other believers. It is written of the first church, "Now all who believed were together" (Acts 2:44). In apostolic days, when people trusted Christ and were born again, they took the next step in their spiritual walk and were baptized and identified with the church. They never heard the slogan "Jesus, yes—the church, no!"

that was popular in the sixties; and if they had heard it, they would have ignored it. After all, if the church is the body of Christ, of which He is the Head, how can you have one without the other?

What did the believers do when they met together? "And they continued steadfastly in the apostles' doctrine and fellowship, in the breaking of bread, and in prayers . . . praising God and having favor with all the people. And the Lord added to the church daily those who were being saved" (Acts 2:42, 47). They worshiped and prayed together, heard the Word together, ate together, gave their offerings together,[1] and witnessed together; and the end result was the daily increase of the church as people were converted.

The New Testament knows nothing of solitary saints who devote themselves exclusively to their own spiritual development and ignore other believers or a lost world. Nor does it endorse the popular brand of "commercial Christianity" that permits people to go to church and get what they want but never make any contribution to the needs of others.

We are *called out*, and therefore, we are a separated people. We are *called together*, and therefore, we are a worshiping and fellowshipping people. But we are also *called forth* as a witnessing people, and this defines our relationship with the billions of lost people in the world today. As the church worships and fellowships, God speaks and calls from the family the men and women He chooses to carry His message abroad in a special way. Jesus said, "As the Father has sent Me, I also send you" (John 20:21). Here's what happened in the church at Antioch:

> As they ministered to the Lord and fasted, the Holy Spirit said, "Now separate to Me Barnabas and Saul for the work to which I have called them." Then, having fasted and prayed, and laid hands on them, they sent them away. So, being sent out by the Holy Spirit, they went (Acts 13:2–4).

If Christians' only goal is to separate from the world system and meet together to enjoy fellowship and worship, then the church will become ingrown and fail to fulfill its purpose in the world. We are debtors (Rom. 1:14) to share the good news wherever we are and to send others to share the good news wherever we aren't.

When I think about what it means to be called out, called together, and called forth, I get excited and realize what a great privilege it is to be a part of God's church. And then when I stop to consider that one day we shall be *called up,* I get even more excited! Jesus Christ will return and take His people to Himself, and we shall be with Him forever!

So, don't lose the wonder of what it means to be a part of "the called of Jesus Christ." With all of its imperfections and weaknesses, the church is still God's people in this world; and the church needs you, and you need the church.

THE CIRCULATORY SYSTEM OF THE BODY

One of the church fathers compared the professing church of his day to Noah's ark. "If it weren't for the judgment on the outside," he said, "nobody could ever stand the smell on the inside!"

In spite of its high and holy calling, the church isn't all that God wants it to be. Yes, believers are called out, but some believers are like Lot (Gen. 19) and Demas (2 Tim. 4:10) and live for this present evil world. Believers are called together, but many professed Christians are careless about obeying Hebrews 10:25: "Not forsaking the assembling of ourselves together." God's people are called forth, but many believers have no concern for a lost world. I'm told that the average church allocates 5 percent of its budget to evangelism, and many Christians don't witness where they are, let alone send missionaries to other places. And as for looking for the Lord Jesus Christ to return, too many professed believers would rather that His coming be delayed because it might interrupt their plans.

The church is not all that it ought to be or all that it can be, but that's no reason for us to abandon it and look for substitutes. The families that you and I grew up in weren't perfect, but somehow they helped to bring us where we are today. The places where Christians work aren't perfect; but they remain loyal, do their work faithfully, and try to make things better. Marriages aren't perfect, but husbands and wives stay together, raise families, and find a lot of joy in spite of their imperfections. Society is a mess, but we stick it out instead of heading for isolation in a mountain retreat or a desert refuge.

Why not take that same attitude toward the church? Seeing the wonder of the church is the first step toward relating properly to God's people, but the second step must follow: honestly facing the imperfections and faults of the church and loving God's people in spite of their faults. After all, they have to put up with our faults, too! And remember, Christians grow in an atmosphere of love.

Dr. Howard Hendricks of Dallas Theological Seminary has called love "the circulatory system of the body of Christ," and I agree with him. The phrase "love one another" is found in at least a dozen places in the New Testament,[2] and the emphasis on love permeates all twenty-seven books.

In the three key passages that discuss the "body life" of the church—Romans 12, 1 Corinthians 12—14, and Ephesians 4—you can't miss the priority given to love. At the heart of Romans 12 you read, "Let love be without hypocrisy. . . . Be kindly affectionate to one another with brotherly love, in honor giving preference to one another" (vv. 9–10). People call 1 Corinthians 13 "the beautiful hymn to love" and read it at weddings, but its main purpose was to encourage the Corinthian believers to stop showing off and start serving one another in love. In Ephesians 4, Paul mentions love three times, and these statements are significant:

With all lowliness and gentleness, with longsuffering, bearing with one another in love (v. 2).

But, speaking the truth in love, may grow up in all things into Him who is the head—Christ—from whom the whole body, joined and knit together by what every joint supplies, according to the effective working by which every part does its share, causes growth of the body for the edifying of itself in love (vv. 15–16).

Love enables us to bear with one another patiently, speak to one another honestly, and serve one another sacrificially; and this results in the building up of the church. We grow in an atmosphere of love; and where that love is lacking, the body becomes weak and sick and stops growing.

The kind of love that edifies the church isn't mere human love that enables us to get along with the people we like. It's divine love that enables us to care for and work with people we may not like. Loving only those we like and who like us will manufacture a clique, but loving all of God's people and serving them will build a church. Remember, Christian love means we treat one another the way God treats us; and God receives all of His children and accepts us in Christ. Although He has His intimates, He doesn't play favorites.[3]

All believers are "taught by God to love one another" (1 Thess. 4:9). God the Father taught us to love by giving His Son (John 3:16), and God the Son taught us to love by giving us the new commandment of love (John 13:34–35) and then demonstrating it by dying on the cross (1 John 3:16). God the Spirit teaches us to love one another by pouring out a river of love in our hearts (Rom. 5:5) and producing in us the fruit of the Spirit, the first of which is love (Gal. 5:22). First John touches on this issue: "We know that we have passed from death to life, because we love the brethren" (3:14); "He who does not love does not know God, for God is love" (4:8).

THE HEALTH OF THE BODY

When the circulatory system of love is working properly, the health of the church is demonstrated by three distinctive features, all of which are explained in Ephesians 4:1–16: unity (vv. 1–6), diversity (vv. 7–11), and maturity (vv. 12–16).[4] These three qualities are essential to the health and growth of the church and give evidence that the circulatory system of love is working properly. Even if Ephesians 4:1–16 is familiar to you, you would benefit from pausing to read it again.

Please note that all three elements are important. Unity without diversity becomes uniformity, and uniformity is deadening and boring. But diversity without unity usually becomes anarchy, "everyone [doing] what [is] right in his own eyes" (Judg. 17:6; 21:25); and anarchy is dangerous and destructive. Uniformity produces a citadel church that never changes, but anarchy produces a chameleon church that is always changing. Uniformity is safe and comfortable, but dull; anarchy is exciting but threatening.

Fortunately, we don't have to make a choice because both unity and diversity are necessary. Many images of the church found in the New Testament illustrate the significance of diversity in unity and unity in diversity. The church is a family, made up of diverse individuals who share the same kinship. The church is an army (Eph. 6:10–20; 2 Tim. 2:3–4), fighting a common enemy and obeying a common Commander; but each individual soldier has his or her own job to do. The church is a holy temple and a holy priesthood (1 Peter 2:5, 9), each stone in its own special place, each priest doing the work God assigned.

But the one image that expresses this truth most vividly is that of the body, because each of us has a body and we understand from experience what it means to have individual parts functioning in unity. When one part of the body "decides" to become independent, we experience pain and develop problems; and sometimes drastic steps have to be taken to restore health. As a member of the body of Christ, I must discover what function the Spirit has chosen for me in the ministry of the body; and I must be faithful to do it. But I must do it in love because apart from love, the body can't grow as it should.

Maturity keeps unity and diversity in balance and prevents them from destroying each other and the church, but maturity is characterized by love. In that great chapter on love, Paul wrote, "When I was a child, I spoke as a child, I understood as a child, I thought as a child; but when I became a man, I put away childish things" (1 Cor. 13:11). He also wrote, "Brethren, do not be children in understanding; however, in malice be babes, but in understanding be mature" (1 Cor. 14:20). In the Ephesians 4 passage, the unity of the Spirit and the gifts of the Spirit are for the purpose of maturity,

> for the equipping of the saints for the work of ministry, for the edifying of the body of Christ, till we all come to the unity of the faith and the knowledge of the Son of God, to a perfect man, to the measure of the stature of the fullness of Christ; that we should no longer be children . . . but, speaking the truth in love, may grow up in all things into Him (vv. 12–15).

So, the local church is a fellowship of believers whose spiritual leaders help them discover, develop, and use their spiritual gifts so that each person may effectively encourage and enable other believers to serve and thereby build up the body of Christ. But all of this must be done in an atmosphere of love, as Paul expressed it, "speaking the truth in love" (Eph. 4:15).

Now we can better understand why believers individually and churches collectively too often have problems that lead to dissension and division. Selfishness and sin block the circulatory system, and the results are division instead of unity, competition instead of diversity, and childishness instead of maturity. When we should be nurturing unity, diversity, and maturity in the body of Christ, we allow immaturity to produce competition and competition to cause disunity.

Children are often competitive and don't handle diversity and unpredictability too well. There is security in sameness—the same bedtime story, the same favorite toy, the same blanket. They're happy when things are going their accustomed way, and childish adults are just like them. The older we get, the less we enjoy change; and so diversity becomes a threat to us. The only way we can enjoy church is to keep everything uniform; and if we have to declare war to get things our way, well, we'll declare war!

THE TRUTH IN THE BODY

We, as God's people, grow and become more like Christ as we are nourished by truth that is shared in love. Not truth alone, but truth ministered in love. It has well been said that truth without love is brutality, but love without truth is hypocrisy; and we don't want to be guilty of either sin. When I'm waiting to be introduced to speak at a meeting, I sincerely pray to the Father, "Please, fill my mind with truth and fill my heart with love. Help me to speak the truth in love." I hope He has always answered that prayer.

The enemy of unity is division, and the professing church today is divided. When we sing "Onward, Christian Soldiers!" we bravely harmonize the words, "We are not divided/All one body we"; but everybody knows better. Yes, from God's point of view, the church is indeed one body and one army. We don't manufacture unity; we maintain it

(Eph. 4:3). But from the world's point of view, the church is a divided army and, even worse, an army at war with itself.[5]

Tradition tells us that the first-century pagans beheld the members of the apostolic church and exclaimed, "Behold, how they love one another!" But by the time of the reign of the emperor Julian (361–63), the situation had changed; and the pagans could honestly say, "Behold, how they fight one another!" According to the fourth-century historian Ammianus Marcellinus, the emperor "had learned that the hatred of wild beasts for man is less than the ferocity of most Christians toward one another."[6]

If Christians don't speak the truth in love, then they speak lies with malice and hatred. Love builds, but hatred destroys. Truth brings people together, but lies shatter togetherness. When we believe the truth, the Spirit of truth can go to work in us and through us and edify the church; but when we believe a lie, we open the door for Satan to work in our fellowship and produce division and destruction.

During my years of ministry, I've preached in churches that were orthodox and proud of it; but while I was with them, I didn't sense the family love that should accompany devotion to God's truth. I've also preached in churches that have boasted of their love, but you would have had to use a magnifying glass to find any truth in their fellowship, either doctrinal or personal. The people were practicing a form of religious flattery that prevented them from being lovingly honest with one another and with the Lord. To sacrifice integrity for unity and then call it love is to abandon truth and cultivate hypocrisy.

There is a kind of cultic church that's dangerous to true spiritual growth because it teaches biblical truth but doesn't do it in an atmosphere of love. Instead of unity, there is a uniformity that comes from strong control at the top, an almost totalitarian management of people's minds and lives. Diversity isn't permitted; the leaders, who are pretty much isolated from the people, know God's will and everybody must submit. While the members of the church grow in knowledge because the Bible is taught, they don't grow in grace. The legalistic atmosphere of the church keeps them dependent. The ministry in these churches majors on guilt, not grace; and those who leave the fellowship for another church are branded as traitors and treated like lepers.[7]

Unfortunately, some cultic churches grow because they attract many people who have deep, hidden needs that must be met. These people are frightened by changes in their world, and they're looking for security; they're lonely and inadequate and need identity; and they're angry at life and need some acceptable way to vent their hostility. The cultic church provides all that they need: strong, omniscient leaders give frightened people security; membership in something successful gives inadequate people identity; and the "we/they" approach to the Christian faith gives angry people opportunity to express their hostility against everybody who disagrees with them. It isn't the ideal atmosphere for spiritual growth, and yet enough biblical truth is taught (but not in love) to maintain the veneer of evangelical respectability.

DIVERSITY IN THE BODY

Some pastors in America are trapped in a ministry time warp, especially those who were trained in the forties and fifties. For some reason, they refuse to deal with diversity and will not take the lead in bringing constructive changes into the church. Now all they can do is watch their local body hemorrhage and die as people escape to other fellowships. If they were "speaking the truth in love," they would be making the eternal truth relevant to the needs of people today; and they'd also be encouraging their people to express their faith in ways that are meaningful and mature. Remember, as a family grows, its members must make changes.

God gave me and my wife four wonderful children; and as these children matured, we had to make adjustments in our home. There were menu changes, schedule changes, budget changes, furniture changes (you don't expect a teenager to sleep in a crib), and even changes in the way we exercised our authority as parents. When you love your children, you show that love by practicing and applying the truth in ways that encourage the children to mature.

The local church is a family composed of spiritual children at various stages of maturity, and each of these precious children of God deserves loving personal attention. "But we were gentle among you," wrote Paul to a group of new believers, "just as a nursing mother cherishes her own children . . . as you know how we exhorted, and com-

forted, and charged every one of you, as a father does his own children"
(1 Thess. 2:7, 11). You can preach to people by the acre; but if you want
to really minister to them and help them grow, you need that personal
touch. Jesus and Paul had time for individuals, and so should we.

There are at least forty-five "one another" statements in the New
Testament, including a dozen "love one another" statements;[8] and if
we obeyed these admonitions, our churches would experience fewer
problems.

Take, for instance, the vexing problem of maintaining church unity
when Christians disagree over religious practices, such as what to eat,
what to wear, how to celebrate special days, what kind of music to
encourage in the church, which translation of the Bible to use, and so
on. These practical matters aren't as important as doctrine, yet they've
been the cause of much dissension and division among God's people
and have even become tests of spirituality and of fellowship.

In one church where I was to speak, an older gentleman approached
me and said, "I notice that in your books, you sometimes quote ——,"
and he named a popular paraphrase of the Bible.

"When I write," I replied, "I quote whatever translation best says
what I want to teach at that point in the book. When I quote from any
book, it doesn't mean I approve of everything in it."

"Well, I'm not going to sit and listen to a man who has no convictions about the Word of God!" he almost shouted, and he turned and
stormed out of the church in anger, disobeying the very Bible he
thought he was defending. I wish he had stayed around long enough for
us to talk quietly about the matter of translations. We might have
helped each other.

When I was ministering over the international "Back to the Bible"
radio network, the staff and I had constant problems with some listeners' responses to broadcast music. Some listeners thought it was too traditional, while others said it was too "contemporary and worldly" and
wanted us to drop orchestrations and go back to piano and organ
accompaniment. When we introduced a synthesizer, you would have
thought we'd denied the virgin birth. A few listeners wrote, "I'll never
again listen to your program or support your work!"

But the first step toward solving problems that arise over diversity is to recognize the fact that God has wisely put diversity into His church, as He has into the human family and the human body, so that the church can be a living body that grows and matures, and not an embalmed corpse that has a name saying it's alive but is dead. Without diversity and differences, faced honestly and handled lovingly, no family, marriage, industry, or church could ever mature. It would remain stagnant.[9]

When you read Romans 14—15, you discover that Paul prescribes some "one anothers" to help us mature and not destroy diversity for the sake of uniformity. "Receive one another" (14:1; 15:7) instructs us not to make these minor differences a test of fellowship. The Jewish believer who still shuns pork must not be criticized by the gentile believer who understands that all foods are lawful. We don't make days and diets a test of church membership or of personal fellowship.

Then Paul admonishes us not to judge one another (14:4, 10–13). We can't see our brother's or sister's heart as God can, and we'll have enough to do to give our own account to the Lord. We should bear with one another (15:1) and seek to please one another (15:2).

Paul encourages us, "Therefore let us pursue the things which make for peace and the things by which one may edify another" (14:19). The whole reason for loving those we disagree with is so that all of us will be able to be edified, to grow up and enjoy the privileges of Christian maturity. We don't pamper weak Christians so they'll stay weak or coddle immature Christians so they'll remain childish. Rather, we love them and protect them so they'll have time to mature in the Lord and come to appreciate and be able to handle the freedom they have in Christ.

Some people in the church have read Romans 14—15 in a mirror and gotten the whole thing backward. They think that strong Christians are the nitpickers who are afraid of freedom, who maintain the traditional practices, while weak Christians are the ones who appreciate diversity and have learned to live with it. Just the opposite is true. Weak Christians can't handle freedom, must have inflexible rules to obey, and are threatened by diversity. The weak criticize the strong, but the strong must be careful not to despise the weak. Dealing with diversity helps all of us grow *if we love one another.*[10]

LOVE

Here are a few "one another" statements that we can obey and thereby manifest Christian love toward one another:

Be kindly affectionate to one another (Rom. 12:10).

Admonish one another (Rom. 15:14).

Through love serve one another (Gal. 5:13).

Be kind to one another (Eph. 4:32).

Forgiving one another (Col. 3:13).

Exhort [encourage] one another (Heb. 3:13).

Do not grumble against one another (James 5:9).

Pray for one another (James 5:16).

Put these—and all the others—together, and they add up to "love one another." We grow in an atmosphere of love.

Chapter 11

CHRISTLIKENESS: BECOMING MORE LIKE JESUS

"**Y**ou will be like God!"

That was Satan's promise to our first parents (Gen. 3:5), a promise that is still believed by most of the world today. Whether in the corridors of government, the halls of ivy, or the latest New Age seminar, frightened people continue to grasp desperately for anything that will help them get control of life. Though this promise comes from the pit of hell, millions are hoping it will lift them to the gates of heaven.

God's answer to Satan's "You will be like God" is this: "We shall be like Him [Jesus], for we shall see Him as He is" (1 John 3:2).

MORE LIKE JESUS

"The true nature of a thing," wrote Aristotle, "is the highest that it can become."

That statement encourages me when I grudgingly sweep the autumn acorns off my driveway. As I sweep, I remind myself that these pesky seeds aren't acorns at all; they're potential oak trees, like the three that grace our front yard. I must remember that when the neighborhood children disturb my nap or threaten my wife's garden, because one of them might be a future president of the United States. The professor who bowed respectfully to his students each morning as he entered the classroom was doing a wise thing. For all he knew, in that room might sit another Churchill, Mozart, Amy Carmichael, or Dorothy Sayers.

If you and I had been watching God at work on the sixth day of creation, we might not have been impressed with what He did when He created the first human. After all, Adam was made out of clay, which isn't the most beautiful or valuable material available, and he was created to exist only a breath away from death. He didn't have the mighty powers given to the angels, and unlike the angels, he had to eat and sleep to survive. But our first parents had something that belonged to no other creature in the universe, including the angels: *they were created in the image of* God.[1]

The implications of this fact are staggering. For one thing, it ought to humble us when we realize the high position God has given us in His creation. No wonder David asked, "What is man that You are mindful of him, and the son of man that You visit him?" (Ps. 8:4). We have fragile bodies, finite minds and, because of Adam's fall, sinful and rebellious hearts; and yet God pays attention to us! Why? The answer is plain: we are made in the image of God, and this means that we have the potential for one day sharing His likeness!

Realizing that we're made in the image of God not only should humble us, but it should also encourage us to seek the God who made us and who alone can meet the needs of the inner person. Being made in the image of God means that we are basically *spiritual* beings. Like the God who made us, we have a mind to think with, emotions to feel with, and a will for making decisions. We possess a spirit within[2] that can't be satisfied by the things that so easily gratify the body. What God provided on earth can sustain and satisfy our physical nature—air, water, food, sunshine, shelter—but they won't sustain the inner person. Augustine was right when he wrote on the first page of his *Confessions,* "Thou hast formed us for Thyself, and our hearts are restless til they find rest in Thee."

The most fulfilling challenge God's children can experience in this life is the challenge of becoming more like Jesus Christ.

THE GLORY OF GOD

Some people are shocked to discover that Jesus didn't die on the cross simply to forgive our sins, solve our problems, and one day take us to heaven. Although all these blessings and much more are included in

CHRISTLIKENESS

God's great plan of redemption, the overriding purpose of it all is *the glory of God*. In his great hymn of praise to the Trinity in Ephesians 1:3–14, Paul reminds us of this purpose three times: "to the praise of the glory of His grace . . . to the praise of His glory . . . to the praise of His glory" (vv. 6, 12, 14).

God's great eternal purpose is that one day God's people shall be "conformed to the image of His Son" (Rom. 8:29) and glorify God for ever. This will happen when Jesus Christ returns and gives us glorified bodies. Scripture describes this momentous event like this:

Beloved, now we are children of God; and it has not yet been revealed what we shall be, but we know that when He is revealed, we shall be like Him, for we shall see Him as He is (1 John 3:2).

And as we have borne the image of the man of dust, we shall also bear the image of the heavenly Man (1 Cor. 15:49).

For our citizenship is in heaven, from which we also eagerly wait for the Savior, the Lord Jesus Christ, who will transform our lowly body that it may be conformed to His glorious body, according to the working by which He is able even to subdue all things to Himself (Phil. 3:20–21).

For the trumpet will sound, and the dead will be raised incorruptible, and we shall be changed (1 Cor. 15:52).

With wonderful glorified bodies, we'll be able to dwell forever in a glorious new home, a city so magnificent that the apostle John almost reached the limits of human language as he described it (Rev. 21—22). One approach he took was to tell us what *wouldn't* be there: pain, tears, darkness, death, sorrow, and the curse that has blighted creation ever since Adam sinned. He wrote, "They shall see His face. . . . And they shall reign forever and ever" (Rev. 22:4–5). What a future!

Please keep in mind that these indescribable blessings won't be provided by God just to make us eternally comfortable. The Christian vision of heaven is much greater than that. All that John described—

new bodies, a new heaven and earth—is part of God's eternal purpose that everything will redound "to the praise of the glory of His grace" (Eph. 1:6).

THE FULLNESS OF CHRIST

The fact that we're created in the image of God should elicit two responses from our hearts. First, we should be humbly grateful to the Lord for giving us such a privilege; and second, we should go only to the Lord for all that we need to satisfy the inner person. There is a third response: we should begin now to glorify the Lord by becoming more and more "conformed to the image of His Son" (Rom. 8:29). The return of Christ should motivate us to become like Him today: "And everyone who has this hope in Him purifies himself, just as He is pure" (1 John 3:3); "Therefore, since all these things will be dissolved, what manner of persons ought you to be in holy conduct and godliness?" (2 Peter 3:11).

God wants us to become like Jesus Christ because there is no higher purpose or goal for us to realize. We have His divine nature within (2 Peter 1:4). Paul called this goal "the measure of the stature of the fullness of Christ" (Eph. 4:13). So, becoming like Jesus Christ is not just our ultimate destiny; it's also our immediate responsibility. It's something that should claim our devotion day after day for the rest of our lives.

No matter how many people we may admire in this life, and even may want to imitate, none can take the place of Jesus Christ. The heroes of faith described in Hebrews 11 encourage us by their examples, but our responsibility is to keep "looking unto Jesus" (Heb. 12:2). That means keeping our eyes of faith on Him through the Word and allowing the Spirit of God to reproduce His image in us: "You have put off the old man with his deeds, and have put on the new man who is [being] renewed in knowledge according to the image of Him who created him" (Col. 3:9–10); "Therefore be imitators of God as dear children" (Eph. 5:1).

When he wrote his first epistle, the apostle John was concerned that his readers grasp the fact that God expected them to live like Jesus Christ. As you read his letter, you notice the phrase "as He is" repeated four times:

But if we walk in the light as He is in the light, we have fellowship with one another (1:7).

Little children, let no one deceive you. He who practices right-eousness is righteous, just as He is righteous (3:7).

But we know that when He is revealed, we shall be like Him, for we shall see Him as He is (3:2).

Because as He is, so are we in this world (4:17).

Just as Jesus Christ abides in the Father's love as He intercedes for us in heaven, so His people here on earth abide in Him and in His love; and this enables us to walk as He walked. Our Christlike life comes not so much from imitation as from identification with Christ. Because we abide in Him, we can depend on the Holy Spirit to help us become conformed to Christ's image both in character and in conduct.

This means *serving as He served*: "If I then, your Lord and Teacher, have washed your feet, you also ought to wash one another's feet. For I have given you an example, that you should do as I have done to you" (John 13:14–15). It also means *suffering as He suffered*: "For to this you were called, because Christ also suffered for us, leaving us an example, that you should follow His steps" (1 Peter 2:21). Paul called this "the fellowship of His sufferings" (Phil. 3:10).

A pastor friend, now in heaven, phoned to tell me that his church had asked for his resignation. He was physically challenged and ministered from a wheelchair; and he knew that, at his age, it would be difficult to get a call from another church.

"Well, my friend," I said, "you've been promoted to share in the fellowship of Christ's sufferings, and that's a pretty big promotion. When we start living the way Jesus lived, we're treated the way He was treated."

Christ is also our example in *sacrificing*: "For you know the grace of our Lord Jesus Christ, that though He was rich, for your sakes He became poor, that you through His poverty might become rich" (2 Cor. 8:9). We don't give to the Lord only because He commands it, or because it's an expression of Christian love, but because it's Christlike. If we want to walk as He walked, we must sacrifice as He sacrificed.

Paul admonishes us to follow His example of *submission* and to think as Jesus thought: "Let this mind [attitude] be in you which was also in Christ Jesus" (Phil. 2:5). Our Lord's example of humble submission and death—"even the death of the cross" (Phil. 2:8)—makes all our pride and religious pretense nothing but rubbish. He became a servant; too often we expect others to serve us. He emptied Himself; we frequently go around asking, "What will I get?" He "made Himself of no reputation" (Phil. 2:7); we tend to worry about what people think of us. We have a long way to go when it comes to thinking as Jesus thought and submitting as He submitted.

We ought to follow Christ's example in *sanctification*, setting ourselves apart to do the Father's will: "And for their sakes I sanctify Myself, that they also may be sanctified by the truth" (John 17:19). He has set Himself apart in heaven where He intercedes for us and perfects us to do His will (Heb. 13:20-21). We must set ourselves apart for God so that we can do His will and serve others.

The beatitudes (Matt. 5:3–12) and the fruit of the Spirit (Gal. 5:22–23) summarize the kind of Christlike character and conduct that ought to mark our lives. Add to these the many admonitions in Scripture that tell us how to think, speak, and act, and you have a portrait of the child of God who is being "conformed to the image of His Son" through the power of the indwelling Spirit of God.

Read Matthew, Mark, Luke, and John, and see what kind of life Jesus lived when He was here on earth. Discover how He ministered to both friends and enemies, how He answered false accusations, how He dealt with threats, how He shared God's love with sinners, and how He accepted suffering and death. This is the example you and I are to follow: "For it is God who works in you both to will and to do for His good pleasure" (Phil. 2:13).

"Few things are harder to put up with than the annoyance of a good example," wrote Mark Twain; but he was smiling as he wrote it. Twain knew full well that good examples encourage good character. "Example is the school of mankind," said Edmund Burke, "and they will learn at no other."

Several of our grandsons have decorated their rooms with the pictures of people they admire, mostly athletes. They watch the games to see what their heroes will do; and I don't doubt that this exposure, if properly handled, can motivate them to want to excel. Their parents wouldn't want pictures of cheap celebrities on their walls, because celebrities are manufactured by press agents. Real heroes, people worth emulating, are grown, not manufactured; and they know the meaning of discipline, hard work, and sacrifice, qualities that all of us ought to cultivate.

What the boys do with athletes, I do with preachers and writers. I have in my study and library pictures of some of my favorite preachers and writers, and seeing their faces day after day encourages me to do my best. I don't think they even know that their photographs are on my shelves and that they're quietly influencing me in my ministry, but they are. Some of them are already home in heaven, but they're still encouraging me.

"A holy life will produce the deepest impression," said evangelist D. L. Moody. "Lighthouses blow no horns; they only shine."

TOOLS OF GROWTH

The process of making us more like Jesus Christ involves a number of tools, the most important of which is the *Word of God.* I've quoted 2 Corinthians 3:18 before in these pages, but it's such a fundamental verse that I want to remind you of it again: "But we all, with unveiled face, beholding as in a mirror the glory of the Lord, are being transformed into the same image from glory to glory, just as by the Spirit of the Lord."

Before we can become like Christ, we must see Him in the Word. "Beholding" and "becoming" go together, and both require time. If you're in a hurry, you may run ahead of God and miss what He has for you. The Holy Spirit wants to show you the glory of the Savior in the Scriptures and give you your own daily "transfiguration" experience.

But please resist the temptation to follow Peter's suggestion to stay on the mountain, basking in the glory (Matt. 17:4). God blesses us so we can be blessings to others; He changes us so we can become change agents in a needy world. Unless the truth of the Word is translated into obedient service, we haven't really learned what the Spirit wanted to teach us. The blessing comes to us (and to others through us) not when we *hear* God's truth, but when we *do* it (James 1:22–25). "Christianity knows no truth which is not the child of love and the parent of duty," said Phillips Brooks; and he was right.

Another tool God uses is *people,* some of them loving and kind, some of them difffficult and abrasive. The first Christian in a family often creates division. "Do you suppose that I came to give peace on earth?" asked Jesus. "I tell you, not at all, but rather division" (Luke 12:51). The first Christian in an office or a schoolroom invites opposition, sometimes even a declaration of war. But our task is to love people and pray for them, especially the ones who oppose us, and do what Jesus would do.

If we look at difffficult people as obstacles, we'll miss the best God has for us. But if we see them as opportunities God gives us for growth, then something wonderful can happen. Unsaved spouses or children, unbelieving fellow employees or supervisors, ungodly neighbors, all of them can either tear us down or build us up, depending on how we relate to them. Joseph forgave his hateful brothers and willingly worked for the keeper of the prison, and Paul stopped the jailer (who beat him) from committing suicide. Jesus prayed for those who crucified Him, and Stephen asked God to forgive those who were stoning him. No wonder Stephen's face glowed with the glory of God!

Difficult circumstances can also become tools in God's hands to make us more like Christ. A faith that can't be tested can't be trusted, so God permits us to go through the furnace of testing to strengthen and purify our faith (1 Peter 1:3–9). "But He knows the way that I take," said suffering Job. "When He has tested me, I shall come forth as gold" (Job 23:10).

When we kind ourselves in difficult circumstances, we must ask, "Am I here because I'm obedient or disobedient to the Lord?" Jonah got into a storm because he disobeyed God, but the disciples sailed into a storm because they obeyed what Jesus told them to do (Matt. 14:22–23). If we're obeying the will of God, then the storm can't harm us, and the Lord will work out His perfect plan.

However, sometimes the Lord permits His faithful and obedient children seemingly to fail. Hebrews 11:4–35 records the experiences of people who saw God do miracles because they trusted Him; but right in the middle of verse 35, the picture changes: "Others were tortured, not accepting deliverance. . . . Still others had trial of mockings and scourgings, yes, and of chains and imprisonment. They were stoned . . . sawn in two . . . slain with the sword" (vv. 35–37). These believers appeared to be losers, but they were just as much men and women of faith as the people who experienced miracles. God didn't choose to deliver them; instead, He gave them the grace to endure pain and to triumph in the midst of seeming defeat.

When trouble comes, many of God's children find encouragement in quoting Romans 8:28—"And we know that all things work together for good to those who love God, to those who are the called according to His purpose"—but they should go on to verse 29 to remind themselves that "His purpose" is that they might "be conformed to the image of His Son, that He might be the firstborn among many brethren." The glory in the future gives us the strength we need to endure the suffering in the present.

But for difficult circumstances to make us like Christ, we must respond to them as Christ did:

Who for the joy that was set before Him endured the cross (Heb. 12:2).

Who, when He was reviled, did not revile in return; when He suffered, He did not threaten, but committed Himself to Him who judges righteously (1 Peter 2:23).

He was oppressed and He was afflicted,
Yet He opened not His mouth.
He was led as a lamb to the slaughter,
And as a sheep before its shearers is silent,
So He opened not His mouth (Isa. 53:7).

What they did to Jesus was illegal, and He endured it; but that may not be God's plan for all of us. For instance, the apostle Paul used his

Roman citizenship to protect himself, his associates, and the reputation of the gospel. In Philippi (Acts 16:35–40) and in Jerusalem (Acts 22:22–29), his Roman citizenship turned the tables on his persecutors; and in Caesarea, Paul used his citizenship to save his life and get him to Rome (Acts 25:1–12). So, there are times when believers submit to unjust laws and willingly suffer; but there are also times when they use their rights to protect and to further the gospel. But they must beware of breaking the law in order to promote the work of God: "But let none of you suffer as a murderer, a thief, an evildoer, or as a busybody in other people's matters" (1 Peter 4:15). The end does not justify the means.

AN ALTERNATE PLAN

Satan's boast was, "I will be like the Most High" (Isa. 14:14).[3] But no angel, including Satan, can ever become like the Most High; therefore, Satan rigorously opposes those who strive to obey God and become like Christ. He offers them his alternate promise and plan: "You will be like God" (Gen. 3:5).

What does Satan's plan involve? Genesis 3:1–5 tells us.

First, *he wants us to abandon the Word of God.* Satan questions the truth of God's Word when he asks, "Has God indeed said . . . ?" (v. 1). If the enemy can get us to doubt the Scriptures, he knows that before long we will start to neglect the Scriptures; and the next step will be to disobey the Scriptures. A survey of several hundred ministers who had fallen into immorality revealed that they came to the place in their lives where they stopped having a daily devotional time. It's dangerous to ignore your Bible. The Book of Proverbs emphasizes,

When wisdom enters your heart,
And knowledge is pleasant to your soul,
Discretion will preserve you;
Understanding will keep you (2:10–11).

Second, *Satan demands that we believe his word instead of God's Word.* He particularly wants us to think that there are no consequences to our disobedience. "You will not surely die" (v. 4) is his promise. When Satan tempts us, he whispers, "You can get away with this!" If we listen to him and then sin, he begins to accuse us and to shout, "You will never get away with this!" If we don't want to hear him shout, we must pay no attention to his whisper.

The world today pays little attention to consequences and lives as though sowing isn't ultimately followed by reaping. The bad things you read about in the newspapers happen to somebody else. Neither the possibility of pregnancy nor the fear of disease can keep people from indulging in illicit sex; in fact, society now says there is no such thing as illicit sex because it claims there are no moral absolutes.

It used to be that the people who broke God's moral law were called sinners, but today they're called victims. That means somebody else is to blame. Not only have we abandoned God's moral law, but we've completely done away with accountability.

Third, *we determine for ourselves what's good and what's evil*. Satan declares, "Your eyes will be opened, and you will be like God, knowing good and evil" (v. 5). "What's good is what you feel good after; what's bad is what you feel bad after." That was said by a famous American novelist who closed his career by committing suicide, but many people who read his books agree with him. According to Satan's philosophy, objective truth is replaced by subjective feeling; and each person has the right to decide what's good and what's evil.

The magic words today are *pluralism* and *tolerance*. We live in a pluralistic society in which many things are legal that are not moral or scriptural, but it isn't politically correct to pass judgment on people you disagree with. Unmarried couples can legally live together, and people of the same sex can legally be married and even adopt children, but you dare not criticize them. "After all," say the apostles of tolerance, "it's their business what they do; and we all have the privilege of deciding for ourselves what's good and what's bad."

The upshot of following this satanic philosophy is that each person becomes his or her own god, deciding what's right and wrong and not worrying about the consequences, for there are no consequences. If this philosophy were applied to any other area of life—science, medicine, mechanics, banking—it would lead to unmitigated disaster. But it's permissible to apply it to human beings who will spend eternity either in heaven or in hell.

A MASQUERADE

Satan is a deceiver, a counterfeiter, a masquerader. Paul declared, "But I fear, lest somehow, as the serpent deceived Eve by his craftiness, so your minds may be corrupted from the simplicity that is in Christ" (2 Cor. 11:3). He deceives people by pretending to give them what they can get only from God.

If God plants good wheat ("the sons of the kingdom"), then Satan plants tares ("the sons of the wicked one" [Matt. 13:38]). If God offers sinners the righteousness of Christ, Satan offers them religious self-righteousness (Rom. 10:1–13; Phil. 3:4–11). If God's witnesses proclaim a gospel of salvation, so does Satan! Paul commented, "I marvel that you are turning away so soon from Him who called you in the grace of Christ, to a different gospel" (Gal. 1:6). There is only one saving gospel, and it's stated clearly in 1 Corinthians 15:1–8, but Satan has his counterfeit gospels.

God has ministers, but so does Satan:

> For such are false apostles, deceitful workers, transforming themselves into apostles of Christ. And no wonder! For Satan himself transforms himself into an angel of light. Therefore it is no great thing if his ministers also transform themselves into ministers of righteousness, whose end will be according to their works (2 Cor. 11:13–15).

The important word in that last quotation is *transform*. It isn't the same word Paul uses in Romans 12:2 or in 2 Corinthians 3:18. In those references, Paul uses the word that gives us our English word *metamorphosis*, an outward change that comes from within. When a caterpillar changes into a beautiful butterfly, the change comes from within as a part of its genetic structure. When Jesus was transfigured on the mountain, the glory came from within. The angels didn't shine a spotlight on Him! When Christians change and become more like Christ, the change comes from within by the working of the Holy Spirit.

The word translated "transform" in 2 Corinthians 11:13–15 means "to change in fashion or appearance." It describes merely an outward change, a masquerade that has nothing to do with the inner person. In other words, Satan appears to be an angel of light, but his basic nature hasn't changed. It's only a masquerade. His ministers appear to be ministers of righteousness, but this is only an outward show. Their hearts are still with the enemy.

To pretend to be something that we really are not is a form of hypocrisy. For example, Judas pretended to be a believer, a faithful disciple, and even a lover of the poor, but he was not a true believer or a faithful disciple (John 6:66–71; 12:1–8; 13:10–11, 18). Satan entered into Judas because Judas belonged to him (John 13:26–29). Judas betrayed Christ and then went and hanged himself. "You will be like God" and even exercise the power of life and death!

As God's children, we have the privilege of experiencing the true transfiguration (metamorphosis) that makes us "conformed to the image of His Son." As the Spirit transforms your mind, you don't want to be conformed to this world (Rom. 12:2). You will obey Colossians 3:2: "Set your mind on things above, not on things on the earth."[4]

We grow to a predetermined image, the image of Jesus Christ. Don't be deluded into a counterfeit transfiguration. Be sure that day by day the Holy Spirit is using God's Word to transform you and make you more like Jesus Christ in all that you are and all that you do.

Chapter 12

GLORY: MAGNIFYING HIS NAME

The main reason we want to mature as God's children is that we might bring glory to our heavenly Father, not only during our life on earth, but throughout eternity, for He saved us "to the praise of His glory" (Eph. 1:12).

As we obey Him and serve others, whatever blessings we experience are only by-products of the greater blessing of honoring and magnifying the Lord. One day, we all want to be able to say to the Father what Jesus said, "I have glorified You on the earth. I have finished the work which You have given Me to do" (John 17:4).

But what does it mean to "glorify God"? And how can frail creatures of clay ever glorify a God whose "greatness is unsearchable" (Ps. 145:3) and who dwells in "unapproachable light" (1 Tim. 6:16)? What do we have to offer Him?

HONOR TO THE MASTER

Glorifying God means making God look good before a disobedient and unbelieving world. It also means bringing joy to the holy angels who watch us and anger to Satan and his demons who hate us. As far as our frailty is concerned, the weaker the servant, the greater the honor to the Master: "But we have this treasure in earthen vessels, that the excellence of the power may be of God and not of us" (2 Cor. 4:7).

Glorifying God is young David shouting to the giant Goliath, "I come to you in the name of the LORD of hosts, the God of the armies of Israel, whom you have defied" (1 Sam. 17:45); and then slaying him with a single stone.

Glorifying God is Mary saying to Gabriel, "Behold the maidservant of the Lord! Let it be to me according to your word" (Luke 1:38). It's Stephen asking God to forgive his murderers (Acts 7:60), and Paul and Silas singing hymns of praise at midnight in a Roman prison (Acts 16:25).

Glorifying God is Amy Carmichael in India rescuing children from bondage and managing the whole enterprise from a sickbed. It's William Wilberforce in Parliament fighting to outlaw the slave trade. It's Martin Luther saying, "Here I stand! I can do no other!" It's blind Fanny Crosby writing beautiful songs for Christians to sing. And it's Joni Eareckson Tada bringing hope to physically challenged people around the world, and doing it from a wheelchair.

But glorifying God is also that weary mother caring for her growing family, and that older husband standing by his wife of many years as she suffers from Alzheimer's disease. It's that lonely widow sacrificing to support a missionary, and that missionary sacrificing to take the gospel to a forgotten people. It's millions of anonymous Christians manifesting Christ's love in difficult places and doing the impossible day after day because they love God and want to please Him.

I once received a letter from a radio listener with a five-dollar bill enclosed to be used for world missions. The writer explained that she was a widow, living alone on a meager pension, but that she was able to save money to give to God's work by having no hot water in her little house, taking no newspapers or magazines, having no telephone, and being careful in her shopping for the few food items she felt she needed.

I'm still deeply moved when I think of that letter and how I had to do some serious heart-searching of my own before I could answer it. I felt like David holding that cup of water in the cave and knowing how much it cost (2 Sam. 23:13–17). I don't even remember that woman's name, but God knows her; and He will honor her for honoring Him. That five dollars surely accomplished some great things for God! The writer to the Hebrews tells us, "For God is not unjust to forget your work and labor of love which you have shown toward His name, in that you have ministered to the saints, and do minister" (6:10).

We glorify God when, by His grace, we do what people don't expect us to do, things they wouldn't do for us; and we do it because we love Jesus. Paul described it best:

> We are hard pressed on every side, yet not crushed; we are perplexed, but not in despair; persecuted, but not forsaken; struck down, but not destroyed—always carrying about in the body the dying of the Lord Jesus, that the life of Jesus also may be manifested in our body. For we who live are always delivered to death for Jesus' sake, that the life of Jesus also may be manifested in our mortal flesh (2 Cor. 4:8–11).

Glorifying God means living for the eternal, living by faith, willing to endure the "sufferings of this present time" (Rom. 8:18) because we know the Father's "Well done!" will be heard one of these days. Glorifying God means willing to become nothing that Christ may be everything.

THE HUMBLE BUSH

Moses saw the glory of God in a burning bush that wasn't consumed (Ex. 3). The fire represented God's glory,[1] but what did the bush represent? Perhaps it represented the children of Israel, for the presence of God's glory was one of the special blessings God gave them (Rom. 9:4). But I think that the humble bush represented Moses himself and that God was showing Moses that he could accomplish the tasks God would assign him if he would put the glory of God first in his life.

Consider Moses' situation at that time, a situation you may have been in yourself. I've been there, and I'm grateful for God's patience with me when I saw only my own unfitness for the task and not the greatness of a God who can ignite a little bush.

Moses had spent forty years in Egypt receiving the finest education a leader could have in that day; but in his zeal to help his people, he had killed a man (probably in self-defense) and fled the country. Then he spent forty more years as a shepherd, a strange occupation for a man who was "learned in all the wisdom of the Egyptians . . . mighty in words and deeds" (Acts 7:22). Talk about being overqualified!

Moses was sure that he was a failure, that all his training in Egypt had been wasted, and that he'd be a shepherd for the rest of his life. But God had other plans for him. It's as though the Lord said to him, "Moses, do you see that bush? Of itself, it's weak and ordinary, but joined to My power and glory, it's something extraordinary. That's what I want to do with you. I want to ignite you and use you to accomplish great things that will glorify My name. I want you to deliver My people from the bondage of Egypt."

At that point, Moses took his eyes off the burning bush, looked at himself, and asked, "Who am I?" as he began to argue with God. That's a dangerous thing to do. When God calls us to serve Him, the weaker we are, the more we can glorify His name; but we must look at His greatness, not our weakness. Peter made the same mistake when he said to Jesus, "Depart from me, for I am a sinful man, O Lord!" (Luke 5:8). Peter lived long enough to be thankful that his prayer went unanswered.

God had already told Moses who and what he was: he was a weak bush that could become a flaming servant and accomplish mighty works for God. If we're to glorify God, it's important that we see ourselves as God sees us. Gideon was hiding in a winepress when God said to him, "The LORD is with you, you mighty man of valor!" (Judg. 6:12). And Saul of Tarsus was a blind, hungry, broken man when God called him "a chosen vessel of Mine" (Acts 9:15). What really counts is what God says about us, not what we think about ourselves.

Make up your mind now that, no matter how much you may have failed in the past or how weak and insignificant you may feel, God can use you to glorify Him. Let Him ignite the bush. You won't be consumed, but He will be glorified.

AN EXAMPLE TO UNBELIEVERS

Glorifying God begins with salvation, an experience that Paul compared to God's creation work in Genesis 1: "For it is the God who commanded light to shine out of darkness, who has shone in our hearts to give the light of the knowledge of the glory of God in the face of Jesus

Christ" (2 Cor. 4:6). We heard God's "Let there be light" (Gen. 1:3), we believed, and we became new creations in Jesus Christ. The glory moved in.

Glorifying God begins with salvation, but it continues with sanctification, submitting to the work of God in our lives. After causing the light to shine in the darkness, God then *formed* and *filled* what He had created because "the earth was without form, and void" (Gen. 1:2). He formed land and filled it with animals and vegetation; He formed seas and filled them with aquatic creatures; and He formed the heavens and filled them with stars and planets. In response to the word of God ("Let there be!"), the Holy Spirit brought order where there was chaos and fullness where there was emptiness; and He can do that in our lives. As the character of Jesus Christ is formed in us, we bring glory to the Father.

But the same God who works in us also works *through* us; like Jesus, we become servants:

> Let your light so shine before men, that they may see your good works and glorify your Father in heaven (Matt. 5:16).

> Having your conduct honorable among the Gentiles [unbelievers], that when they speak against you as evildoers, they may, by your good works which they observe, glorify God in the day of visitation (1 Peter 2:12).

Peter wrote to Christians in five Roman provinces who were having a difficult time with their unbelieving neighbors. He told them that *doing good* was the best way to get the attention of the unbelievers and gain opportunities for witness (1 Peter 2:14–15, 20; 3:11, 13, 16–17; 4:19). It takes more than conducting services, passing out literature, leading protests, and opposing sin to convince a pagan world that God loves sinners and can forgive them and make them His children. It also demands demonstrating that love by means of good works. Jesus "went about doing good" (Acts 10:38), and we should follow His example. After all, we have been "created in Christ Jesus for good works, which God prepared beforehand that we should walk in them" (Eph. 2:10).

What would happen if the available believers in a church would go to their local city hall and volunteer to help in any way they were needed? Are there parks that need cleaning up, school crossings that need guarding, older people who need assistance with their shopping, children who need watching? Aren't these good works that can be done in the name of Jesus Christ and to the glory of God? Although they aren't a substitute for a direct witness of Christ and the gospel, good works certainly make it easier to share God's love with the lost.

Christians can even glorify God by their death. Jesus said that the death of His friend Lazarus was "for the glory of God, that the Son of God may be glorified through it" (John 11:4); and He informed Peter "by what death he would glorify God" (John 21:19). Stephen, the man with the "face of an angel" (Acts 6:15), glorified God in the way he died; and he left such a powerful witness behind that it touched the heart of Saul of Tarsus (Acts 7:54–60; 22:20).

THE LITTLE THINGS

God probably won't call most of us to glorify Him as David did, by slaying a giant, or to be like Joshua and open up rivers and shout down city walls. But if we ask ourselves how we can do each day's work to the glory of God, then we'll be following in their train. And we'll be heeding this admonition: "Therefore, whether you eat or drink, or whatever you do, do all to the glory of God" (1 Cor. 10:31).

You can even purchase fuel for your car to the glory of God. Years ago, an evangelist friend told me about a friend who was driving him to a meeting when he discovered the gas gauge was very low. They passed several filling stations, and my friend wondered why the man didn't stop at one of them; but he just kept saying to himself, "Okay, Lord, not this one or this one." Then they came to a station that was really only a shack; and his driver said, "Okay, Lord, this is it!" and pulled in.

The man who came out to serve them had a tumor that so disfigured his face that it was difficult to look at him. But the driver got out of the car and chatted with the man while he pumped the gas. He went into the shack with him to pay the bill but didn't come out for several minutes. When he did come out, he announced, "Well, he trusted the Lord! That's why the Lord brought us here!"

You can even mow the lawn to the glory of God. One Saturday, I noticed that a new neighbor was having trouble with his power mower. I walked across the street and asked how I could help. I offered to mow his lawn while he went to get his mower fixed, or he could use my mower until his own was repaired. From this contact, I had the privilege of later seeing him come to Christ, and I had the joy of baptizing him and receiving him into our fellowship.

You can even be friendly to the glory of God. While visiting an acquaintance in the hospital, I noticed a teenage boy in the room with his leg in an elevated cast. He was looking very glum, so before leaving the room, I stopped to chat.

"Sorry to see you're trussed up like that," I said. "At least you don't have to go to school."

"I'd rather be in school," he replied sullenly.

"What's your name.?"

"Daniel."

"Are you like Daniel in the Bible?" I asked.

"I'm not like *anybody* in the Bible!" he answered. "But I wish I could be."

With a reply like that as an opener, it didn't take long to explain the gospel and lead Daniel to faith in Christ. God had prepared him, and I was grateful I'd taken time to be friendly.

We don't always get to witness to everybody we help, and we don't always have the joy of seeing everybody we witness to receive Christ; but that shouldn't discourage us. Our kindness and our witness to the glory of God will prepare those people to meet the next Christian God brings across their path, and who knows what may happen?

FROM CREATION TO ETERNITY

It's interesting to trace the glory of God in the Bible.

God's glory was first manifested in creation: "The heavens declare the glory of God" (Ps. 19:1). Moses and the people of Israel saw God's glory at Mount Sinai when God gave them His law (Ex. 19). When Moses dedicated the tabernacle, the glory of God moved in (Ex. 40:34–35; Lev. 9:22–24). Sad to say, the people of Israel sinned, and there came a day of defeat when Ichabod, "the glory has departed," described their spiritual plight (1 Sam. 4:21).

Solomon built the temple; and when it was dedicated to God, the glory once more moved in (2 Chron. 7:1–3). But once again the people sinned, and the prophet Ezekiel watched God's glory depart from the temple (Ezek. 8:1–4; 9:3; 10:4, 18; 11:22–23). Ezekiel also had a vision of the day when God's glory would once again return (43:1–5).

The glory of God came to earth when Jesus was born (Luke 2:8–14). John summed it up this way: "And the Word became flesh and dwelt among us, and we beheld His glory, the glory as of the only begotten of the Father, full of grace and truth" (John 1:14). Sinful men took the Lord of glory and nailed Him to a cross (1 Cor. 2:8); He arose from the dead; and then He ascended to heaven.

On earth today, the glory of God resides in God's people individually (1 Cor. 6:19–20) and the church collectively, which is God's temple (John 17:22; Eph. 2:21–22). When God's children gather for worship, the glory of God ought to be so evident that it brings fear and conviction to any unbeliever who happens to attend the service (Acts 5:11–14). Paul painted this picture of the unbeliever: "And thus the secrets of his heart are revealed; and so, falling down on his face, he will worship God and report that God is truly among you" (1 Cor. 14:25).

Our destiny is the heavenly Jerusalem where the glory of God will bathe the city in eternal light: "The city had no need of the sun or of the moon to shine in it, for the glory of God illuminated it. The Lamb is its light" (Rev. 21:23). This will be in answer to our Lord's request, "Father, I desire that they also whom You gave Me may be with Me where I am, that they may behold My glory which You have given Me" (John 17:24). As Paul expressed it, we "rejoice in hope of the glory of God" (Rom. 5:2).

THE BRIGHT SIDE OF TRIBULATION

Meanwhile, as we wait for our Lord to return, our task is to reveal His glory on this earth wherever He puts us and by whatever means He gives to us. In the Christian life, there is no such thing as secular and sacred. Whatever we do in the will of God, we can do to the glory of

God (1 Cor. 10:31). It really doesn't matter what people do to us, think of us, or say about us. The important thing is that the name of the Lord be glorified.

One special way we can glorify the Lord is through personal suffering, particularly when we're persecuted because of our faith in Christ. Peter declared, "Yet if anyone suffers as a Christian, let him not be ashamed, but let him glorify God in this matter" (1 Peter 4:16). And the apostles had firsthand experience: "So they departed from the presence of the council, rejoicing that they were counted worthy to suffer shame for His name" (Acts 5:41).

Godliness and suffering go together: "All who desire to live godly in Christ Jesus will suffer persecution" (2 Tim. 3:12). If your desire is for godliness, and I hope it is, then your destiny is to go through the furnace of suffering because an ungodly world doesn't appreciate the example of a holy life. The world treats us the way it treated Jesus: "If the world hates you, you know that it hated Me before it hated you. If you were of the world, the world would love its own. Yet because you are not of the world, but I chose you out of the world, therefore the world hates you" (John 15:18–19).

Whether it's personal physical suffering—and God's people have their share of the common burdens of life—or suffering because of the faith, the vital thing is that God be glorified. Like Paul, I should have the desire that "Christ will be magnified in my body, whether by life or by death" (Phil. 1:20). Suffering today for the sake of Christ means glory tomorrow in the presence of Christ: "For our light affliction, which is but for a moment, is working for us a far more exceeding and eternal weight of glory" (2 Cor. 4:17). No matter how much we may hurt, we can have the confidence of Job: "But He knows the way that I take; when He has tested me, I shall come forth as gold" (Job 23:10).

"The right side is not always the bright side immediately," said Vance Havner, "but it will be ultimately. 'In the world you will have tribulation'—that is the dark side. 'But be of good cheer, I have overcome the world'—that is the bright side."[2]

When you and I by faith see "the bright side" of suffering, then the lost world will see the glory of God in our lives. Stephen saw Jesus in heaven, and his face radiated the glory of God (Acts 6:15; 7:54–60).

Stephen is a good example for us to follow: he looked up and saw Jesus, he prayed for his persecutors, and he submitted to the will of God. The result? The chief persecutor eventually was converted!

Part 3

THE MATURING CHRISTIAN

*Till we all come to the unity of the faith
and the knowledge of the Son of God,
to a perfect man, to the measure of the
stature of the fullness of Christ.*
Ephesians 4:13

Chapter 13

MATURITY: REACHING THE GOAL OF CHRISTIAN LIVING

A child's first maturing experience is probably that of weaning, and a difficult experience it is. David describes it in Psalm 131:

LORD, my heart is not haughty,
Nor my eyes lofty.
Neither do I concern myself with great matters,
Nor with things too profound for me.
Surely I have calmed and quieted my soul,
Like a weaned child with his mother;
Like a weaned child is my soul within me.
O Israel, hope in the LORD
From this time forth and forever.

David shares three practical principles concerning this painful experience called weaning: (1) God's goal for His children is maturity; (2) God's method in maturing His children is weaning; and (3) God's desire in this weaning process is that His children submit to Him.

GOD'S GOAL FOR US

Let's start with that first principle: *God's goal for His children is maturity.*

A veteran missionary once said to me, "I'm tired of working with mature people!"

Somewhat surprised, I asked, "Would you rather be working with immature people?"

He laughed. "No, my preference is for *maturing* people, people 'on the grow,' people like Paul who know they haven't arrived yet."[1]

There is a vast difference between age and maturity. Age is a quantity of years, while maturity is a quality of experience. Novelist F. Scott Fitzgerald wrote about people who "go from one childhood to another," and that kind of person is with us today.[2] They don't know the difference between being childlike and being childish, and they go through life trapping people into becoming surrogate parents whose main task is to pamper and protect them. Consequently, they never really grow up; they just grow old.

What are the characteristics of maturing people? For one thing, they know themselves and accept themselves, and therefore don't build their lives on illusions. ("LORD, my heart is not haughty, nor my eyes lofty.") Maturing people are themselves—their best selves—and don't try to make other people think they're something that they really aren't. ("Neither do I concern myself with great matters, nor with things too profound for me.") They come to understand their feelings better and are sensitive to the feelings of others, and they keep their feelings under control without becoming less than human. ("Surely I have calmed and quieted my soul.")

We'd be greatly disappointed if our children or grandchildren failed to mature properly because we know how much they would miss in life. To be sure, the road of maturity is a rough one; but as the big brother told his sister when she complained about the bumps on the mountain path, "The bumps are what you climb on!"

Maturing people know themselves. Their self-image is an honest one, not an imaginary composite of all the people they admire and imagine themselves to be. Though they constantly strive to be better and do better, there is still a consistency about the image they have of themselves. Paul had this in mind when he wrote "that we should no longer be children, tossed to and fro and carried about with every wind of doctrine, by the trickery of men, in the cunning craftiness of deceitful plotting" (Eph. 4:14).

Honest relationships are mirrors that help us see ourselves as we really are, beginning with our relationship with the Lord through His Word. I can't fully explain how it happens, but as I read the Bible and meditate on its truth, I get deeper insight into what I'm really like deep inside. The Bible is indeed "a discerner of the thoughts and intents of the heart" (Heb. 4:12). God knows me perfectly, and He is willing to share what He knows if I'm willing to accept the truth and honestly act on it.

A well-known comedian likes to joke about his annual checkup at the doctor's office. "The surgeon wanted me to have a ten-thousand-dollar operation," says the comedian, "but I saved myself the trouble and the money. I just had them retouch the X ray!" But changing the X ray won't solve the problem; and it's a basic law of life that if you can't face the truth, you'll have to face the consequences.

Our relationships with other people are also mirrors in which we can see ourselves. Of course, not everybody responds honestly in a relationship: some people lie to us; some flatter us, which is a form of lying; some try to exploit us; but some sincerely accept us as we are and help us become what we ought to be. Again, Paul touched on this truth: "But, speaking the truth in love, may grow up in all things into Him who is the head—Christ" (Eph. 4:15). Sometimes "truth in love" hurts, but it never harms.

How we respond to the circumstances of life helps us see ourselves in a clearer way. We tell what we are by what makes us laugh, what makes us weep, and what makes us get angry. Adolph Hitler wept when he saw a wounded animal, but he felt no sorrow or guilt when he had aged and infirm people "put to sleep" and millions of Jews put to death in gas chambers. "Hitler's insensitivity to the torments and tortures he inflicted on others was absolute," writes one of his biographers. "He had not the slightest interest in any human suffering except his own."[3]

Maturing people also accept themselves. They may not be happy about everything they know about themselves. They may recognize that there is room for improvement. But they're willing to be what they are, make the most of it, and not complain. As I mentioned in the beginning of the book, when I was in grade school, I carried on a feud with myself and the Lord because I had neither athletic nor mechanical ability, although I didn't have any trouble handling my studies and getting good grades. I would have had a much happier childhood if I had accepted myself, warts and all, and quit complaining.[4]

AN APPETITE FOR THE TRUTH

Important spiritual dimensions to maturity must also be considered. As we mature in the Lord, not only do we become more stable and more discerning (Eph. 4:14) and able to speak "the truth in love" (Eph. 4:15), but we grow in our appetite for the truth of the Word and are able to teach it to others. The writer to the Hebrews discussed this subject:

> For though by this time you ought to be teachers, you need someone to teach you again the first principles of the oracles of God; and you have come to need milk and not solid food. For everyone who partakes only of milk is unskilled in the word of righteousness, for he is a babe. But solid food belongs to those who are of full age, that is, those who by reason of use have their senses exercised to discern both good and evil (5:12–14).

The "milk" of the Word represents "the first principles of the oracles of God," the basic truths of the Christian life, the work that Jesus Christ did on earth: His birth, life, teaching, death, and resurrection. As you read elsewhere in Hebrews, you discover that the "meat" of the Word represents what Jesus Christ is now doing in heaven for His people on earth: "Called by God as High Priest 'according to the order of Melchizedek,' of whom we have much to say, and hard to explain, since you have become dull of hearing" (5:10–11).

Ask the children in almost any Sunday school class to give you the basics of our Lord's life on earth, how He came, what He taught, and what He did; and they will do it. But ask them about Melchizedek and the heavenly priesthood of Jesus Christ, His ministry as mediator, and His "perfecting" of His people (Heb. 13:20–21), and you'll get a respectful silence. Ask the same question of most adult believers, and you'll probably get the same silence.

Many of God's people are still in spiritual childhood and haven't grown in their knowledge of Christ's present priestly ministry in heaven. What Paul wrote to the Corinthians, the Lord could say to many people in churches and Sunday school classes: "I fed you with milk and not with solid food; for until now you were not able to receive it, and even now you are still not able" (1 Cor. 3:2).

My friend Dr. John DeBrine, host of "Songtime" radio ministry, says that Christians will either "grow in grace or groan in disgrace," and he is right. God's children should enjoy hearing the gospel story and should never abandon the "pure milk of the word" (1 Peter 2:2), but we shouldn't stop with the milk. The appeal in the epistle to the Hebrews is "let us go on to perfection [maturity!]" (6:1). What Jesus did "in the days of His flesh" (Heb. 5:7) is tremendously important, but it was a launching pad and not a parking lot: "Even though we have known Christ according to the flesh, yet now we know Him thus no longer" (2 Cor. 5:16).[5] Even unbelievers can get sentimental over the gentle Carpenter of Nazareth, but that's not the same as worshiping the exalted Christ and allowing Him to mature us.

Maturing spiritually means seeing the total work of Christ as it relates to us today, allowing Christ to apply the blessings of His atonement to us personally, and thus becoming more like Him in character and conduct. This involves reading His Word and accepting by faith all that it says about Him and about His people. Paul calls this "reckoning" (Rom. 6:11).[6]

Maturing Christians have an appetite for the solid food of the Word, and they know what Christ is doing for them today as He reigns on the throne. They rejoice in His ministry of making them "complete in every good work to do His will, working in [them] what is well pleasing in His sight" (Heb. 13:21); and they are able to share this teaching with others.

The Importance of Teamwork

Of all the problems that abounded in the Corinthian church, the basic problem was the spiritual immaturity of the people. The church was supposed to be like a fruitful field filled with harvesters and a holy temple filled with beauty (1 Cor. 3:9). Instead, it was more like a noisy playpen filled with children competing with each other for attention.

Paul had to write them:

And I, brethren, could not speak to you as to spiritual people but as to carnal, as to babes in Christ (1 Cor. 3:1).[7]

However, we speak wisdom among those who are mature (1 Cor. 2:6).

Brethren, do not be children in understanding; however, in malice be babes, but in understanding be mature (1 Cor. 14:20).

"When I was a child," wrote Paul, "I spoke as a child, I understood as a child, I thought as a child; but when I became a man, I put away childish things" (1 Cor. 13:11). That was the problem with the Corinthian believers: they were playing with toys instead of working with tools, competing with each other instead of cooperating with each other. Like children, they were saying, "That's mine!" and protecting their own interests instead of looking out "for the interests of others" (Phil. 2:4). What they needed was *teamwork*.

People who don't know much about farming or building probably know something about sports, which may explain Paul's frequent athletic images in his letters. Paul called his two friends Euodia and Syntyche "women who labored with me in the gospel" (Phil. 4:3), and the word translated "labored" can be translated "were athletes [teammates] together with me."[8] When you're a member of a team, you work together to win the game because it's the team that gets the trophy, not one member of the team. If there is a "glory hound" on the team who has to make all the scores, then the team will probably lose. After picturing the Christian life as a footrace, Paul wrote, "Therefore let us, as many as are mature, have this mind" (Phil. 3:15). Teamwork is a matter of maturity.

Maturing people are serious about life and the work God has given them to do, and they're able to work together with others in getting the job done. It was a liberating experience to me when I discovered that God could bless people I disagreed with. For years, I'd sheltered myself behind a "wall of conviction," which was in reality a "wall of convenience" that protected me from the rigors of having to grow up and face the challenge of diversity. I finally learned to pray this anonymous prayer:

From the cowardice that shrinks from new truth,
From the laziness that is content with half-truths,
From the arrogance that thinks it knows all truth,
    O God of truth, deliver us!

THE MATURING OF OTHERS

As Christians, we have the obligation to help one another mature in the Lord. Sometimes we do this by being problems that challenge people's patience, and other times by being resources from which people can gain strength. Of course, the Lord and our friends prefer the second option; and we do, too.

Christian workers and Christian parents especially know the struggle that's involved in leading people from childhood to maturity. "Him we preach," wrote Paul, "warning every man and teaching every man in all wisdom, that we may present every man perfect [mature] in Christ Jesus. To this end I also labor, striving [agonizing] according to His working which works in me mightily" (Col. 1:28–29). That was Paul's personal experience of Christ's present heavenly ministry (Heb. 13:20–21).

Helping others mature involves praying for them. Paul commented, "Epaphras, who is one of you, a bondservant of Christ, greets you, always laboring fervently [agonizing] for you in prayers, that you may stand perfect [mature] and complete [fulfilled] in all the will of God" (Col. 4:12). I find it helpful during my quiet time to use the prayers of the Bible as a basis for praying for myself and my Christian friends, and I recommend this practice to you.[9]

Commonplace as it may seem, we also help one another mature by being faithful in participating in public worship: "And let us consider one another in order to stir up love and good works, not forsaking the assembling of ourselves together, as is the manner of some, but exhorting [encouraging] one another, and so much the more as you see the Day approaching" (Heb. 10:24–25). When Jesus Christ returns, we'll go to the gathering whether we want to or not; but if we're faithful to our local assembly now, we'll be ready to meet Him then.

Attending public worship may seem like a routine thing to us, but it's an influential ministry. For one thing, when we leave the house on the Lord's Day, Bibles in hand, we're bearing witness to our unsaved neighbors that Jesus Christ is alive and we're going to church to worship Him. When we walk into the church building and become a part of the congregation, we announce our agreement with all the people there that Jesus Christ is worthy of our praise and adoration, and thus we affirm the decision they made to attend public worship. If you attend a megachurch, you might think that your absence wouldn't be noted by people on earth, but it would certainly be noted by God in heaven. The average church in the United States has about one hundred members, all of whom need to attend church so the Lord can encourage them and they can encourage others.

Staying away from church because of something (or somebody) we don't like is dangerous to our spiritual health and threatening to the Holy Spirit's maturing process in our lives. "Wherever we see the Word of God purely preached and heard, and the sacraments administered according to Christ's institution, there, it is not to be doubted, a church of God exists," wrote John Calvin. "The principle extends to the point that we must not reject it [a local church] so long as it retains them [the marks of a true church], even if it swarms with many faults."[10]

The Corinthian congregation was swarming with faults and failures and public scandals, yet Paul addressed the people as "the church of God which is at Corinth" (1 Cor. 1:2). A "pure church" is a wonderful ideal, in fact, something that Jesus prayed for (John 17:17); but it's an ideal that can be realized only when the church gets to heaven (Eph. 5:25–27; Jude 24). Meanwhile, as long as the churches are still composed of sinful human beings, we'll all have to do our part, with the Lord's help, to build up the body and make it more like Jesus Christ (Eph. 4:1–16).

A MATTER OF THE WILL

Maturing people depend less and less on their moods and feelings and more and more on God, who works in them "both to will and to do for His good pleasure" (Phil. 2:13). Maturing Christians do what's right because it is right and because they're responsible to do it, not because they feel like doing it. Few things are as treacherous as "religious feelings." This verse sums up the idea:

The heart is deceitful above all things,
And desperately wicked;
Who can know it? (Jer. 17:9).

To say, "I don't feel like doing it!" may be an evidence of honesty, but it certainly isn't a mark of maturity. Neither is refusing to do something because of the person or persons with whom you must work. In the process of growing up and serving God, everybody experiences disagreements with people and gets hurt by them at one time or another; but these are the facts of life that we simply have to accept. "The turning point in the process of growing up," writes Max Lerner, "is when you discover the core of strength within you that survives all hurt."[11]

One reason the Book of Psalms is in the Bible is to remind us that nobody has to feel good either to worship God or to serve God. The psalms run the gamut from the deepest pain to the most ecstatic joy; and the key to it all is the fact that the psalmists always admit honestly just how they feel, but they don't make their feelings the center of their experience. No matter how much they've been abused, misunderstood, and hurt, no matter how much danger they're in or how many burdens they carry, the writers focus on the Lord and not on themselves.

One of my favorite preachers, George H. Morrison, writes these helpful words about the experiences and emotions of life:

> It is not by exceptional providences that we live. It is not by exceptional joys we are enriched. It is not by anything rare or strange or singular that we are fashioned under the hand of God. It is by sorrows that are as old as man, by trials that a thousand hearts have felt, by joys that are common as the wind is common that breathes on the palace and on the meanest street. By these things do we live; by these we grow; by love and tears, by trials, by work, by death; by the things that link us all into a brotherhood, the things that are common to ten thousand hearts.[12]

We know we're maturing when we stop saying, "Nobody knows how I feel!" and we stop acting like we're the only ones who ever walked the path of suffering before. Peter encouraged the afflicted saints of his day by reminding them that "the same sufferings are experienced by your brotherhood in the world" (1 Peter 5:9). To be sure, there can be a painful loneliness attached to some suffering; but loneliness doesn't confer uniqueness, unless we go on an ego trip and decide to use our pain as a weapon instead of a tool. Knowing that others have been in the same furnace, and that some are in it now, assures us that God hasn't singled us out for punishment, that others are praying, and that God is at work in His church around the world, accomplishing His special purposes, even through suffering.

Living the Christian life involves the whole person—body, mind, will, emotions—but Christian living is primarily a matter of the will. Christian love is choosing and willing that we shall treat others the way God treats us. Christian service, too, is an act of the will, although certainly the intelligence and the emotions aren't ignored ("doing the will of God from the heart" [Eph. 6:6]). However, we must try not to make the way we feel the main test of our walk with God or our work for God. When He was dying on the cross, the Lord Jesus was obeying the Father's will implicitly; and yet His suffering was intense.

Sometimes people say to me, "I just don't feel like I'm close to God."

"What does it feel like to be close to God?" I ask.

"You're joyful and bubbly and full of power," one believer replied. "You have a deep and abiding peace," said another. "You feel like you could face anything and lick the world!" said a third. Certainly, these spiritual experiences are possible to Christians who abide in Christ,[13] but nowhere in Scripture are we told that these emotions are tests of our relationship with the Lord. Samson awoke and felt like he could "lick the world," but his power had left him (Judg. 16:20). Peter felt very confident of his courage, but he denied the Lord three times (Luke 22:31–34). Our feelings are treacherous; we dare not ignore them, but we dare not build on them.

The poet and hymn writer William Cowper had his share of traumatic emotional experiences, yet he wrote,

God moves in a mysterious way,
His wonders to perform;
He plants His foot-steps in the sea,

And rides upon the storm.

Ye fearful saints, fresh courage take;
    The clouds ye so much dread
Are big with mercy, and shall break
    In blessings on your head.

Judge not the Lord by feeble sense,
    But trust Him for His grace;
Behind a frowning providence
    He hides a smiling face.

"Judge not the Lord by feeble sense" is good counsel. Seek the Lord with a humble and sincere heart, and wait for His purposes to be fulfilled. His ways are beyond our thoughts, and our feelings aren't the test of His love.

A SENSE OF FREEDOM

Maturing Christians should experience a growing sense of freedom. Physical maturity is a pilgrimage from bondage to freedom, and so is spiritual maturity. As we noted earlier, the life of a baby is one of confinement: first the womb; then the crib; then the playpen; then limited freedom under the constant watchfulness of parents, siblings, and other guardians. Paul declared, "Now I say that the heir, as long as he is a child, does not differ at all from a slave, though he is master of all" (Gal. 4:1).

In the Christian life, freedom isn't the privilege of doing whatever we please because living to please only ourselves would be the worst bondage possible. Rather, freedom means life controlled by truth and motivated by love. We not only speak "the truth in love" (Eph. 4:15), but we seek to live the truth in love by the power of the Spirit of God.

Children who are fortunate enough to live in a home surrounded by truth and love will grow into a life of responsible freedom as outward discipline gradually becomes inward direction. A similar process takes place when you learn to swim, play the piano, drive a car, or run a computer: the rules become principles that become a part of you.

Before long, you don't even think about the rules as you play the piano or drive the car.

When our family lived in Wheaton, Illinois, I often drove past the college football field and saw the players scrimmaging under the hot August sun, repeatedly going over the same plays. Their coaches wanted to be sure that the signals and plays the team had committed to memory would become a part of their nerves and muscles as well. If they were to play their best and win the game, they had to have the freedom that comes when you love what you're doing and you're possessed by inner laws that are second nature to you.

When believers are filled with (controlled by) the Spirit of God (Eph. 5:18) and the Word of God (Col. 3:16), God's truth takes possession of the mind and heart; and we experience freedom. Christian freedom is not independence because no Christian can be independent and survive. Rather, it's a *responsible* freedom that liberates us from the old life and enables us to enjoy the new life by serving others and glorifying God.

Whoever wrote Psalm 119 expressed it this way: "Your statutes have been my songs in the house of my pilgrimage" (v. 54). Imagine turning laws into songs! If a choir announced a concert program consisting of the city traffic code set to music, people would attend only out of curiosity, not because they expected to hear beautiful lyrics. Laws are written to be obeyed, not to be sung; but when God's laws are in your heart, they set you free to serve and give you a song to sing! David expressed this beautifully when he wrote, "I delight to do Your will, O my God, and Your law is within my heart" (Ps. 40:8).

The most wonderful freedom in the world is the freedom to experience all that God has planned for us and to glorify Him as we enjoy it. It isn't enough just to know God's will and do it. We must come to the place in life where His will delights us and nourishes us (John 4:34). Only then are we enjoying the freedom that God planned for us to enjoy.

Too many times we act like the elder brother in Christ's parable: we dutifully obey the Father's will and do the Father's work, but we don't bring joy to the Father's heart (Luke 15:11–32). The elder brother was a drudge. He did his job because he had to, not because he wanted to; and in his heart he had a secret desire to do something else. The prophet Jonah had the same wrong attitude: he went to Nineveh, not because he loved God or the lost people who were there, but because he didn't want to take another trip to the bottom of the sea. Both Jonah and the elder brother were angry, and they were angry because they didn't get what they wanted. If they had put God's law into their hearts instead of nurturing their hidden ambitions, both Jonah and the elder brother would have been better men.

When duty becomes delight, when labor is motivated by love, statutes become songs, and life becomes an exciting experience of freedom and maturity.

Chapter 14

WEANING: REPLACING MILK WITH MEAT

God's goal for our lives is maturity, and one of God's tools for maturing us is weaning. David stated,

> Surely I have calmed and quieted my soul,
> Like a weaned child with his mother;
> Like a weaned child is my soul within me (Ps. 131:2).

Our English word *wean* comes from a root that means "to get accustomed." The weaned child has to get accustomed to feeding himself or herself and no longer nursing at the mother's breast. The Hebrew word translated "to wean" is much richer. It means "to recompense, to treat kindly" and carries the idea of "completeness." The word was used to describe the ripening of fruit. Weaning is a process of ripening and completing; it's a necessary experience on the difficult journey of life that leads to maturity.

In Old Testament days, a child was usually weaned at the age of three on a specific date that marked the official end of this first phase of childhood. (See Gen. 21:8.) Weaning meant more freedom for the child, but it also demanded a new and deepening relationship for the mother (at least that was what she hoped). Feeling rejected, the child might become bitter; feeling independent, the child might begin to act rebellious. It isn't always easy to learn to handle freedom, your own or somebody else's.

TRUST IN THE LORD

Life is one long process of weaning until we get to the end, and then all we have is God. But that's the whole idea behind weaning: to bring us to the place where all we want and all we need is God.

The child is weaned from the mother's breast but is still at home and under parental guidance. Then the child starts attending school, and an emotional weaning takes place. Children away from home start making new friends, and these friends exert a powerful influence over them. The weaning process continues: summer camp, high school graduation, a move to a university dormitory, a job away from home, a girl-friend or boyfriend, a wedding, the establishment of a new home, parenthood, and then the weaning process starts all over again.

But weaning is God's idea, and there is no reason for us to fear it or resist it. Weaning may hurt us (and others), but it will never harm us if we learn to cooperate with God's will. God made life like this because it's the best and wisest way for Him to keep us maturing. Each step in the weaning process prepares us for the next stage in life and encourages us to grow up as we grow older. At each critical stage, we lay down old toys, pick up new tools, and bravely face the challenge.

You can see this weaning process at work in the life of Abraham (Gen. 11:27—25:11). When Abraham departed from Ur, God told him to leave his family behind; but he took with him Terah, his father, and Lot, his nephew. Terah died in Haran. When Abraham started for Canaan, Lot was still with him, so God had to separate Lot and Abraham (Gen. 13).

Abraham disobeyed God and fathered a child by his wife's maid, Hagar. "Oh, that Ishmael might live before you!" was Abraham's prayer; but God had to get Ishmael out of the home, a very painful weaning experience for Abraham. Then He gave Abraham and Sarah the promised son, Isaac; and when Isaac was a young man, God commanded Abraham to give him back (Gen. 22)! Throughout this process, God was saying, "Don't depend on your father, yourself, your wife, your son Ishmael, or even your son Isaac. Depend on Me!"

You see this weaning process at work also in the life of David as God removed every human crutch on which David might be tempted to lean: his beloved friend Jonathan, his mentor Samuel, his sons, even his faithful counselor Ahithophel. It certainly isn't wrong to have friends and counselors, but it's wrong to trust them instead of trusting the Lord. The psalmist cried out, "Loved one and friend You have put far from me, and my acquaintances into darkness" (Ps. 88:18).

THE MOTHERHOOD OF GOD

The subject of weaning introduces us to the neglected but important theme of the motherhood of God.[1] Though God is called "Father" in both Old and New Testaments,[2] there are ways in which His character is best described by comparing Him to a mother.

Like a mother, God is *unchanging in His love*:

> But Zion said, "The LORD has forsaken me,
> And my Lord has forgotten me."
> "Can a woman forget her nursing child,
> And not have compassion on the son of her womb?
> Surely they may forget,
> Yet I will not forget you" (Isa. 49:14–15).

This marvelous truth is to be experienced, not explained.

Like a mother, God is *unfailing in His comfort*:

> As one whom his mother comforts,
> So I will comfort you;
> And you shall be comforted in Jerusalem (Isa. 66:13).

When children need comfort, they usually run first to their mother. This doesn't mean that their father is incapable of comforting them. Children from birth are accustomed to their mother's arms, kisses, and words of assurance.[3]

Our English word *comfort* means "with strength." God doesn't pamper us because that would make us weaker; He comforts us and makes us stronger: "God is our refuge *and strength*" (Ps. 46:1, italics mine). He "hugs" us that He might help us and shelters us that He might strengthen us. Once we've been comforted by God, it's our responsibility to go out and comfort others. Paul summarized this point: "[God] comforts us in all our tribulation, that we may be able to comfort those who are in any trouble, with the comfort with which we ourselves are comforted by God" (2 Cor. 1:4).

Like a mother, God is *unsparing in His joy:*

In that day it shall be said to Jerusalem:
"Do not fear;
Zion, let not your hands be weak.
The LORD your God in your midst,
The Mighty One, will save;
He will rejoice over you with gladness,
He will quiet you with His love,
He will rejoice over you with singing" (Zeph. 3:16–17).

What a remarkable picture, almighty God singing to His children![4] Though fathers also sing to their children, we commonly think of the mother sharing a lullaby to a fretful but weary child and bringing calm to his troubled heart. God rejoices over His children and enjoys "mothering" them! To be quieted by His love is a wonderful experience.

Like a mother, God is *unwilling in His punishment:* "How often I wanted to gather your children together, as a hen gathers her chicks under her wings,[5] but you were not willing!" (Matt. 23:37). My mother was very patient with my misbehavior and tolerated a great deal of nonsense for which I should have been disciplined immediately. But eventually the hour of reckoning came, and I got what I had coming to me. Fathers can also be patient in this way:

As a father pities his children,
So the LORD pities those who fear Him.
For He knows our frame;
He remembers that we are dust (Ps. 103:13–14; also see vv. 8–10).

Our God is patient with us and with unbelievers who reject His salvation, for God is "not willing that any should perish but that all should come to repentance" (2 Peter 3:9).

This brings us back to Psalm 131: like a mother, God is *unyielding in His purpose*. He will see to it that His children mature, for their sake, for the sake of others, and for His sake so He can enjoy fellowshipping with mature sons and daughters. Whatever it takes, God will see to it that there are no spoiled brats in His family.

Realizing two facts should bring peace to the weaned child's heart: (1) weaning is an expression of the mother's love, and (2) weaning takes away something good in order to give something better.

Weaning doesn't mean that the mother is punishing the child any more than pruning means that the vinedresser is punishing the branches. The vinedresser cuts away *good* wood in order to improve the quality of the branches that remain, and the mother weans the child in order to improve the quality of his or her life. The child's future happiness and usefulness depend on this new relationship with the mother. I can agree with Paul: "When I became a man, I put away childish things" (1 Cor. 13:11). They were good things, but I outgrew them.

ONLY ONE TRUE HERO

When I was a youngster, my playmates and I would frequently debate the merits of our favorite radio heroes—the Lone Ranger, the Green Hornet, the Shadow, the Whistler, and others. On Saturdays, we'd argue about movie cowboys like Ken Maynard, Tom Mix, Hopalong Cassidy, and Gene Autry. Sometimes our debates would get so heated that we'd get angry and even stop playing together. Fortunately, the hostilities didn't last very long.

Because the members of the church at Corinth were immature in the faith, they acted like children and boasted about their heroes. To foster church unity, Paul wrote,

> Now I plead with you, brethren, by the name of our Lord Jesus Christ, that you all speak the same thing, and that there be no divisions among you, but that you be perfectly joined together in the same mind and in the same judgment. . . . Now I say this, that each of you says, "I am of Paul," or "I am of Apollos," or "I am of Cephas," or "I am of Christ." Is Christ divided? Was Paul crucified for you? Or were you baptized in the name of Paul? (1 Cor. 1:10, 12–13).

Paul was the founder of the church at Corinth (Acts 18:1–11); Apollos succeeded him (Acts 18:24–28); and at some point, Peter (Cephas) got involved in the ministry there. Here are three men, different in personality, different in style of ministry, and yet all men of God and all doing God's work in building the church. Each of them won people to Christ; but, alas, some of their converts attached themselves to the servants instead of to the Master.

It certainly isn't wrong to love and appreciate the people who led us to Christ or who taught us the Word in our formative years. "For though you might have ten thousand instructors in Christ," Paul wrote, "yet you do not have many fathers; for in Christ Jesus I have begotten you through the gospel" (1 Cor. 4:15). Nor is it wrong to show our appreciation to faithful, hardworking spiritual leaders in the church (1 Thess. 5:12–13). But no servant of God must come between the believer and the Savior and "play God" in another believer's life.

The goal of spiritual leaders must be to encourage their people to follow Christ; but one mark of cultic leaders is a desire to possess people and control them. Paul didn't have that attitude. He saw his work as that of a spiritual parent, caring for a growing family (1 Thess. 2:7–12); and his goal was to mature the believers, not master them. Paul stated, "Not that we have dominion over your faith, but are fellow workers for your joy; for by faith you stand" (2 Cor. 1:24). Christians can play follow the leader only when they know for sure that the leader is following Christ (1 Cor. 11:1).

I am no man's disciple, and I want no man to be my disciple. I agree with Scottish novelist George MacDonald: "I believe that no teacher should strive to make men think as he thinks, but to lead them to the living Truth, to the Master Himself, of whom alone they can learn anything, who will make them in themselves know what is true by the very seeing of it."[6] If all spiritual leaders would relate people to the Lord Jesus in a mature way, and stop basking in the glow of their fan clubs, the church would enjoy more unity and manifest more maturity.

Maturing believers must resist the temptation to imitate and follow other Christians whom we admire, no matter how godly they are. When we imitate others, we usually copy the accidentals, not the essentials—how they walk and talk, what kind of Bible they use, how they pray—and this robs us of being ourselves and becoming what Christ wants us to become.

One young pastor I know listened to the sermon tapes of a well-known preacher, memorized the messages, and even tried to imitate the man's voice and style of delivery. The result was disappointing both to him and to his people. He was an echo, not a voice; and the Spirit couldn't use his uniqueness to make the Word living and powerful through his life. Others can encourage and inspire us, but we must always be ourselves.

Imitating outstanding Christians is dangerous, but so is conforming to the general mediocrity of the average Christian in the average church. I once heard Vance Havner say, "Things are so bad in the church that a person has to backslide in order to have fellowship with anybody!" It may not be that bad in the church you attend, but the warning is still a valid one: it's much easier to drift and sink than it is to climb. A proverb makes this distinction: "He who walks with wise men will be wise, but the companion of fools will be destroyed" (Prov. 13:20).

We relate to different people in different ways at different times, always seeking to be consistent in our own character and conduct. Some people are friends; others are merely acquaintances. Some of them build us up; others we seek to build up. A few people, we should probably avoid altogether, even if they profess to follow the Lord. Paul saw this danger and said about it, "Now I urge you, brethren, note those who cause divisions and offenses, contrary to the doctrine which you learned, and avoid them" (Rom. 16:17). It takes a great deal of spiritual discernment to know how to relate to people, but growing in discernment is one evidence that we're maturing in the Lord.

BELIEVERS AND THE LAW

While window-shopping one day, I saw a T-shirt with beautiful butterflies printed on it, accompanied by this solemn pronouncement in large letters: BUTTERFLIES ARE FREE! "Sure, butterflies are free!" I said to myself. "They're free to be butterflies. But they aren't free to be jet planes!"

I want to focus on the "free" part of the slogan because weaning has to do with freedom. We noted in the previous chapter that mature freedom isn't independence or the right to do whatever we please. For the Christian, freedom means a life motivated by love and controlled by truth. It's turning God's statutes into songs and singing our way along the pilgrim path of life.

To find peace, the weaned child has to accept both truth and love: the truth that what his mother did was right and for his own good, and she did it out of a heart of love. She knows far better than the child all that's involved in this step toward maturity. Yes, there will be joys and privileges because of this new freedom, but there will also be responsibilities and trials. "You will be like God!" Satan will promise him (Gen. 3:5), offering him what many immature people crave: freedom without responsibility. But freedom without responsibility is lawlessness, and lawlessness is destructive. Adolph Hitler was accountable to nobody; and for every word in his book *Mein Kampf (My Struggle)*, 125 persons died in World War II! "Success is only achieved by the individual conqueror," he wrote in a chapter entitled "The Strong Man Is Mightiest Alone."[7]

Besides lawless independence and foolish imitation, there is a third danger that must be avoided when we begin to experience freedom, and that's legalism. Some people are actually afraid of freedom and of their ability to handle it, so they deliberately put themselves into bondage to avoid having to be free. They want security, not identity; but the security they get is that of the child and not of the adult. What they're really avoiding is having to grow up.

One of the first theological battles the early Christians had to fight[8] dealt with the question of the place of the law in the church: "Must a Gentile become a Jew in order to become a Christian?" You find the record in Acts 15. Many of the legalistic Pharisees said, "Yes!" but Paul and Barnabas and Peter said, "No!" The legalists lost the debate, but the battle went right on. The first shot may have been fired in Jerusalem, but it was soon heard around the Roman world as the legalists proceeded to invade the churches that Paul had founded among the Gentiles.

One result of this struggle was Paul's epistle to the Galatians, the main theme of which is, "Stand fast therefore in the liberty by which Christ has made us free, and do not be entangled again with a yoke of bondage" (Gal. 5:1). This matter of Christian freedom is an issue not of differing personalities ("Well, you're the legalistic type!") or of church preferences ("I like worship services that are more spontaneous!") but of Jesus Christ and what He did on the cross.[9]

In this fiery epistle, Paul makes at least seven dogmatic assertions about what the law cannot do:

1. The law cannot justify the sinner:
   "Knowing that a man is not justified by the works of the law but by faith in Jesus Christ" (2:16).

· 2. The law cannot give righteousness:
   "I do not set aside the grace of God; for if righteousness comes through the law, Christ died in vain" (2:21).

3. The law cannot give the gift of the Holy Spirit:
   "This only I want to learn from you: Did you receive the Spirit by the works of the law, or by the hearing of faith?" (3:2).

4. The law cannot give believers an inheritance:
   "For if the inheritance is of the law, it is no longer of promise; but God gave it to Abraham by promise" (3:18).

5. The law cannot give life to dead sinners:
   "For if there had been a law given which could have given life, truly righteousness would have been by the law" (3:21).

6. The law cannot impart the grace of God:
   "You have become estranged from Christ, you who attempt to be justified by law; you have fallen from grace" (5:4).[10]

7. The law cannot make a person free:
   "Stand fast therefore in the liberty by which Christ has made us free, and do not be entangled again with a yoke of bondage" (5:1).

There is something about the old nature that enjoys trying to obey religious rules and reach the spiritual goals that we set for ourselves. For one thing, we become quietly proud when we do obey the rules and meet the goals; and when life is a collection of rules and goals, spirituality becomes easy to measure. We know exactly how many prayers we've prayed, people we've witnessed to, Bible chapters we've read, and meetings we've attended.

There is nothing wicked about following standards and setting goals, but two things are true: (1) we must never think that achieving the goals is the same as becoming more like Jesus Christ; and (2) we must never depend on our own strength to accomplish either one. All the activities listed above are good if our doing them is evidence of "faith working through love" (Gal. 5:6). But if instead of faith, there is fleshly self-effort, and if the motive is competition and pride rather than love, then what we're doing is legalistic and we're in bondage.

After all, the Pharisees in Jesus' day attended meetings, won converts, obeyed rules, lived by high standards, and studied the Scriptures; yet Jesus called them hypocrites, whitewashed tombs, and children of the devil (Matt. 23; Luke 18:9–14).

The law is a yoke from which believers have been delivered (Acts 15:10; Gal. 5:1). It's a guardian (baby-sitter) who isn't needed by people who have been adopted by God and have an adult standing in His family (Gal. 4:1–7). The law is a slave girl like Hagar who could never give birth to a free child (Gal. 4:21–31); a bond of indebtedness that has been fully paid for us (Col. 2:14); a shadow that vanished because the true Light appeared (Col. 2:16–17); and a husband who died so that we could be "married to Christ" and set free (Rom. 7:1–4). The Christian's relationship to the law is expressed in one word: *FREE!*

A LAWFUL USE OF THE LAW

But this blood-bought freedom doesn't give Christians the right to reject the law of God and deliberately disobey it. The word for this is *antinomianism*—"against the law." Legalism is bad enough, but antinomianism is worse, for it turns liberty into license and makes God's law our enemy instead of our servant. There is a lawful use of the law in the Christian life, for in the law we see Jesus Christ and the righteousness of God revealed. "Therefore the law is holy, and the commandment holy and just and good," Paul confessed. "For I delight in the law of God according to the inward man" (Rom. 7:12, 22). In this, Paul agreed with the psalmist who wrote, "Oh, how I love Your law! It is my meditation all the day" (Ps. 119:97).

When I was ministering over the "Back to the Bible" broadcast, I did a series of Old Testament studies and received an irate letter from a listener that said (and I paraphrase): "Why are you spending so much time in the Old Testament? It's been fulfilled in Christ! It doesn't apply anymore! Let's study the New Testament, because that's where Christians live."

I wrote to the brother and explained that (1) all Scripture, including the Old Testament, is inspired and is profitable for God's people (2 Tim. 3:16–17); (2) Jesus Christ is seen in both Testaments (Luke 24:27); (3) the only Scripture the early church had was the Old Testament, and they managed to witness to the then-known world; and (4) Jesus commanded us to feed on "every word that proceeds from the mouth of God" (Matt. 4:4). He never wrote back.

The external old covenant law has been replaced by God's Word written internally—on our hearts—by the Spirit of God (2 Cor. 3:1–3). God's children have the living Holy Spirit within, and He gives us the power to obey God's will and please Him. Paul declared, "The law of the Spirit of life in Christ Jesus has made me free from the law of sin and death. . . . That the righteous requirement of the law might be fulfilled in us who do not walk according to the flesh but according to the Spirit" (Rom. 8:2, 4). Note the passive voice in Romans 8:4. We don't fulfill the law in our own strength; the Holy Spirit fulfills the righteousness of the law in and through us as we walk in the Spirit.

You don't produce life or encourage life by passing laws. As we discovered in the first part of this book, life follows the laws that are built into it. If the corn isn't growing in Iowa, the legislature can pass all the laws it wants to, but that won't make the corn grow. If the baby isn't growing properly, the pediatrician can make rules and issue threats and penalties, but none of these efforts will make the baby grow. Growth comes from within.

"My prayer life is languishing," a church member said, "but I've determined to spend at least an hour a day in prayer, starting next Sunday."

I opened my Bible to Romans 7[11] and read to him: "For the good that I will to do, I do not do; but the evil I will not to do, that I practice. . . . I find then a law, that evil is present with me, the one who wills to do good" (vv. 19, 21).

"Whenever we determine to do a good thing," I explained, "we're in danger of moving from grace to law and from faith to self-effort. We may succeed in reaching our goal for a time, but then a reaction sets in; and before long, we're back where we started and feeling very frustrated.

"My suggestion is that you take time to pray about your praying, and ask the Holy Spirit to work in you to give you a heart for prayer. That's what one of the apostles did: 'Lord, teach us to pray.' Prayer is communion with God, and you don't regulate or motivate communion with laws. It comes from life, life motivated by love. The more we love God, the better we'll pray; and that love comes from the Spirit of God within."

Now, let me balance this with what we learned in Chapter 8 about spiritual exercise. While it's true that the Holy Spirit is the only One who can fulfill the righteousness of God's law in us, it's also true that we must exercise discipline and cooperate with the Spirit in what He wants us to do. Paul calls this "walking in the Spirit" (Rom. 8:1, 4). I like the New International Version's translation of Galatians 5:25: "Since we live by the Spirit, let us keep in step with the Spirit."

God's commandments are still God's enablements. If the Lord commands us to pray, and if we have a desire to pray, then let's set aside time for prayer and trust the Holy Spirit to help us. Paul reminds us, "For it is God who works in you both to will and to do for His good pleasure" (Phil. 2:13). Swimmers can't practice swimming unless they dive into the water, and we Christians can't grow in our prayer life unless we pray: "Thus also faith by itself, if it does not have works, is dead" (James 2:17).

RELEVANT QUESTIONS

How can I tell if I'm drifting into legalism and in danger of falling from grace? The honest answers to some personal questions can help me find out.

1. *Am I satisfied with my spiritual walk?* If I am, either I'm ignorant of

what the Bible teaches about the Christian walk, or my Christian life is an empty routine that I can follow without having to depend on the Lord. Christ's words to the believers in Laodicea are pertinent: "Because you say, 'I am rich, have become wealthy, and have need of nothing'—and do not know that you are wretched, miserable, poor, blind, and naked" (Rev. 3:17).

People in prison don't face too many challenges (unless they're planning to break out), and life is pretty much a routine. But people who are free face new challenges every day and find their faith and love tested, but this is the way they grow.

2. Am I afraid of diversity? We learned in Chapter 10 that God has built both unity and diversity into His church, and maturity keeps them working together harmoniously. But legalists must have uniformity; diversity is a threat to them, and they don't have the maturity necessary to handle it. They're unable to cope with new music in worship and new approaches to evangelism or Christian education. They vote against changes in the church;[12] and if the church changes, they change churches. Remember, you can be orthodox in theology and devoted to the Lord but still be in the bondage of legalism.

3. Am I threatened and angered by people who disagree with me? This is a corollary of the second question. Legalists must always be right and must never seriously consider the merits of differing viewpoints. They read only approved literature and listen only to approved speakers. Once you have all the truth, what more is there to learn? They forget Paul's statement: "Now I know in part" (1 Cor. 13:12).

Historians are sure the story is apocryphal, but it illustrates this inflexible mind-set. When Muslim conqueror Amr ibn Al-As asked what he should do with the parchments left in the great library at Alexandria, the caliph replied, "If these writings of the Greeks agree with the Book of God [the Koran], they are useless, and need not be preserved; if they disagree they are pernicious, and should be destroyed."[13]

When they meet new people, legalists are prone to be suspicious. Instead of discovering where they and the new acquaintance agree, they try to find out where they disagree. Charles Spurgeon warned his pastoral students to beware of believers who "walk around with a revolver in their pockets."

4. Am I critical of other believers, and do I feel superior to them? Jesus spoke a "parable to some who trusted in themselves that they were righteous, and despised others" (Luke 18:9). God may enable us to see some truths more clearly than others see them, and obey His precepts more faithfully; but that doesn't give us the right to belittle our friends or boast about ourselves. Rather, we should "pursue the things which make for peace and the things by which one may edify another" (Rom. 14:19).

5. Is my spiritual life predictable? When I was serving in Youth for Christ, Bob Cook and Ted Engstrom would tell us at prayer meetings, "Let's pray around the circle and all get rid of our favorite prayers; then we can really get down to business and pray." It worked! We'd all pray and get the cold ashes off the altar; then God would kindle a fresh fire, and we'd pray with compassion and fervency.

I pray about some things every day, but I hope my prayers aren't boring to God. I would certainly be unhappy if my children and grandchildren never changed their conversations with me. I can't teach God anything; but if He commands me to sing "a new song" (Ps. 96:1), I suspect He'd be happy to hear me pray a new prayer.

We've already learned that we need system, order, and discipline for an effective devotional life; but that doesn't mean we can't make changes occasionally. It's good to be systematized as long as we aren't paralyzed. Maybe I need to read a new translation of the Bible or follow a different reading schedule. Perhaps I need to evaluate my prayer list in the light of changing circumstances. How much of my praying do I devote only to my interests? "The unexamined life is not worth living," Socrates told Plato. I wonder how that statement applies to the devotional life.

6. Do I live under a cloud of guilt? Very often, the life of the legalist is negative and secretly unhappy. Legalists set such high standards for themselves and try to reach such challenging goals that they're constantly praying, "O wretched man [or woman] that I am! Who will deliver me from this body of death?" (Rom. 7:24). They're like the elder brother (Luke 15) who would rather argue with his father than forgive his brother and go in to enjoy the feast! Or like angry Jonah, sitting outside the city, hoping God will destroy it!

As God's children, we should maintain a sensitive conscience and be quick to confess our sins; but we shouldn't cultivate a negative view of the Christian life and think that constant guilt is a mark of consecration. Christians live in the sphere of grace (Rom. 5:1–5) and really don't have to prove anything to the Father. As we have more need, He gives more grace (James 4:6). The Father wants to love us into more freedom; and He will if we let Him.

7. *Am I a blessing to others?* It's worth noting that Jesus attracted sinners, while the scribes and Pharisees repelled them (Luke 15:1–2). Legalists usually attract other legalists, and together they form a defensive cultic fellowship that's better at building walls than building bridges.

In 1757, John Newton, composer of "Amazing Grace," wrote a letter to George Whitefield, part of which makes a good conclusion to this chapter:

The longer I live, the more I see of the vanity and the sinfulness of our unchristian disputes; they eat up the very vitals of religion. I grieve to think of how often I have lost my time and my temper in that way, in presuming to regulate the vineyards of others, when I have neglected my own; when the beam in my own eye has so contracted my sight that I could discern nothing but the mote in my neighbor's. . . . I allow that every branch of gospel truth is precious, that errors are abounding, and that it is our duty to bear an honest testimony to what the Lord has enabled us to find comfort in, and to instruct with meekness such as are willing to be instructed; but I cannot see it my duty, nay, I believe it would be my sin, to attempt to beat my notions into other people's heads. . . . When our dear Lord questioned Peter, after his fall and recovery, he said not, Art thou wise, learned and eloquent? nay, he said not, Art thou clear and sound, and orthodox? But this only, "Lovest thou me?" An answer to this was sufficient then; why not now?[14]

Chapter 15

SUBMISSION: CHOOSING TO LET GOD LEAD

God's goal for our lives is maturity, and He uses weaning to help us mature. But if weaning is to accomplish His purposes, His children must submit to Him. As David declared, "Surely I have calmed and quieted my soul, like a weaned child with his mother" (Ps. 131:2). When the will is committed, the heart will be calm.

SUCCESS IN A HOSTILE ENVIRONMENT

The more I study it, the more convinced I am that 1 Peter is an especially relevant document for the church today. Like the saints who first received that letter, God's people today are scattered across the earth, and like those early believers, they face pressures from culture, society, government, and the sheer paganism that surrounds them. How can the church succeed in such a hostile environment?

Peter's answer is in one powerful word: *submit*. He counsels all believers to submit to government authorities and to do good works (2:11–17). He tells servants to submit to their masters (2:18–25) and Christian wives to submit to their husbands (3:1–7). Finally, he admonishes all the believers in the local assemblies to submit to one another and minister to one another (3:8–12), and this includes the younger members submitting to their elders (5:5). In other words, if God's people are good citizens, good employees, good spouses, and good church members, zealous to do good works, God will bless them and use them, no matter where they live or what pressures they face. In a world filled with rebellion, God's children should model submission.

The word Peter used that we translate "submit" ("subject" in KJV) is a military term that means "to rank under." It has nothing to do with the character or worth of the people involved; it simply describes order and organization. The buck private may be a better man than the sergeant, but he obeys the sergeant because that's the order of command. Submission isn't subjugation, the demeaning and destroying of people; rather, it's the acceptance of God's order in the home, the church, and human society. Christ is first, others second, self last.

Many people aren't in the family of God because they won't submit to the righteousness of God (Rom. 10:1–3). The cause of many church splits is the absence of submission to spiritual leaders and to one another (James 4:1–7). Family problems arise when parents won't submit to God and to one another (Eph. 5:18–21) and when children refuse to submit to their parents. Jesus submitted to Mary and Joseph during His formative years (Luke 2:51) and one day heard the Father say, "You are My beloved Son; in You I am well pleased" (Luke 3:22).

RULES FOR WEANING

The image of submission given in Psalm 131 is that of the child submitting to the mother. I want to begin with this image and then consider several other images of submission found in Scripture.

It's difficult for children to pass this first maturity milestone that we call weaning. Says Dr. Benjamin Spock to parents: "Think how you'd feel if a big bossy giant who had you in his power and who didn't understand your language kept trying to take your coffee away and make you drink warm water out of a pitcher."[1] Hmmm.

During the weaning process, children think that the mother has deserted them and doesn't love them anymore; and no amount of reasoning or bribing will convince them otherwise. (Remember, they don't understand our language, or at least they act like they don't understand.) Telling them that weaning is opening the door for their future doesn't persuade them because they want to hold on to the past; and they don't understand maturity anyway. But before we criticize innocent children too harshly, let's review our lives and see how we've responded when we've gone through the weaning process.

There is a difference between losing something and giving something away. How easy it would be if the child would only say to himself or herself, "My mother loves me and wants me to give up nursing (or the bottle) and start drinking from a cup. I won't let her *take* this from me; I'll willingly give it up to her." Some children naturally wean themselves and that's a good example for us to follow.

So, the first rule for successful weaning is: *don't let God take anything good from you; willingly give it to Him*. That's what Abraham did on Mount Moriah (Gen. 22), and God blessed him for it. If we presented to Him as a loving sacrifice everything good God weaned from us, what a difference it would make in the way we feel and the rate of our spiritual maturity.

The second rule is: *remind yourself that weaning isn't the end; it's the beginning*. Junior no longer has that regular special attention from Mother (although he hasn't lost Mother's love). So what? Now he is free to have lunch with the neighbors, go to the park for a picnic, and spend the rest of his life discovering a variety of gastronomical delights. That makes it worthwhile! At every turn in the maturity road, we lose something in order to gain something. We need to adopt the attitude of Job: "The LORD gave, and the LORD has taken away; blessed be the name of the LORD" (Job 1:21).

The third rule says: *remind yourself that the submission required in weaning is a mark of strength and not weakness*. Submission is not subjugation or domination. It's not the quivering slave at the feet of the master, fearing the future, but the quiet, confident child in the loving arms of the mother, anticipating the future. Every good thing that God takes from us makes our hands free to receive something better; and as the Christian life progresses, God even takes away the better so that He can give us the best.

The fourth rule is: *remember that the goal is maturity, not security*. You're never more secure than when you're in the will of God, submitted to His love and His purpose. As we mature, His love deepens in our hearts, and "perfect [complete, mature] love casts out fear" (1 John 4:18).

APPROACHES TO THE WILL OF GOD

When our Lord was arrested in the Garden of Gethsemane, something took place there that I see as a microcosm of the way people act in our present world. Here's the text:

> And while He was still speaking, behold, a multitude; and he who was called Judas, one of the twelve, went before them and drew near to Jesus to kiss Him. But Jesus said to him, "Judas, are you betraying the Son of Man with a kiss?" When those around Him saw what was going to happen, they said to Him, "Lord, shall we strike with the sword?" And one of them struck the servant of the high priest and cut off his right ear. But Jesus answered and said, "Permit even this." And He touched his ear and healed him (Luke 22:47–51).

> So Jesus said to Peter, "Put your sword into the sheath. Shall I not drink the cup which My Father has given Me?" (John 18:11).

You see three persons—Judas, Peter, and Jesus—and you see each of them taking a different approach to the will of God.

Judas, though an apostle, *pretended to do God's will*; and his weapon was a hypocritical kiss.[2] Peter *opposed God's will*, and in his hand was a sword. Jesus *submitted to God's will*, and in His hand was a cup.

A kiss, a sword, a cup: three different approaches to the will of God. Like Judas, you can fake God's will; like Peter, you can fight God's will; or like Jesus, you can fulfill God's will.

Judas had been organizing his mob and Peter had been sleeping when Jesus was praying, "Father, if it is Your will, take this cup away from Me; nevertheless not My will, but Yours, be done" (Luke 22:42). Although in Scripture the drinking of a cup is often a picture of judgment (Jer. 25:15; Rev. 14:10), willingly taking a cup and drinking it pictures obedience and submission.[3] The cup that Jesus drank was for us: He tasted the wrath of God against the sins of the world and was made sin for us. No wonder His holy soul abhorred what was about to happen to Him! No wonder He asked for deliverance!

According to John 8:44, Satan is both a liar (the kiss) and a murderer (the sword). Peter in his fervency was just as much a servant of the evil one as was Judas in his treachery and hypocrisy. If Peter had been holding a cup in his hand, he wouldn't have nearly killed a man; a cup is something you drink from, not something you fight with. "All who take the sword will perish by the sword," warned Jesus (Matt. 26:52); but those who willingly take the cup will be invincible until their work is done.

No child of God should be afraid to take the cup because what's in it has been prepared by the Father. Yes, sometimes it's difficult to pray, "Nevertheless, not what I will, but what You will" (Mark 14:36); but the alternative is even more difficult: "Father, what I will, not what You will." Do we know the future better than God does? Can we plan our lives better than He can? Will our selfishness and blindness give us a happier and holier life than His love and grace can give us? Remember, the greatest judgment God can send us in this life is to let us have our own way.

We can't *take* the cup until we put down the sword.

We can't *drink* the cup until we stop our hypocritical kissing.

We can't overcome until we submit. As George Matheson expressed it:

Make me a captive, Lord,
And then I shall be free;
Force me to render up my sword,
And I shall conqueror be.

A LIVING SACRIFICE

The sacrifice on the altar is another picture of submission, especially the burnt offering (Lev. 1:1–17; 6:8–13). "All on the altar" (Lev. 1:9) is the key phrase, because everything was given to God. The parallel for believers today is Romans 12:1: "I beseech you therefore, brethren, by the mercies of God, that you present your bodies a living sacrifice, holy, acceptable to God, which is your reasonable service." (We discussed this passage in Chapter 8.)

The burnt offering was a sweet savor sacrifice (Lev. 1:9, 13, 17), which means that, like a fragrant perfume, it was well pleasing to God:

"Christ also has loved us and given Himself for us, an offering and a sacrifice to God for a sweet-smelling aroma" (Eph. 5:2). Presenting our bodies to God is our "spiritual act of worship" (Rom. 12:1 NIV); it makes us like Jesus, and it pleases the Father.

Had they known what was about to happen to them, the animals would have resisted; but in their brutish ignorance, they submitted. But ours is to be "an act of *intelligent* worship" (Rom. 12:1 PHILLIPS, italics mine). The Jerusalem Bible reads, "In a way that is worthy of thinking beings." The more we think about the mercies of God, the more we should want to give our all to Him and live for Him. Our submission must be intelligent and voluntary.

But note that God is seeking living sacrifices, not dead ones. Some of His people may be called to lay down their lives for Him, but *all* of us are called to live our lives for the sake of Christ and the gospel. We must surrender our lives and give our all to Him, knowing that "whoever desires to save his life will lose it, and whoever loses his life for My sake will find it" (Matt. 16:25).

Two living sacrifices in Scripture illustrate what this means: Isaac (Gen. 22) and our Lord Jesus Christ. Isaac didn't rebel against his father Abraham but was willing to give his life if that was what God wanted. A ram died in Isaac's place, but Isaac died and was raised from the dead "in a figurative sense" (Heb. 11:19). He became a living sacrifice!

When Jesus was raised from the dead, He had a glorified body that could pass through locked doors, but that body still bore the wounds of Calvary (Luke 24:36–43). Jesus is alive today, but His body shows that He gave Himself as a sacrifice for us; and today He ministers to His church from heaven as a living sacrifice. Like Isaac, He was obedient to His Father, *but no other sacrifice took His place!* No other sacrifice was good enough.

A living sacrifice isn't one that is bound to the horns of the altar, waiting to be slain (Ps. 118:27). It's one that has been placed on the altar, slain, and raised to "walk in newness of life" (Rom. 6:4). Paul urged, "Present yourselves to God as being alive from the dead, and your members as instruments of righteousness to God" (Rom. 6:13).

A LOVING RELATIONSHIP

The loving submission of wife and husband to each other is another picture of what it means for Christians to yield to God. Paul instructs, "Wives, submit to your own husbands, as to the Lord. . . . Husbands, love your wives, just as Christ also loved the church and gave Himself for her" (Eph. 5:22, 25).

Contrary to what the pop psychologists teach, marriage is not a fifty-fifty proposition. If it's really going to succeed and honor the Lord, marriage demands 100 percent from both spouses: total dedication to the Lord and total devotion to each other. Our submission to Christ is a loving relationship; and the longer we cultivate this relationship, the deeper it should become.

The marriage relationship has its hours when you're on an incredible emotional summit; but it also involves many days when you're trudging on the plain, doing routine things, and even its valley experiences that are painful and stressful. However, no matter how you feel, you're still married, your commitment to each other hasn't vanished, and there is no reason why your love for each other should evaporate because circumstances are tough. Spouses who separate or divorce because they "don't have the same feeling for each other" that they used to have didn't have much to build their marriage on to begin with.

Transfer this to your experience with Jesus Christ. There are hours when your heart is filled with love and praise, and you're quite sure this feeling will last forever. But it doesn't because every summit introduces a valley. The test of our devotion to Christ isn't our occasional triumphing on the mountain so much as our patient trudging on the plain and courageous struggling through the valley. Note the sequence given in Isaiah 40:31:

> But those who wait on the LORD
> Shall renew their strength;
> They shall mount up with wings like eagles,
> They shall run and not be weary,
> They shall walk and not faint.

Once we make our commitment to the Savior, to love Him and live for Him, the relationship is settled and secure, no matter how we feel from day to day; and He will love us and care for us even if we occasionally neglect Him or even resist Him. We shouldn't do those things, of course, because our delight should be to please Him. But if we do grieve Him, we must remember that His love for us doesn't depend on what we do or how we feel. Our enjoyment of His love is conditional (John 14:21–24), but His love toward us is unconditional.

The Christian life is a loving relationship between the believer and Christ, a relationship that must be cultivated; but like human marriage, it's a relationship that has its ups and downs. Jesus never has to apologize,[4] nor does His love ever change. The problem lies with us, not with Him. He always has more love to share if we can receive it.

THE POTTER AND THE CLAY

The potter and the clay also illustrate what it means to be submitted to God:

> The word which came to Jeremiah from the LORD, saying: "Arise and go down to the potter's house, and there I will cause you to hear My words." Then I went down to the potter's house, and there he was, making something at the wheel. And the vessel that he made of clay was marred in the hand of the potter; so he made it again into another vessel, as it seemed good to the potter to make. Then the word of the LORD came to me, saying: "O house of Israel, can I not do with you as this potter?" says the LORD. "Look, as the clay is in the potter's hand, so are you in My hand, O house of Israel!" (Jer. 18:1–6).

The application in Jeremiah's day was to the people of Judah, a reminder to them of God's sovereign control over the nations. But it was also a message of sovereign grace, for though Judah was a disobedient nation, God offered to make the people again if only they would submit to Him. His purpose wasn't to destroy, but to heal.[5]

Jeremiah's experience with the potter was a living parable showing him (and us) a God-centered philosophy of life. Clay without a potter has potential, but it takes the potter's hands and the spinning of the wheel to make the clay into something beautiful and useful. Inert clay can't mold itself, but you and I can make decisions that deeply affect what happens to us. Clay can't really resist a potter's skill; but as human beings, we're capable of resisting God in many ways. Our God is almighty and can do anything, but He will never violate our freedom and force Himself on us. When God isn't allowed to rule, He will overrule and still accomplish His great purposes; but if we fail to obey, we are the losers.

God controls the wheel of life and throughout our lives uses the pressures of many hands to mold us: parents, siblings, teachers, mentors, pastors, bosses, friends, enemies, even total strangers. *To resist the pressure is to resist the Potter.*[6] If we didn't see and sense the hand of God at work, our lives would become unbearable, and we'd feel like quitting. This doesn't mean that God is to blame for the way people act, but that what people do to us can be used of God to make us what He wants us to be. This outlook kept Joseph going. "You meant evil against me," he said to his brothers, "but God meant it for good" (Gen. 50:20). This is the Old Testament version of Romans 8:28.

We must confess that we're only clay and that we'll never fulfill our potential unless we yield to the Potter. If we're in control, the clay will amount to very little as far as eternity is concerned; but in God's hands, we become very valuable indeed as we share in His eternal plan. If we resist Him and fail, He can make us again, as He did David, Elijah, Jonah, and Peter.

Mary of Bethany's broken vessel left fragrance behind (John 12:1–8), and Jesus memorialized her around the world (Mark 14:9). Judas, the man who criticized Mary, left a cemetery behind as his memorial, a potter's field filled with broken vessels, among them Judas (Matt. 27:3–10).

Adelaide A. Pollard dealt with this subject by proclaiming,

Have Thine own way, Lord! Have Thine own way!
Thou art the Potter; I am the clay.
Mold me and make me after Thy will,
While I am waiting, yielded and still.

This is the prayer of the maturing Christian.

Chapter 16

FAITH: PLACING
CONFIDENCE IN HIM

My fellow Hoosier, Elbert Hubbard, author of the famous essay "A Message to Garcia," once defined *faith* as "the effort to believe what your common sense tells you is not true." He is wrong, of course, although that would make a good definition of *superstition*.

The people who jest about faith don't realize how big a part it plays in everyday affairs. It takes faith to get married, because marriage vows are basically promises. It takes faith to send children off to school. It takes faith to get a prescription filled (pharmacists do make mistakes) and to take the medicine when we get it (doctors also can make mistakes). It takes faith to eat in a restaurant, deposit money in a bank, sign a contract, drive on the highway, or get on an airplane or an elevator. Faith isn't some kind of religious experience for the elite; it's the glue that helps hold people's lives together, from the infant nursing at her mother's breast to the senior citizen waiting for a pension check.

But remember, faith is only as good as its object. If we trust people, we get what people can do; if we trust money, we get what money can do; if we trust ourselves, we get what we can do; if we trust God, we get what God can do. But what does it mean to "trust God"?

FOUR FACTS ABOUT FAITH

When you read Hebrews 11, the great faith chapter of the Bible, you discover four basic facts about faith.

1. Faith begins with a revelation from God. What these heroes of faith did was in response to what God said to them, because "faith comes by hearing, and hearing by the word of God" (Rom. 10:17). Faith isn't psyching ourselves up so that we're confident God is on our side. Faith is listening to what God says in His Word and acting on it.

2. Faith grows out of a relationship with God. Let's suppose you're shopping in a department store and a total stranger approaches you and says, "I think you should loan me five hundred dollars so I can buy a new washing machine."

My guess is you'd either ignore him or say, "I'm sorry, but I don't do business that way."

Obviously offended, he would probably reply, "What's the matter? Don't you trust me?"

I can hear your answer: "Trust you? I don't even *know* you!"

Trust is a relationship that can be built only over a period of time. To hand five hundred dollars to a total stranger and expect to get it back isn't faith; it's presumption. The people whose faith is described in Hebrews 11 were people who walked with God and had a growing relationship with God. They knew that His character was such that His word could be trusted.

3. Faith motivates us to do the will of God. Note the verbs in Hebrews 11: Abel offered an acceptable sacrifice; Noah prepared an ark; Abraham went out; Abraham offered his son; Moses chose Israel over Egypt; and so on. True faith isn't feeling good about what God says; it's *doing* what God says. Faith isn't discussing the will of God; it's obeying the will of God. James asked, "But do you want to know, O foolish man, that faith without works is dead?" (2:20).

4. Faith, when acted upon, gives us the witness of God. "For by it [faith] the elders obtained a good testimony [witness]" (Heb. 11:2)— this means that they received God's approval for what they did. God witnessed to Abel that his sacrifice had been accepted (Heb. 11:4), and to the martyrs that their faith was accepted and rewarded (Heb. 11:39). True faith rests on the *objective* Word of God, but it is witnessed to *subjectively* by the Spirit of God. Faith is "the evidence of things not seen" (Heb. 11:1), and the word translated "evidence" means "conviction." When we have true biblical faith, it produces the inner conviction that God will do what He says. In fact, the very presence of this faith in our hearts is proof that God wants us to trust Him for the miracle.

When you put it together, you discover what it means to trust God. Trusting God means thinking and acting according to God's Word in spite of circumstances, feelings, or consequences. The object of our faith is God—not our feelings, not faith itself, but almighty God. Remember, faith is only as good as the object.

I fear that contemporary society knows nothing about true faith. People sing about faith ("I believe for every drop of rain that falls/A flower grows")[1] and talk about faith ("You just gotta believe, that's all!") but don't personally know the faithful God or "the word of faith" (Rom. 10:8) that He has given us. It's a kind of masquerade people play to bolster their spirits and encourage one another. How strange that they can have faith in faith and faith in feelings, but they can't have faith in the Word of the living God!

GROWTH IN FAITH

Maturing in the Christian life depends on our growing in faith. The Christian life begins with faith ("For by grace you have been saved through faith" [Eph. 2:8]), and it can develop only through faith. We walk by faith ("For we walk by faith, not by sight" [2 Cor. 5:7]), and we stand by faith ("For by faith you stand" [2 Cor. 1:24]). So serious is this matter of believing God that Paul warns us, "For whatever is not from faith is sin" (Rom. 14:23). The writer to the Hebrews observed, "But without faith it is impossible to please Him" (11:6).

One of the key verses in Scripture is Habakkuk 2:4: "But the just shall live by his faith." So important is this verse that the Holy Spirit wrote three New Testament books to explain it: Romans, Galatians, and Hebrews. Habakkuk 2:4 is quoted at the beginning of Romans (1:17), in the middle of Galatians (3:11), and near the end of Hebrews (10:38); and each book deals primarily with one phrase from Habakkuk 2:4. Romans tells us who "the just" are; Galatians describes how the just "live"; and Hebrews emphasizes that they live "by faith." (The phrase "by faith" is found nineteen times in Hebrews.)

So, we aren't just saved by faith; we also live by faith. Paul understood this truth: "And the life which I now live in the flesh I live by faith in the Son of God, who loved me and gave Himself for me" (Gal. 2:20).

But how can we tell when we're really living and acting by faith? By asking ourselves four questions based on four texts from Romans, and answering these questions honestly.

1. Is what I'm doing based solidly on God's Word? Paul summed it up, "So then faith comes by hearing, and hearing by the word of God" (Rom. 10:17). Faith is our obedient response to God's revelation to us. It doesn't matter how we feel, what the circumstances are, or what the consequences may be. We obey God because we have confidence in His Word. Whether it's Noah building an ark, Abraham offering up his son, Moses and Israel crossing the Red Sea, or Joshua taking a city, the faith sequence is the same: relationship with God, revelation from God, response of obedience, and reward from God.

God doesn't speak to us today in the same ways He spoke to the patriarchs and prophets. We have His unchanging written Word that we can read, study, and meditate on; and Peter tells us that the written Word is better than marvelous experiences with the Lord (2 Peter 1:16–21). On the Mount of Transfiguration, Peter, James, and John beheld Christ's glory, saw Moses and Elijah in glory, and heard the Father's voice out of the glorious cloud; but Peter affirms that the Word of God is superior even to this glorious experience.

For one thing, exciting experiences with God come to only a select few, and the memory of these experiences will fade; but the Word of God can come to anyone who will receive it, and the Word will endure. Men die, and their experiences die with them; but the Word of God "lives and abides forever" (1 Peter 1:23–25). You can't franchise a spiritual experience, but you can give people the Bible and trust the Holy Spirit to teach them.

The Word of God and the Word of God alone is the basis for our faith. It reveals the character of God and records His mighty works, both of which encourage us to believe and obey. The precepts of God reveal His will, and we can obey them by faith because God's commandments are still God's enablements. The promises of God are dependable: "Not a word failed of any good thing which the LORD had spoken to the house of Israel. All came to pass" (Josh. 21:45); "And now, O Lord GOD, You are God, and Your words are true" (2 Sam. 7:28). Anything that we do contrary to Scripture is sin because we can't disobey the Word of God by faith.

2. Am I willing to wait? "For the Scripture says, 'Whoever believes on Him will not be put to shame'" (Rom. 10:11)—that quotation is from Isaiah 28:16 where it reads, "Whoever believes will not act hastily." Since the Holy Spirit authored both verses, He has the right to change and expand them; and it doesn't take much insight to discover the relationship between the two: whoever acts hastily will end up being ashamed! When God leads you to do something by faith, He'll give you the patience to wait on His time. You'll be among "those who through faith and patience inherit the promises" (Heb. 6:12). The God of patience gives us patience and encouragement through the Scriptures (Rom. 15:4–5).

Children are usually known for their impatience, but patience is a mark of a maturing person. James commented, "But let patience have its perfect work, that you may be perfect [mature] and complete, lacking nothing" (1:4). Start off on vacation with your children, and when you stop at the first stoplight, one of them will ask, "Are we there yet?" Faith not only does God's will, but it does it in God's time.

If I find myself impatient and anxious to rush ahead, I can be sure that what I'm doing is not in the will of God. When Jesus received the urgent message that His beloved friend Lazarus was sick, He stayed where He was for two days (John 11:6) because He lived on the Father's divine timetable. "Are there not twelve hours in the day?" He asked His worried disciples (John 11:9).

The late J. Oswald Sanders visited us at "Back to the Bible" some years ago, and in response to a question he asked, I told him what a full schedule I was carrying as radio teacher, writer, magazine editor, conference speaker, and member of several boards. He listened patiently, smiled benignly, and said quietly, "Brother, there's always time for the will of God." It was just the loving rebuke I needed.

There's an urgency about God's will, so our waiting on His timing must never become complacency or inactivity. For believers walking by faith, waiting is always preparation for the next step. It's a time for watching and praying, seeking to discern what Satan may be doing, making our plans, and taking inventory of our resources. Four months passed between the day Nehemiah began to pray for Jerusalem and the day he actually asked the king for help (Neh. 1:1; 2:1); but during that time, he got himself and his plans ready for the time God would send him on his way.

3. *Do I have joy and peace?* Paul offers this encouragement: "Now may the God of hope fill you with all joy and peace in believing, that you may abound in hope by the power of the Holy Spirit" (Rom. 15:13). Although faith doesn't depend on how we feel, true biblical faith does bring with it inner peace and joy that belie the circumstances we're in or the consequences we may be facing. At a time when they could have been at their lowest, the apostles "departed from the presence of the council, rejoicing that they were counted worthy to suffer shame for His name" (Acts 5:41). God's Spirit gives to God's believing people a peace "which surpasses all understanding" (Phil. 4:7), a calm in the midst of the storm, an inner confidence in the heart of the battle.

George H. Morrison defined *peace* as "the possession of adequate resources." This explains the courage and confidence of those who walk by faith. It isn't the arrogance that could come from experience, training, or ability; rather, it's the boldness that comes when you know God is on your side. Peter and John had it: "Now when they [the members of the Jewish council] saw the boldness of Peter and John, and perceived that they were uneducated and untrained men, they marveled. And they realized that they had been with Jesus" (Acts 4:13).

4. *Will what I do glorify God?* Paul said of Abraham: "He did not waver at the promise of God through unbelief, but was strengthened in faith, giving glory to God" (Rom. 4:20). One reason the Lord waited twenty-five years to give Abraham and Sarah the promised son Isaac was to allow them to be "as good as dead" so they couldn't claim any credit for themselves. Jesus allowed Lazarus to die because raising him from the dead would glorify the Son of God (John 11:4).

We've already discussed this important subject in Chapter 12, but we should deal with *why* faith especially brings glory to God.

During my five years as a seminary student, I heard many chapel messages; but most of them I've forgotten. However, Vance Havner spoke in chapel one day and gave a message I can never forget. The text was Hebrews 11:23–29, the faith of Moses; and his outline was: "By faith, Moses chose the imperishable, saw the invisible, and did the impossible."

Faith takes ordinary people (including failures like Moses) and enables them to do extraordinary things. That's why faith glorifies God! The choice Moses made was contrary to human nature, for who would give up an easy and honorable position in Egypt for the tough job of molding a mob of slaves into a nation and leading them to their promised inheritance? Who would reject the pleasures and treasures of Egypt for hardship in the wilderness? When because we see the invisible we choose the imperishable, then we can do the impossible; and God gets the glory. I hear again the words of Dr. Bob Cook: "If you can explain what's going on, God didn't do it."

VIVID EXAMPLES OF FAITH

These four tests should help maturing believers distinguish between faith and presumption; but just to make it even clearer, I want to illustrate these tests from the lives of Abraham and Sarah (Gen. 16), David (2 Sam. 7), and Paul (Acts 27).[2]

When Abraham was seventy-five years old and his wife sixty-five, God promised them a son (Gen. 12:1–3); and He reaffirmed that promise at least twice (Gen. 13:14–17; 15:1–21). They waited ten years, but no son was born. So Sarah suggested that Abraham marry her maid Hagar and have a son by her. It was a perfectly legal procedure in that day, but it wasn't in the will of God. Hagar did bear a son, Ishmael, but the fact that she was a mother and Sarah was barren brought trouble into the home. Eventually, both Hagar and her son had to leave (Gen. 21).

Let's ask Abraham our four test questions.

"Was marrying Hagar a decision based on the word of God?"

"No, I did it to please my wife. God never spoke to me and told me to marry Hagar. On other occasions, it was always the word of God that guided us in what we did, but not this time."

"Were you willing to wait?"

"That was the whole problem! We got impatient after ten years and tried to help God fulfill His promises. We were in a hurry, and we ended up being ashamed."

"Did what you did bring joy and peace?"

"Just the opposite! We had nothing but trouble in our home, both before Isaac was born and after he was weaned."

"Did what you did bring glory to God?"

"No, it didn't. Everybody in our camp knew that Hagar and I had done the whole thing in our own power. There was nothing supernatural about the conception and birth of Ishmael."

Now for King David (2 Sam. 7). After David had consolidated his kingdom, he got a burden to build a temple for God and get the ark of the covenant out of the tent he had pitched for it. It was a noble desire, but it wasn't in the will of God. He told his court chaplain Nathan what he wanted to do, and Nathan encouraged him to go ahead.

But that night, God kept Nathan awake long enough to tell him that he'd made a mistake, and that he had to visit the king the next morning and tell him that David's son Solomon would build the temple. It was bad news for David, who for years had been collecting the spoils of war to devote to building the house of God. So, God gave David the good news that the Lord would build a "house" (family) for David and give him a throne forever (2 Sam. 7:16). The promise was ultimately fulfilled in Jesus Christ (Luke 1:32, 69; 22:30).

Let's interview David and Nathan.

"Brethren, was your decision about the temple based on the word of God?"

"I'm afraid not," says David. "I just had this feeling down inside that it would be a good thing to do. Israel was at peace, I was living in my own house, and I felt guilty that the ark was living in a tent. I'd gathered all that wealth from my battles, and I wanted to use it for the Lord."

"As for me," says Nathan, "I thought it was a good idea, but I should have told the king to pray about it and wait for God's direction. I was wrong to give the impression that God had already given

His approval. God rebuked me when He asked, 'Wherever I have moved about with all the children of Israel, have I ever spoken a word to anyone . . . saying, "Why have you not built Me a house of cedar?"' Of course, He never had, so I was wrong to run ahead of the Lord."

"*Your Majesty, were you willing to wait?*"

"I'm afraid not. If God hadn't intervened and sent Nathan with that message, I would have started the next day."

"*Did you have joy and peace?*"

"I was embarrassed," Nathan replies. "Here I am, chaplain to the king, and I gave him wrong counsel. It made me uneasy."

"Until Nathan gave me the additional word about God building a house for me," says David, "I was a deeply disappointed man. After all, I'd risked my life in many a battle to get wealth for the Lord's treasury. But once I prayed to God, I felt better about the whole thing."

"*Did your decision bring glory to God?*"

"Ultimately," says David, "but not immediately. I must confess that perhaps my motives were mixed. I'd always wanted to build a temple for the Lord, but God had other—and better—plans. It was when I sat before the Lord and prayed that I realized His glory was the main thing, not my desires. Then I was able to say, 'So let Your name be magnified forever'" (2 Sam. 7:26).

Our third interview is with Paul (Acts 27).

"*Paul, you were a prisoner on the way to Rome when you faced a crisis of faith. Did that ship leave port because God's word told the pilot to do so?*"

"Absolutely not!" says Paul. "My friends and I told them not to leave, but the centurion got expert advice from the pilot and the owner of the boat. Just to make sure, he took a vote; and the majority advised him to set sail. So much for expert counsel and statistics!"

"*Wasn't the centurion willing to wait?*"

"Quite the contrary: he was anxious to sail. So when the south wind began to blow softly, he assumed that it was the right time to leave. That south wind turned into a stormy wind."

"*Did you experience joy and peace?*"

"Joy and peace!" says the apostle. "Never! We experienced two weeks of a storm so violent that it wrecked the ship, destroyed the cargo, and would have drowned the passengers if God hadn't been merciful to us. Because I believed God's word, I had peace in my heart and was able to encourage the others."

"Did the voyage bring glory to God?"

"Only in a negative sense," says Paul. "I was able to say to the passengers and crew, 'I told you so! You should have listened to what God said to me!' The fact that God brought all two hundred and seventy-six people through safely was an honor to His name, but it would have been better had we obeyed His word at the beginning."

As you consider the experiences of these believers, you can come to some general conclusions about walking by faith. The first is that *our feelings can be deceptive and lead us astray.* Both David and Nathan felt good about David building the temple, but God vetoed the idea. When the south wind began to blow softly (Acts 27:13), the centurion felt good about setting sail, but the ship sailed right into a storm. Sarah felt good about her husband taking a second wife and begetting a son, but the Lord frowned on the whole enterprise. There is a difference between feeling good and having God's joy and peace in your heart.

Second, *believers must not test their spiritual decisions the way the world tests its decisions.* The fact that the experts approve of a decision doesn't make the decision right, for experts have been known to be wrong. The fact that a majority of the people involved consider the facts and vote a certain way is no guarantee it's the right way. If your closest relative or dearest friend advises you to do something, it doesn't mean that God is pleased with the advice. In many things, it's right and proper to please the people we love, but not when it comes to matters of faith.

Which leads us to a third conclusion: *the way of faith is often a lonely way.* Rather than be unpopular and hurt our loved ones, we seem to think it's easier to take the scientific approach and walk by sight. It *is* easier—until we start reaping the harvest of our foolish decisions. Sarah told Abraham what to do and then blamed him and God for the problems her suggestion created! It's not easy to walk by faith in a world (and a church) that prefers to walk by sight.

DEGREES OF FAITH

One mark of the maturing Christian is the development of stronger faith. Consider these statements of our Lord to various people, and note that there are degrees of faith in the Christian life:

Why are you so fearful? How is it that you have no faith? (Mark 4:40).

Why are you fearful, O you of little faith? (Matt. 8:26; see 14:31).

Assuredly, I say to you, I have not found such great faith, not even in Israel! (Matt. 8:10).

O woman, great is your faith! (Matt. 15:28).

No faith. Little faith. Great faith. And how strange that the great faith belonged not to orthodox Jews but to a Roman centurion and a Gentile mother!

How can we encourage faith to grow?

Let's start with the obvious: *faith grows when we feed on the Word of God.* Paul stated, "So then faith comes by hearing, and hearing by the word of God" (Rom. 10:17). The Word of God generates faith, and when we believe and obey, it releases power: "For no word of God shall be void of power" (Luke 1:37 ASV [1901]). Jesus commanded the man with the disabled hand to stretch out his hand; and the command gave him the power to do it, and he was healed (Matt. 12:10–13). Our Lord commanded the man at the pool of Bethesda to take up his bed and walk, and he did it (John 5). God's Word is living and powerful (Heb. 4:12), and faith releases that life and power.

Second, *faith grows when we pray.* The apostles said to Jesus, "Increase our faith!" (Luke 17:5). Jesus didn't rebuke them for their prayer, but He did teach them that quality of faith helps to determine quantity. He compared faith to a mustard seed, not because that particular seed is small, but because, though it is small, the little seed has life in it and can produce remarkable results. When the seed of faith is "watered" with prayer, it will increase and enable us to do exploits that will honor the Lord.

Paul prayed for the believers in Thessalonica and asked God that he might be able to visit them again and perfect what was lacking in their faith (1 Thess. 3:10). God didn't send Paul back to Thessalonica, but He did answer his prayer for the church. When he wrote his second letter, Paul was able to say, "We are bound to thank God always for you, brethren, as it is fitting, because your faith grows exceedingly" (2 Thess. 1:3). Prayer can help our faith to grow.

Third, *faith grows when we endure trials*. James declared,

My brethren, count it all joy when you fall into various trials, knowing that the testing of your faith produces patience. But let patience have its perfect work, that you may be perfect [mature] and complete, lacking nothing (1:2–4).

You don't learn to swim just by watching videos and reading books. You dive into the water and start moving! Trials are to our faith what exercises are to our muscles: they help them develop. Satan tempts us to bring out the worst in us, but the Lord tests us to bring out the best in us. God is wise in the way He tests us, always suiting the test to the needs of the believer; and He is loving and gracious in how He tests us, giving us just what we need to endure and to overcome. He keeps His eye on the clock and His hand on the thermostat; He knows just how long and how much.

Fourth, *faith grows when we consider the example of godly spiritual leaders*. The writer to the Hebrews urged, "Remember those who rule over you, who have spoken the word of God to you, whose faith follow, considering the outcome of their conduct" (13:7). The ministry and memory of faithful spiritual leaders ought to stimulate the faith of the people to whom they had ministered.[3]

My favorite literature is biography and autobiography. I have hundreds of these volumes in my library, some of which I've read many times. I find that reading the lives of God's spiritual giants increases my faith and encourages me to do better. J. Hudson Taylor,

Amy Carmichael, Fanny Crosby, Charles Spurgeon, William Carey, Jim Elliot, Lottie Moon, Martin Luther, Robert Murray M'Cheyne, and a host of others have ministered to me over the years and helped my faith to grow. When I hear missionary speakers tell what God is doing around the world, my faith grows.

Christians with no faith or little faith are fearful people who doubt God's Word and do a great deal of worrying. Consequently, they can't really minister to others or give a strong witness to the lost. Instead of walking by faith and claiming their inheritance in Christ, they're wandering in the wilderness of unbelief and missing God's best for their lives. We should heed Jesus' words: "According to your faith let it be to you" (Matt. 9:29).

Chapter 17

OBEDIENCE: DOING HIS WILL

"**O**nly he who believes is obedient; only he who is obedient believes." That was written by the German pastor and martyr Dietrich Bonhoeffer, and it's a statement that shows insight into the relationship between personal faith in Christ and obedience to the will of God. We've just thought about what it means to live by faith; now let's consider what it means to obey by faith and do the will of God.

The familiar phrase "the will of God" may elicit a negative response from some believers, especially those who have experienced an overdose of legalism and an undersupply of love. When they think of the will of God, they have frightening nightmares of bowing before a cruel master, becoming an emotionless robot, or maybe falling into the cogs of a grinding machine that's run by a cunning computer. They can't understand why Jesus said, "My food is to do the will of Him who sent Me, and to finish His work" (John 4:34). To them, the will of God is punishment, not nourishment.

Four principles should govern our attitude toward the will of God: (1) the will of God is planned from the heart of God; (2) the will of God is for the glory of God; (3) the will of God is revealed through the Word of God; and (4) we appreciate the will of God more as we trust Him and obey what He tells us to do.

FROM THE HEART OF GOD

The will of God comes from the heart of God: "The counsel of the

LORD stands forever, the plans of His heart to all generations" (Ps. 33:11).

Note that phrase "the plans of His heart." It takes care of any nightmares you may have about merciless masters, heartless robots, and faceless machines. If the will of God comes from the heart of God, then His will is the expression of His love. Rebellious nations see God's will as chains to be broken, and they shout in unison, "Let us break Their bonds in pieces and cast away Their cords from us" (Ps. 2:3). But God doesn't shackle His children with chains; He draws us "with gentle cords, with bands of love" (Hos. 11:4). God wants to guide us like children, with His counsel and His eye, not like animals, with a bit and a bridle (Ps. 32:8–9).

The will of God isn't a faceless machine that comes to a sudden halt if I disobey the Lord. The will of God is a living relationship between me and the Lord. What He has willed proves His love for me; my obedience to that will proves my love for Him, "and His commandments are not burdensome" (1 John 5:3).

God's will is more like a warm human body than like a piece of cold machinery. If one part of my body rebels, the rest of my body compensates for it until the doctor and I can get the malfunctioning part fixed. When my gallbladder declared war on me a few years ago, I became a very sick man; but my heart kept beating and my breathing didn't stop. Within a week, my rebel gallbladder had been taken out, and I was on the mend.

But the big problem isn't that we have pain when we disobey the will of God, because we expect disobedience to be punished. Sin usually brings its own pain with it, and sometimes the Father has to chasten us to bring us to our senses. The problem comes when we have pain because we obey the will of God, like the pain Abraham must have felt when he told his son Ishmael that he had to leave home, or the pain he felt when he offered his beloved son Isaac on the altar.

The apostle Paul received 39 stripes five times (that's 195 stripes), was stoned once, spent a night and a day in the sea waiting to be rescued, suffered hunger and thirst, was hounded like a criminal by his enemies, and closed his life writing, "At my first defense no one stood with me, but all forsook me" (2 Cor. 11:22–33; 2 Tim. 4:16); yet he spent his life doing the will of God! And what about the pain Jesus felt when He did the will of the Father and died on a cross? People who think that doing the will of God is a guaranteed escape from suffering and sorrow haven't read very far in their Bibles.

Our problem is that we confuse being hurt with being harmed. Love sometimes brings hurt, but it never brings harm. Maturing believers don't enjoy pain or go seeking it, but they do expect pain and aren't shocked when it arrives. Peter cautioned, "Beloved, do not think it strange concerning the fiery trial which is to try you, as though some strange thing happened to you" (1 Peter 4:12).

So, my first response to suffering in the will of God ought to be, "My Father loves me and knows that I need this pain. Therefore, I'll accept this pain as His gift of love. This experience may hurt me, but by faith I won't allow it to harm me." What life does to us depends largely on what life finds in us. If we have faith in our hearts, knowing that God loves us, then suffering will make us. If we become bitter and resist God's will, then suffering will break us.

FOR THE GLORY OF GOD

The second principle is: the will of God is for the glory of God.

Most of us are prone to think of God's will only as His plan for getting something done. That's why we pray, "Your will be done on earth as it is in heaven" (Matt. 6:10). Getting things done may be the *immediate* purpose of His will, but the *ultimate* purpose is His glory; and the glory of God is the highest purpose that can occupy the human heart and life.

God's immediate purpose in opening the Red Sea was to rescue Israel from the pursuing Egyptian army, but His ultimate aim was to reveal His glory to a pagan nation whose ruler had flippantly asked, "Who is the LORD, that I should obey His voice to let Israel go?" (Ex. 5:2). As they watched the Egyptian army drown, no wonder Israel sang,

I will sing to the LORD,
For He has triumphed gloriously! . . .
He is my God, and I will praise Him (Ex. 15:1–2).

In chapter 12, we discussed what it means to glorify God, so there's no need to repeat it. What I want to emphasize here is that we dare not separate the will of God from the glory of God. Jesus put them together in the Lord's Prayer: "Hallowed be Your name. Your kingdom come. Your will be done" (Matt. 6:9–10). What God has joined together, we dare not put asunder.

Moses made that mistake when he smote the rock instead of speaking to it (Num. 20:1–13). God provided the water that His people needed, but Moses paid a price: he was not allowed to enter the Promised Land. God told him, "Because you did not believe Me, to hallow Me in the eyes of the children of Israel, therefore you shall not bring this congregation into the land which I have given them" (Num. 20:12). When we don't glorify God, we're always the losers.

James and John committed the same blunder when they urged their mother to ask Jesus for special thrones in the kingdom. Salome boldly said, "Grant that these two sons of mine may sit, one on Your right hand and the other on the left, in Your kingdom." Our Lord's reply was, "You do not know what you ask" (Matt. 20:21–22). In seeking the will of God, they had forgotten the glory of God. Would Jesus receive more glory because these two men were sitting next to Him? Or were James and John thinking about how *they* would be honored?

When Moses on the mount interceded for Israel, his greatest concern wasn't the nation he loved or even himself as their leader. His greatest concern was the glory of God. Listen to his plea:

Why should the Egyptians speak, and say, "He brought them out to harm them, to kill them in the mountains, and to consume them from the face of the earth"? Turn from Your fierce wrath, and relent from this harm to Your people. Remember Abraham, Isaac, and Israel, Your servants, to whom You swore by Your own self, and said to them, "I will multiply your descendants as the stars of heaven; and all this land I have spoken of I give to your descendants, and they shall inherit it forever" (Ex. 32:12–13).

Like the prodigal son, too often we want to enjoy our Father's wealth, but we don't want to glorify our Father's name. Our primary prayer is "Father, give me" and not "Father, make me" (Luke 15:12, 19).

Maturing believers aren't content merely to know what God wants them to do; they also want to know how to do it so that God will be glorified. David's desire to bring the ark to Jerusalem was a noble venture, but his first attempt failed because he didn't glorify God (2 Sam. 6). Paul's prayer to be delivered of his thorn in the flesh wasn't answered because having the thorn and depending on God's grace brought more glory to God (2 Cor. 12:7–10). When Mary and Martha sent word to Jesus that Lazarus was sick, He didn't immediately come to their aid. By waiting until Lazarus died, Jesus was able to bring more glory to God (John 11:4, 40).

When the Assyrian army surrounded Jerusalem and threatened to capture it, King Hezekiah prayed to God for help; and when you read his prayer (Isa. 37:14–20), you see that his great burden was the glory of God as opposed to the vanity of the Assyrian idols. He prayed, "You are God, You alone, of all the kingdoms of the earth" (v. 16). Sennacherib sent his army "to reproach the living God" (v. 17). And what a grand climax to his prayer: "Now therefore, O LORD our God, save us from his hand, that all the kingdoms of the earth may know that You are the LORD, You alone" (v. 20). God answered the prayer, delivered His people, and glorified His name.

When our prayers focus on the glory of God, we're in league with all creation, for "the heavens declare the glory of God" (Ps. 19:1). We're also cooperating with God in the great goal of salvation, "to the praise of the glory of His grace" (Eph. 1:6); and we're keeping in step with the Holy Spirit who was given that Jesus might be glorified (John 16:14).

THROUGH THE WORD OF GOD

The third principle is: the will of God is revealed through the Word of God: "Your word is a lamp to my feet and a light to my path" (Ps. 119:105).

Perhaps the psalmist had the nation of Israel in mind when he wrote that statement, for God guided His people by means of a glorious cloud by day and by night (Ex. 13:21; 40:34–38; Neh. 9:12). In times of perplexity, I've wished I had such visible and obvious means of guidance; but then I had to remind myself that God's children can't mature unless we walk by faith and not by sight.

However, we must not think that the Bible is some kind of magical book that reveals the future, like a deck of tarot cards or a cup of tea leaves. Opening the Bible at random and pointing to a verse is gambling, not seeking God's will; and the consequences could be disastrous. It's not the random use of the Bible that gives us guidance but reading the Word daily, systematically, and obediently. "Let the word of Christ dwell in you richly in all wisdom" is God's commandment (Col. 3:16).

Through its admonitions, promises, warnings, and examples, the Bible makes very clear what pleases God and what displeases Him. In fact, some verses state, "This is the will of God." "For this is the will of God, your sanctification: that you should abstain from sexual immorality" (1 Thess. 4:3). Nobody has to pray about committing fornication or adultery because God says these acts are sins and must be avoided. "In everything give thanks; for this is the will of God in Christ Jesus for you" (1 Thess. 5:18). That takes care of our complaining! "For this is the will of God, that by doing good you may put to silence the ignorance of foolish men" (1 Peter 2:15). The best way to handle criticism and slander is to do good works and let God do the rest.

I can't prove it statistically, but I'm sure that 90 percent of the decisions I make daily are covered in the Scriptures; and I don't have to ask God what to do. I've read my Bible enough to know that it's wrong to steal, to lie, to hate, to avenge myself, to gossip, to lose my temper, to harbor resentment, and to be unkind to people. But what about the other 10 percent? Although it gave me plenty of counsel concerning marriage and the Christian home, my Bible didn't tell me exactly the girl I should marry. It didn't name the school I should attend, the city I should live in, or the local church my family and I should attend. How do we handle these everyday practical decisions?

It's here that we trust God for the sanctified common sense that comes from the renewing of the mind (Rom. 12:2). Believers who spend time daily in the Word and prayer gradually develop a spiritual radar, a practical wisdom[1] from the Holy Spirit that gives us direction when we need it. Sometimes that direction comes from a promise or warning in Scripture, sometimes from God's providential working in circumstances, and sometimes from the Spirit's witness in our hearts. Even a chance remark by a friend can be used of God to guide us if our minds and hearts are prepared and we're willing to obey God's leading.

The Bible wasn't written *to* us, but it was written *for* us; and it was written in such a way that the Spirit can use it to teach us, warn us, restore us, and keep us on "the paths of righteousness for His name's sake" (Ps. 23:3). But we must be willing to obey, for God can't direct a saint whose spiritual gears are in neutral. Asking for God's leading while thinking, *And if I like it, I'll do it,* is like getting married while saying to yourself, *And if this doesn't work, I'll get a divorce.* Jesus said, "If anyone chooses to do God's will, he will find out whether my teaching comes from God" (John 7:17 NIV). F. W. Robertson was right: obedience is the organ of spiritual knowledge.

Determining God's will also depends on knowing God's character, and His character is revealed in His Word. It doesn't take long for a child to learn what Mother and Father are really like, and the child's behavior is based on that knowledge. Students study their instructors as much as they study their books, and they try to do the kind of work that will please their teachers the most. That's the way to get a better grade.

It isn't enough to read the Bible and discover what God did; we also need to learn why God did it. God "made known His ways to Moses, His acts to the children of Israel" (Ps. 103:7). The Israelites knew what God did because they saw it happen, but Moses knew why God did it. That's because Moses prayed, "If I have found grace in Your sight, show me now Your way, that I may know You and that I may find grace in Your sight" (Ex. 33:13).

When the Lord revealed Himself to Moses on the mount, He answered Moses' prayer by reciting His glorious attributes: "The LORD, the LORD God, merciful and gracious, longsuffering, and abounding in goodness and truth" (Ex. 34:6). And when Moses interceded for the disobedient nation at Kadesh-Barnea, he reminded God of His holy character and obtained pardon for them (Num. 14:11–25). When you know the character of God, you find it easier to pray in the will of God.

When circumstances or people want to direct us, we must trust the Spirit of God within us to bear witness and give us guidance from the Word. We must always test circumstances by the Word of God;

otherwise, we'll find ourselves going on detours. On two occasions, David had opportunity to kill King Saul, and some of his men encouraged him to do it. But David refused because he knew it was wrong to avenge himself by laying hands on God's anointed leader, even though that leader was rejected by God. (See 1 Sam. 24; 26.) When the south wind blows softly (Acts 27:13), we need great discernment, and that discernment can come only through the Spirit of God using the Word of God.

Please permit me to say it again: this kind of spiritual guidance comes not from a random reading of the Bible but from allowing the Word to "dwell in [us] richly" (Col. 3:16) and making it the daily nourishment of the inner being. It comes when we exhibit the same kind of submission and devotion that David exhibited when he wrote,

Show me Your ways, O LORD;
Teach me Your paths.
Lead me in Your truth and teach me,
For You are the God of my salvation;
On You I wait all the day (Ps. 25:4–5).

AS WE TRUST AND OBEY

Our fourth principle is that we appreciate the will of God more as we trust Him and obey what He tells us to do: "And do not be conformed to this world, but be transformed by the renewing of your mind, that you may prove what is that good and acceptable and perfect will of God" (Rom. 12:2).

The word translated "prove" means "to prove by experience." It describes the testing of metal in the furnace and suggests to us that discerning the will of God is something we learn by practical experience in the furnaces of life. Sometimes children don't believe their parents' warnings or instructions and have to learn the hard way that fire burns, knives cut, too much candy can make you sick, and electricity is dangerous to play with. But Paul isn't advising us to learn the hard way; rather, he is telling us how to learn to discern God's will in the daily experience of life and avoid the problems.

Words like *be transformed* and *renewing* describe an ongoing process rather than something completed. God doesn't hand us the latest road atlas, complete with maps, photographs, and directions. Rather, He gives us a compass and a goal, and we learn the rest along the way.

"The God of our fathers has chosen you that you should know His will" (Acts 22:14). That's where it begins—knowing His will. But it must not stop there because God wants us to *understand* His will: "Therefore do not be unwise, but understand what the will of the Lord is" (Eph. 5:17). This involves getting to know God better, both His character and His ways. This should lead to "doing the will of God from the heart" (Eph. 6:6). The better we know God, the more we should love Him; and the more we love Him, the more we'll be motivated by that love. Jesus said, "If anyone loves Me, he will keep My word" (John 14:23).

This growing experience should lead to *delighting* in the will of God: "I delight to do Your will, O my God, and Your law is within my heart" (Ps. 40:8). Now the statutes have turned into songs because duty has become delight and the whole person is devoted to the will of God. David prayed,

Teach me Your way, O LORD;
I will walk in Your truth;
Unite my heart to fear Your name (Ps. 86:11).

Here you have the mind ("teach me"), the will ("I will walk"), and the heart ("unite my heart") joined together in joyful obedience to the Lord.

God's "good and acceptable and perfect will" is one will and not three. The will of God isn't like a mail order catalog that offers the customer "good—better—best," the only difference being the price and the quality of the merchandise. A young man said to me, "I think I'll settle for God's good will because I don't want to make the sacrifices necessary for His perfect will." But a holy and loving God could never will for His beloved children anything other than what is perfect. If we settle for second best, it isn't God's second best because He wills only what is the very best for us. "The renewal of the mind," writes Leon Morris, "enables the believer to discern what is good, what is pleasing to God, and what is perfect."[2]

If you keep in mind that discerning the will of God means developing a personal relationship with the Lord, not receiving a series of memos from heaven, then you will better understand how this demanding but delightful process works. The better we get to know the Lord, the better we understand His ways and His character and, therefore, the better we know how to please Him. However, at the same time, we get to know ourselves better, and we discover the things that need special attention. It's similar to the kind of personal growth that spouses experience during their first year or two of marriage.

When I was in pastoral ministry, during premarital counseling sessions I would give the man and the woman each a piece of paper and say, "Would you please write down the three things that you enjoy the most, and then the three things you think your prospective mate enjoys the most." The results were sometimes devastating!

"If you two don't know how to please each other now," I'd say, "what will happen after you're married?" Sometimes this led to another counseling session, which I hope led to a happier marriage.

This adventure of getting to know God and ourselves better makes doing the will of God exciting, far more exciting than sinning. When we sin, we become blind to ourselves and to God; and there is no growth in character. Like the prodigal son, we find ourselves lonely and perishing while there is plenty back at the Father's house. What Dr. Theodore Epp called "adventuring by faith" is the most exciting kind of life anybody could ever experience.

QUESTIONS ABOUT GOD'S WILL

We've examined the four principles relating to the will of God. What remains now is to deal with some practical questions that often arise when you discuss this topic.

What if I've prayed, read the Word, and waited on God, but no answer has come? What do I do next?

You keep waiting. If there is no answer, you assume God wants you to stay where you are. Remember that God is more concerned about building the worker than getting the work done. If He wants to grow a mushroom, He can do it overnight; but it takes a few years to build an oak. In our waiting, God works in our lives to prepare us for what He is preparing for us.

What if I make a mistake and start to move out of His will?

It has been my experience that the Lord checks me at some point and lets me know that I need to stop and seriously evaluate the situation. When I was a seminary student, I needed a job, so I consulted the student bulletin board and found one that seemed to fit my abilities and my schedule. Without taking time to pray, I called the phone number given and told the man who answered that I'd take the job. No sooner did I hang up the phone than my heart was very uneasy, and I wasn't able to study. Then I took time to pray, and the Spirit rebuked me for running ahead of the Lord. I had to phone the company again, apologize, and tell the man I couldn't take the job. On other occasions, when I've run ahead of the Lord, He has allowed circumstances to block the way and close the doors. Our Father loves us too much to allow us ignorantly to rush out of His will. If we're stubborn and rebellious, He may let us suffer for it before He pulls us out.

What about putting out a fleece?

What Gideon did was a sign not of faith but of unbelief (Judg. 6:36–40), and I don't recommend that you follow his example. God had already made it clear to Gideon that He would use him to deliver Israel from the Midianites, and there was no need for Gideon to test God's will further. Who are we to tell God *how* He should communicate with us? How do I know that the test I'm proposing is a valid one? I've heard people say, "Well, if I get a phone call by such and such a time, I'll know this is God's will." So we allow the phone company to determine God's will for us! Better to depend on the Word and wait on the Lord. Gideon didn't have a complete Bible as we do, so perhaps we can excuse him. But beware! Use a fleece and the devil may pull the wool over your eyes!

To what extent can I follow the counsel of friends?

To the extent that they're walking with God, following the Bible, and seeking His blessing. However, people who give us advice and counsel really don't have anything to lose if we get into trouble, except perhaps some credibility; and that's soon forgotten. It's wise to have a few confidants with whom we can share our needs; but it's unwise to have too many, or we'll give the impression that we're looking for somebody to agree with what we've already decided to do! Counseling people about major decisions isn't a job for amateurs or strangers. Talk only to people who know you, love you, and will level with you.

I have a friend who determines God's will by taking a card out of her promise box. Is this dependable?

No. I call that religious roulette. The purpose of a promise box is to give us a promise a day that we can carry with us, memorize, and learn to appreciate. But pulling out a card to determine God's will is like opening your Bible at random and pointing to a verse. If you were planning a trip, would you open the road atlas just anywhere and point to a highway? A promise can encourage us *after we've made a decision*, but pulling out a card is a dangerous way to make that decision.

Does God want to guide us in little things or only in big things?

He wants to guide us in everything, but He also expects us to use our common sense. I had a friend who became unbalanced emotionally because he wanted God to tell him what breakfast cereal to eat, what color tie to wear, and what side of the street to walk on. There are no trivial things in the Christian life, but some things are more important than others. God can use a casual word or a new acquaintance to help us determine His will. If we yield ourselves to God each day and ask Him to guide us, we'll have the direction we need when we need it. If we don't, then we wait. God leads in little things and big things because He is making all things work together for good.

Sometimes I get petrified when I think about the will of God and how I could mess up my life if I disobey it. What should I do?

Stop focusing on God's will and start focusing on God. Remember, the will of God is a personal relationship between you and the Lord, and He wants your attention and affection. Don't be like the date who was so worried about how he looked and what he said that he ignored his girlfriend and drove away from the party without her. *We never have to be afraid of the will of God because the will of God comes from the heart of God.* It's one thing to fear the Lord because that can be a mark of humility; but it's quite something else to fear failure because that could be a mark of pride. Nobody wants to fail, but occasionally, we all stumble. It's a part of being human. But don't get so lost in the process that you neglect your Lord and fail to get to know Him better. People who only sit in the car and read the map don't get to enjoy the scenery.

Chapter 18

HOPE: LIVING IN THE LIGHT OF ETERNITY

M ost Christians think of heaven primarily as a destination, the place God's people go when they die or when the Lord returns. They cling to Christ's promise, and a great promise it is: "I go to prepare a place for you. And if I go and prepare a place for you, I will come again and receive you to Myself; that where I am, there you may be also" (John 14:2–3).

But maturing believers realize that heaven is much more than a destination. Heaven is a *motivation*. Because God's children know we're going to heaven, it makes a difference in the way we live right now on earth. "If you read history," wrote C. S. Lewis, "you will find that the Christians who did the most for the present world were just those who thought the most of the next."[1]

Four times in the Gospel of John, Jesus uses the phrase "where I am." He was referring, of course, to heaven. These four passages describe the kind of people we will become when the assurance of heaven becomes a motivation in our lives today.

WITNESSING PEOPLE

To begin with, if we really believe we're going to heaven, we'll be a *witnessing people*. John described this scene:

The Pharisees heard the crowd murmuring these things concerning Him, and the Pharisees and the chief priests sent officers to take Him. Then Jesus said to them, "I shall be with you a little while longer, and then I go to Him who sent Me. You will seek Me and not find Me, and where I am you cannot come" (John 7:32–34).

If there is no heaven, and if death means only extinction, then "let us eat and drink, for tomorrow we die!" (1 Cor. 15:32). But according to Jesus, there is a place called heaven, and there is also a place called hell. Death is not extinction, for "it is appointed for men to die once, but after this the judgment" (Heb. 9:27). If these are the facts—and Jesus is our authority—then the warning of the prophet Amos is appropriate for today's world: "Prepare to meet your God!" (Amos 4:12).

People who know they're going to heaven ought to be motivated to want others to go there with them. That's why Jesus warned the religious leaders of His day that if they didn't trust Him, they'd never go where He was going—to heaven. It was a loving witness, but it was also an uncompromising witness. The alternatives were clear.

In recent years, some Christians have been wavering in their witness because they aren't really sure about heaven and hell. "Can it be," they ask, "that people who have never trusted Christ are really destined to be eternally condemned? Would a God of love and grace do such a thing to sincere people?"

In other words, did Peter know what he was talking about when he said to the highest Jewish religious council, "Nor is there salvation in any other, for there is no other name under heaven given among men by which we must be saved" (Acts 4:12)? Was Jesus telling the truth when He said to the Pharisees, "Therefore I said to you that you will die in your sins; for if you do not believe that I am He, you will die in your sins" (John 8:24)?

There is an exclusiveness about the Christian faith that doesn't fit into our contemporary atmosphere of pluralism. We're told that it's bad manners and politically incorrect to tell our neighbors that the only way to heaven is through faith in Jesus Christ. We Christians ought not to be arrogant in our witness, but we do need to be diligent and declare boldly that Jesus Christ is the only way to heaven, not one of many ways. Salvation isn't a buffet where sinners select what they want. Jesus is the only true Bread of Life, and everybody who rejects Him rejects eternal life.

The story about J. Hudson Taylor and Mr. Nyi, a Chinese business-man, comes to mind. God saved Mr. Nyi and made him a fervent wit-ness to his people. One day, he asked Hudson Taylor, "How long have you had the Glad Tidings in England?" Somewhat embarrassed, Taylor told him, "Several hundreds of years."

"What!" exclaimed Mr. Nyi. "Is it possible that you have known about Jesus so long and only now have come to tell us. My father sought the truth for more than twenty years and died without finding it. *Oh, why did you not come sooner?*"[2]

The words of Scripture make it clear that people who are going to heaven have the responsibility of telling others that they can go with them:

> Go home to your friends, and tell them what great things the Lord has done for you, and how He has had compassion on you (Mark 5:19).

> Go out quickly into the streets and lanes of the city, and bring in here the poor and the maimed and the lame and the blind (Luke 14:21).

> Go out into the highways and hedges, and compel [constrain] them to come in, that my house may be filled (Luke 14:23).

> Go into all the world and preach the gospel to every creature (Mark 16:15).

When I was a teenager and a young Christian, I heard a speaker at a Youth for Christ rally say, "Never forget that little word *go*. It's two-thirds of the word *God*, one-third of the word *gospel*, and half of the word *good*. It's a little word with a big meaning."

SACRIFICING PEOPLE

We'll also become a *sacrificing people*, Our Lord said,

The hour has come that the Son of Man should be glorified. Most assuredly, I say to you, unless a grain of wheat falls into the ground and dies, it remains alone; but if it dies, it produces much grain. He who loves his life will lose it, and he who hates his life in this world will keep it for eternal life. If anyone serves Me, let him follow Me; and where I am, there My servant will be also. If anyone serves Me, him My Father will honor (John 12:23–26).

A seed lives for the future, but it can't experience that future of beauty and fruitfulness unless it's buried in the earth and dies. Seeds kept in a granary have potential, but that potential isn't realized until the seeds are taken out of the bin and planted in the ground. In using this image, our Lord was first of all speaking about Himself and His approaching death on the cross, but the principle involved in this image applies to every believer. Unless we die to self, take up our cross, and follow Him, we will be alone, fruitless, and without the Father's approval. If you lose your life for His sake, you find it; and if you die, you live. A paradox? Indeed, and a very precious one!

"The field is the world," said Jesus, "[and] the good seeds are the sons of the kingdom" (Matt. 13:38). The Lord of the harvest plants His people where He wants them, and there they die to their own plans and bear fruit for His glory. What keeps them going when the going is tough? They know they're going to heaven and will be with Christ where He is. As the songwriter expressed it, "It will be worth it all when we see Jesus!"

But if we think dying to self is difficult for us, consider what Jesus experienced at Calvary. You and I can't begin to imagine what our Lord had to endure when He died for us on the cross. How was He able to do it? "Looking unto Jesus, the author and finisher of our faith, who *for the joy that was set before Him* endured the cross, despising the shame, and has sat down at the right hand of the throne of God"

(Heb. 12:2, italics mine). The Seed would die and be buried, but then He would burst forth in resurrection power and glory and produce a great harvest.

A journalist visiting a jungle mission outpost said to a nurse who was caring for a patient, "It must be difficult to be buried out here."

As she cleansed the patient's ugly wound, the nurse smiled and replied, "I wasn't buried. I was planted."

She had her eyes on heaven.

CONFIDENT PEOPLE

If we know we're going to heaven, we ought to be a *confident people*. You no doubt know these familiar words:

> Let not your heart be troubled; you believe in God, believe also in Me. In My Father's house are many mansions; if it were not so, I would have told you. I go to prepare a place for you. And if I go and prepare a place for you, I will come again and receive you to Myself; that where I am, there you may be also (John 14:1–3).

It shouldn't surprise us that the apostles were troubled. Jesus had told them that one of them was a traitor, and He had warned Peter that he would deny Him before the cock crowed at dawn. Those two announcements would have been enough to discourage them, but He also told them that He was leaving them and going back to the Father. That announcement broke their hearts.

Jesus didn't shelter the apostles from the realities of life, nor did He suggest that they deny the pain they were experiencing in their hearts. The present hour was grim for them, but the future was full of glory; and He focused their attention on the future. It wasn't a nebulous pledge of "pie in the sky by and by" but a divine promise "that where I am, there you may be also."

The destination was meant to be a motivation. The fact that the apostles were going to heaven should have calmed their hearts, dissolved their worries, and given them the peace they needed. Heaven would be their home forever, an eternal home with the Lord Jesus Christ.

Years later, when Peter wrote to the saints in Asia Minor, he used the same approach. They were about to experience a "fiery trial," but Peter knew what would sustain them. He wrote,

> Blessed be the God and Father of our Lord Jesus Christ, who according to His abundant mercy has begotten us again to a living hope through the resurrection of Jesus Christ from the dead, to an inheritance incorruptible and undefiled and that does not fade away, reserved in heaven for you (1 Peter 1:3–4).

A living hope, an eternal inheritance, the Father's house: with all of that to anticipate, God's children should be able to face and endure any trials to the glory of God. But we must not think of heaven only as *escape from;* we should look upon the promise of heaven as *entrance into.* Jesus "for the joy that was set before Him endured the cross" (Heb. 12:2), particularly the joy of presenting His beautiful, faultless bride to His Father (Jude 24).

It's really too bad we emphasize heaven only when somebody dies. After all, the hope we have is a "living hope," and that should give us confidence for living, even when things seem hopeless.

UNITED PEOPLE

Knowing that we're going to heaven should make us a witnessing people, a sacrificing people, a confident people, and a *united people,* loving one another. This is the way Jesus prayed:

And the glory which You gave Me I have given them, that they may be one just as We are one: I in them, and You in Me; that they may be made perfect in one, and that the world may know that You have sent Me, and have loved them as You have loved Me. Father, I desire that they also whom You gave Me may be with Me where I am, that they may behold My glory which You have given Me; for You loved Me before the foundation of the world (John 17:22–24).

What Jesus says here is incredible. First, He tells us that the glory of heaven has already been given to those who belong to Him. That glory hasn't yet been revealed publicly, but it's there; and it's our guarantee of heaven. But that's not all. He also says that the Father loves us—His children—*just as He loves the Son!* Jesus even closes His prayer on that note: "That the love with which You loved Me may be in them, and I in them" (John 17:26).

I say it again: it's incredible! The Father loves us as He loves His Son, and the glory of heaven is already residing in us! We share heaven's love and heaven's glory. That being the case, we ought to be able to love one another here on earth, for after all, *we're going to be in heaven together!* How can we expect the lost world to believe that God loves sinners if there is no evidence of that love even among the saints? If we who share the same spiritual gifts—God's life (John 17:2–3), God's Word (John 17:8, 14), God's glory (John 17:22), and God's love (John 17:23, 26)—can't get along with one another, what right do we have to criticize the people outside God's family for fighting one another?

The unity that Jesus prayed for is a *spiritual* unity, a bond of family love that comes from within, but that doesn't suggest that this unity is invisible. Quite the contrary. It's a *visible* unity that the world can see, a unity that tells the world of God's love. The fact that God's people are all going to heaven ought to encourage that kind of love among churches and individuals today. How wonderful it would be if the watching world would say once again, "Behold, how they love one another!"

So, the next time we have opportunity for witness and we're tempted to be silent, let's remember that we're going to heaven; and the people who aren't going to heaven need to know how to get there. The next time God calls us to sacrifice, let's remind ourselves that we're going to heaven; therefore, He can plant us wherever He desires. The next time we find ourselves fretting and worrying, let's say to ourselves, "We're going to heaven! Why worry about the journey when the road leads home?" Finally, the next time there is danger of a family feud among some of God's people, let's lovingly remind everybody that we're all going to heaven; and we ought to be able to love one another here, even if we do have our disagreements.

BE SERIOUS

The theme of heaven and hope brings up the solemn subject of death, a subject most people want to avoid. A contemporary wit said, "It's not that I'm afraid to die. I just don't want to be there when it happens." I have news for him: he won't know when it will happen, *but he'll be there.* The maturing Christian believer has a balanced biblical view of death that does away with fear but delivers from flippancy.

As God's maturing children, born again to a living hope, we ought to make three responses to the reality of death.

First, death is an enemy, so *we must be serious:* "The last enemy that will be destroyed is death" (1 Cor. 15:26). The first enemy described in Scripture is Satan, who through our first parents introduced sin and death into the human race: "Therefore, just as through one man [Adam] sin entered the world, and death through sin, and thus death spread to all men, because all sinned" (Rom. 5:12). Death now reigns (Rom. 5:14, 17), and only through Jesus Christ can death be finally conquered. Paul wrote,

"O Death, where is your sting?
O Hades, where is your victory?"

The sting of death is sin, and the strength of sin is the law. But thanks be to God, who gives us the victory through our Lord Jesus Christ (1 Cor. 15:55–57).

For the Christian believer, death is a defeated enemy, but still an enemy. Death is highly unpredictable and humanly irreversible. It robs us of loved ones; it cuts down young people and prevents them from enjoying fulfilled lives; it snatches children from their parents' arms; it even enters the womb and turns it into a tomb. Whether we think about it or not, every living thing on earth is fighting death twenty-four hours a day. Queen Elizabeth I of England said, "All my possessions for one moment of time"; and then she died. "Death takes no bribes," said Benjamin Franklin; and that even applies to queens.

For the most part, people today are sheltered from birth and death, the two boundaries of life, both of which used to occur at home. Today, Mother goes to the hospital and comes home with a baby; Grandmother goes to the hospital and doesn't come home.

Well-trained morticians make corpses look as though they're only sleeping, and the people who come to comfort the family are careful not to use the words *die* and *death*. Though a certain amount of tenderness is commendable, "let's pretend" doesn't go very far when somebody is missing at home and never shows up. And those who avoid talking about death, or who jest about death, are often the ones least prepared to face death.

BE WISE

Death is an enemy, and it behooves us to be serious. But, second, death is a teacher, so *we must be wise:* "So teach us to number our days, that we may gain a heart of wisdom" (Ps. 90:12).[3]

Even though we live a day at a time, I doubt that many people actually number their days. We number our years; and at a given point, we even stop revealing the total. In light of eternity, life is brief; and the older we become, the faster time seems to travel:

> For a thousand years in Your sight
> Are like yesterday when it is past,
> And like a watch in the night.
> You carry them away like a flood;
> They are like a sleep.
> In the morning they are like grass which grows up:
> In the morning it flourishes and grows up;
> In the evening it is cut down and withers (Ps. 90:4–6).

The fact that God is eternal but our days are numbered ought to teach us some solemn lessons that, if heeded, should make us wiser and better Christians.

1. Treat life as a treasure to be invested and not to be wasted. You can't trade life in for a new model, the way you get rid of a beat-up used car. Life is a stewardship, and we never know when our time is up and the Master will call for an accounting. Henry David Thoreau, though not a professed evangelical believer, had the right idea about life: "I went to the woods because I wished to live deliberately, to front only the essential facts of life, and see if I could not learn what it had to teach, and not, when I came to die, discover that I had not lived."[4]

2. Live a day at a time in the light of eternity. Accept each day as God's gift to you:

As your days, so shall your strength be (Deut. 33:25).

His compassions fail not.
They are new every morning;
Great is Your faithfulness (Lam. 3:22–23).

Instead of complaining about what we don't have, let's rejoice over what we do have. Someone has said that the average person is being crucified between two thieves: the regrets of yesterday and the worries about tomorrow. Don't make that mistake. Let each day be a new beginning, and live that day in the light of eternity.

3. Treasure the people in your life. We don't know how long we'll have the family and friends that we may be prone to take for granted or even criticize. Are there misunderstandings that have alienated family members? Then get them settled while there is still time. Life is too short for us to be carrying grudges. Have you planned to write that letter or make that phone call, but somehow it just hasn't gotten done? Then do it! It wouldn't hurt if every single day we expressed our sincere appreciation to somebody in our circle who means something to us.

4. Put God first in every area. John stated it this way: "He who does the will of God abides forever" (1 John 2:17). After wrestling with the enigmas of life and death, success and failure, Solomon wrote,

Let us hear the conclusion of the whole matter:
Fear God and keep His commandments,
For this is man's all (Eccl. 12:13).

Let the touch of eternity be on every aspect of life, every decision, every rite of passage, every relationship, every success and failure, every joy and sorrow; and life will be richer and fuller.

5. Share the gospel. Life is short, and you never know when you might be the last person to have the opportunity to speak to somebody about salvation. One room at the Moody Memorial Church in Chicago is named Harper Hall after John Harper, who almost became pastor of the church. A native of Scotland, he preached at Moody Church in 1911 and was so well received that he was invited back the next year when the church was seeking a pastor. He booked passage on the world's greatest liner, the *Titanic,* and was one of those who went down with the ship. But before his death, as he drifted in the icy waters, Harper called to a young sailor, "Are you saved?" and quoted Scripture to him. That sailor was rescued and later trusted Christ, testifying to all, "I am John Harper's last convert."[5]

BE READY

Death is an enemy; therefore, we must be serious. Death is a teacher; therefore, we must be wise. Finally, death is an adventure; therefore, *we must be ready:* "For I am already being poured out as a drink offering, and the time of my departure is at hand" (2 Tim. 4:6).

The word translated "departure" gives us our English word *analysis* and means "to break down into component parts." In Paul's day, the word was used in a variety of ways, each of which has its application to the Christian life.

Soldiers used the word to refer to breaking camp, taking down the tents, and moving on. Paul used a similar image in 2 Corinthians 5:1: "For we know that if our earthly house, this tent, is destroyed, we have a building from God, a house not made with hands, eternal in the heavens." He is not referring to a mansion in heaven but to the glorified body that will swallow up our temporary tent when Jesus returns (2 Cor. 5:2). Death means taking down the tent, but resurrection means receiving a glorified body (1 Thess. 4:15–18).[6]

Sailors used the word to describe loosing the ship's moorings and setting sail. Although nowhere in Scripture are we told that we're going to heaven in a boat, "setting sail" is an ancient and common image for death. Tennyson used it in his poem "Crossing the Bar."[7] Paul saw death as freedom, being loosed from this world and ushered into the presence of God.

Farmers used the word for the unyoking of oxen. "My work is done," said Paul, "and I'm entering into rest." Teachers and philosophers used the word to mean "solving a problem." In this life, we have questions that nobody can answer; but when we see the Lord, He'll make everything clear to us. What Jesus said to Peter, He says to us: "What I am doing you do not understand now, but you will know after this" (John 13:7).

Finally, weavers used the word to mean "taking a weaving off the loom." Life is like a weaving, and we don't always see the pattern God is using. From our point of view, there is no pattern, and there are many dangling threads; but when we see the Lord, the pattern will be complete. After a near death experience, King Hezekiah used the same image when he praised the Lord for his miraculous recovery:

> My life span is gone,
> Taken from me like a shepherd's tent;
> I have cut off my life like a weaver.
> He cuts me off from the loom (Isa. 38:12).

Peter paints a fascinating picture of death in 2 Peter 1:11: "For so an entrance will be supplied to you abundantly into the everlasting kingdom of our Lord and Savior Jesus Christ." The image here seems to be that of an Olympic winner returning to his city and being honored. Sometimes the jubilant populace would construct a new gate in the city wall and name it after their champion. The Christian life is a difficult race, but what a welcome the faithful runner will receive!

When you consider these pictures of Christian death, you can understand why Joe Bayly wrote, "Death is the great adventure, beside which moon landings and space trips pale into insignificance." This doesn't mean that we should get so excited about death that we take it into our own hands because God alone has the privilege of calling us to Himself in His time (Deut. 32:39; 1 Sam. 2:6; Job 14:5; Luke 2:29; 12:20; Acts 17:28; Rev. 1:18).

The best way for a Christian to prepare for death is to be faithful in life and to be able to say with Paul, "I have fought the good fight, I have finished the race, I have kept the faith" (2 Tim. 4:7) or, even more, to be able to say with Jesus, "I have glorified You on the earth. I have finished the work which You have given Me to do" (John 17:4). Quitters don't win, and winners don't quit.

"Most men hope to go to heaven when they die," Bishop J. C. Ryle wrote a century ago,

> but few, it may be feared, take the trouble to consider whether they would enjoy heaven if they got there. Heaven is essentially a holy place; its inhabitants are all holy; its occupations are all holy. To be really happy in heaven, it is clear and plain that we must be somewhat trained and made ready for heaven while we are on earth.[8]

Maturing Christians don't have a morbid curiosity about death, nor do they ignore it or treat it lightly. They take death seriously by taking life seriously. They measure time in the light of eternity and seek to use their God-given opportunities wisely. If your Christian life is an adventure, then your death will also be an adventure; and you have nothing to fear.

On his seventy-fifth birthday, Sir Winston Churchill quipped, "I am ready to meet my Maker. Whether my Maker is prepared for the great ordeal of meeting me is another matter."

God is prepared to meet anybody, and He alone knows when the meeting will take place; but are we ready to meet Him?

Maturing Christians are. They say with David, "As for me, I will see Your face in righteousness; I shall be satisfied when I awake in Your likeness" (Ps. 17:15).

Chapter 19

GENEROSITY: SHARING
HIS GIFTS WITH OTHERS

H ere's my definition of *a Christian wedding*: "a religious ceremony during which a man and a woman confess their love for each other and prove it by putting down their toys and weapons and picking up their tools, promising that, from that time forth, they will work together to build a home, living each for the other and both for the Lord." It's a long definition, I know, and maybe you should read it again; but I think it covers all the essentials.

Since that's the way I feel about marriage, I often gave this last piece of counsel to newlyweds: "Remember, from now on, there's no such thing as *mine* and *yours*; it's *ours*." I hope all the couples I married took that advice to heart.

PRIORITIES

Defending territorial rights may be important in the international arena, but on the personal scene, the practice could be a declaration of war. People who work together or live together certainly ought to enjoy their privacy and their possessions, but they also have the obligation to share themselves and what they have with others. How we respond to the needs of others reveals how far the maturing process has gone in our lives. Are we building walls or bridges? Have we laid down our toys and weapons so that we can pick up our tools and build? Are we guarding or sharing?

I realize that children must learn early to respect both privacy and property. However, the strongest foundation for that respect isn't law; it's love. Law says, "What's mine is mine; I'll keep it." Lust says, "What's yours is mine; I'll take it." But love says, "What's mine is yours; I'll share it." The Christian way is the way of love.

We know we're maturing when we love people and use things instead of following the world's pattern of using people and loving things. In act 3 of *Lady Windermere's Fan*, Oscar Wilde defines a *cynic* as "a man who knows the price of everything and the value of nothing." That definition describes many people who wouldn't call themselves cynics, including some professed Christians. They put pleasing themselves ahead of pleasing God, and getting things is more desirable than loving people.

In Old Testament days, Israel valued things by "the shekel of the sanctuary" (Lev. 27:25), but today's church tends to measure things by the shekel of the marketplace. We've forgotten that Jesus said, "For what is highly esteemed among men is an abomination in the sight of God" (Luke 16:15).

Our Lord's theology of things is explained in what we call the Sermon on the Mount (Matt. 5—7).[1] In this sermon, He tells us how to cultivate true righteousness, the righteousness that characterizes the citizens of His kingdom; and He warns us to avoid the false righteousness of religion, the kind practiced by the scribes and Pharisees of that day (5:20). What He requires is really quite simple: we must be rightly related to God, people, and things.

God comes first: "But seek first the kingdom of God and His righteousness, and all these things shall be added to you" (Matt. 6:33). People come next, even people who don't like us or that we don't like, for we're commanded, among other things, to be merciful, to make peace, to be nonjudgmental, and to be generous and forgiving. This list suggests that some of the people in our lives won't be too easy to live with, but we're supposed to love them and seek to lead them to Christ.

Last on the list is what Jesus calls things, the basics that keep physical life going. Unlike some ascetics and gurus, Jesus doesn't condemn our owning and enjoying things. After all, God made things and called them "very good" (Gen. 1:31); He knows that we need things to survive

(Matt. 6:32); and He "gives us richly all things to enjoy" (1 Tim. 6:17). But Jesus does remind us that we must put God's kingdom first, and if we do, God will take care of providing the things we need.

It's all a matter of priorities: God first, people next, things last. But that was before the world was invaded by power advertising, credit cards, TV shopping channels, and exciting shopping malls with their own theme parks. Far too many people today are prone to put themselves first, things next, and other people last. God is usually left out completely, although many people in North America condescend to give Him an annual nod of appreciation on Thanksgiving Day.

So, the Christian philosophy (or theology) of things is that God made things and shares them with us as a generous Creator and a loving Father. We should receive these gifts as appreciative stewards, enjoy them, and use them wisely for His glory. Note that I said stewards, not owners. A steward owns nothing but has the privilege of managing another's wealth. However, a steward had better be faithful in using that wealth because one day the master will audit the books.

Let's consider some of the gifts the Father has graciously shared with us, and seek to discover how we can share these gifts with others.

THE GIFT OF LIFE

Life itself is a gift from God. "He gives to all life, breath, and all things," Paul told the Greek philosophers on Mars Hill. "In Him we live and move and have our being" (Acts 17:25, 28). Life isn't a goal that we've achieved; it's a gift that we've received. One day we'll answer to God for what we've done with His investment.

What is life? Carl Sagan humbly admits, "A great deal is known about life. . . . Yet despite the enormous fund of information that each of these biological specialities has provided, it is a remarkable fact that no general agreement exists on what it is that is being studied. There is no generally accepted definition of life."[2] All of which boils down to: "We don't know."

How you define life may depend on how you feel about life. The Jewish writer Sholom Aleichem called life "a blister on top of a tumor, and a boil on top of that"; but we must remember that the Jewish people have endured a great deal of suffering. To Samuel Butler, life was "one long process of getting tired." And Clarence Darrow described it as "a span of time in which the first half is ruined by our parents and the second half by our children."[3]

All life comes from life, and all life comes from God, who alone has life in Himself. But life is much more than the body we feed and clothe and protect. "Is not life more than food," asked Jesus, "and the body more than clothing?" (Matt. 6:25). I wish I could shout to the crowd in Times Square or Piccadilly Circus, "Life is more! Life is more!"

The most materialistic atheist would have to agree with Jesus that "life is more." Even atheists occasionally have unforgettable moments of joy and ecstasy that they can't analyze in their laboratories or explain in their lectures. The miracle of the birth of a baby, the drama of sunrise or sunset in the mountains, the holy tenderness of a beautiful wedding, the spontaneous hug and kiss from a grandchild, the rapture of a beautiful symphony—these and many more experiences tell us that "life is more." Though we're made from the dust and need sustaining roots in this earth, there is something in human life that goes beyond food and clothes, something transcendent that links us to the eternal. Solomon gave us the answer: "He has put eternity in their hearts" (Eccl. 3:11).

That explains why life is empty and tasteless for so many people: they've left out the eternal. They've forgotten that "life is more." Leave out the eternal and you must join Solomon's pathetic lament, "Vanity of vanities, all is vanity" (Eccl. 1:2). The Hebrew word translated "vanity" means "futility, nonsense, frustration" and describes the meaningless existence of people who have gained the whole world but lost their souls.

Dag Hammarskjold put it this way: "Is life so wretched? Isn't it rather your hands which are too small, your vision which is muddied? You are the one who must grow up."[4]

SHARING FROM THE HEART

Life is what you are alive to.

Offer me free tickets to a sporting event, and you won't see me generate much enthusiasm. But tell me you have access to a private used-book sale, and I'm ready to go right now. The doorbell chimes, announcing a man who is taking a survey, and I do my best to get out of it. But if that chime announces a surprise visit from a family member or a friend, I'm suddenly very excited. Life is what we are alive to.

That explains why Paul wrote, "For to me, to live is Christ, and to die is gain" (Phil. 1:21). Life to Paul meant Christ, and that's why death to him meant gain. If you start that sentence with "For to me, to live is money or fame or power or possessions" or whatever else the world lives for, then you have to end the sentence with "and to die is to lose everything forever." How can you call that life?

To Paul, living was Christ; therefore, he was able to share himself with others and do it joyfully. He admitted that it was far better for him to go to be with Christ in heaven, *but* "to remain in the flesh is more needful for you" (Phil. 1:24). Here was a man willing to stay out of heaven for the sake of believers who needed his ministry![5] If life is Christ, then life is lived the way Christ lived; and that means sharing life with others.

Sharing life joyfully is a mark of the maturing person. Children must often be reminded, "Now, share your toys!" The children obey reluctantly and usually have to be reminded again. It's the old problem of territorial rights: "What's mine is mine; I'll keep it!"

When we share ourselves with others, we give them the most priceless possessions we have: life and time. If I write a check for a worthy cause, I'm doing a good thing; but I know I can probably earn more money to replace it in my account. If you share the produce of your garden with your neighbors, you're pretty sure that more fruit and vegetables will grow as the season progresses. But when you give someone your precious time, sharing yourself in listening, empathizing, praying, and working, that time can never be recovered. Once time is gone, it's gone; but for the Christian, shared time may be gone, *but it's never lost*. It becomes an investment in eternity that will pay dividends when we see the Savior.[6]

The same principle applies to the words we share, the money we give, the work we do for others. If it's truly the sharing of ourselves, sharing from the heart, then God will bless it, record it, and ultimately reward it, if not in this life, then in the life to come.

GRACE LIVING

For maturing believers, living is giving; and the motivation behind both the living and the giving is *the grace of God*. We don't give because we want to receive;[7] we give because we have *already* received. We've studied 2 Corinthians 8—9[8] and know what it means to live by the grace of God.

Sharing ourselves with others is much more than a responsibility or even a privilege; it's a grace. In 2 Corinthians 8—9, Paul used nine different words to describe the special offering he was gathering for the Jewish believers, but the word he used most was *grace*. Grace means that God does something in and through us for His glory, not that we do something for God and get credit for it.

Grace living begins when we give ourselves to the Lord and to others: "And not only as we had hoped, but they first gave themselves to the Lord, and then to us by the will of God" (2 Cor. 8:5). This decision doesn't depend on the circumstances we're in, the way we feel, or the reward we may receive. Grace living doesn't calculate or speculate; it comes from the heart, prompted by the Spirit of the Lord. To the world, this kind of living is irrational; to the grace-motivated believer, it's the only sane way to live because it's so Christlike. Festus shouted, "Paul, you are beside yourself! Much learning is driving you mad!" (Acts 26:24). But Paul was the only sane one in the auditorium!

The greatest example of grace living and grace giving is Jesus Christ: "For you know the grace of our Lord Jesus Christ, that though He was rich, yet for your sakes He became poor, that you through His poverty might become rich" (2 Cor. 8:9). The phrase "He became poor" refers to His incarnation, when Jesus Christ wedded Himself to sinless human nature that He might die on a cross and bear on His own body the sins of the world (1 Peter 2:24). When He arose from the dead, His body was glorified so that there is today a glorified Man in heaven who will exist forever in that glorified body with His glorified people.

The point that Paul makes is that, during His earthly ministry, Jesus not only shared precious gifts with needy people—sight to the blind, food to the hungry, healing to the sick, even life to the dead—but Jesus gave Himself for all people so that anybody who trusted Him would share the riches of His grace. Furthermore, He didn't simply take away the bad and replace it with the good. Jesus took on Himself all that was bad in us, including our sins, so that He might share with us all the good that is in Him. "Surely He has borne our griefs and carried our sorrows" to the extent that "the LORD has laid on Him the iniquity of us all" (Isa. 53:4, 6)[9]

Ordinary Deeds

Most of us have read or heard stories about poor little rich kids who received everything they wanted from their parents except the thing they wanted most: their parents. But Father was too busy making money and Mother was too busy spending it, so the children grew up living on substitutes. When they finally established their own homes, after very expensive weddings, they treated their spouses and children the same way they had been treated; and the family generated conflict, unhappiness, and then divorce. When their children grow up, the cycle may be repeated.

"Your children don't want your gifts," pediatricians and psychologists shout to us, "they want you!" I've had to learn that lesson many times.

I was busy writing a book when our younger daughter, then in her early teens, stopped at the study door and asked, "Could I talk with you a minute about something?"

I kept on typing (I didn't use a computer in those ancient days) and, without even looking up, replied, "I have just a couple of pages to finish. Do you mind waiting?"

She stood at the door for perhaps thirty seconds, and then quietly said, "You took the time to *have* me. Why can't you take the time to *listen* to me?"

I stopped typing, apologized, and listened.

During a family Christmas celebration, one of our grandsons asked me to play a table game with him, a game I didn't understand and wasn't really interested in learning. Before long, he could tell that Grandpa was only going through the motions of playing and that what I really wanted to do was get involved in the interesting conversation going on in the kitchen.

Suddenly, he said, "That's okay, Grandpa. I'll play by myself." He picked up the board and pieces and walked up the hall to his room to finish the game. About five minutes later, he stuck his head out the door and called, "Grandpa, *you lost!"*

He was right: I lost; and what I lost, I can't get back. I lost the opportunity to give of myself and my time to a little boy who treasured them more than the gifts his grandma and I had brought him. I lost the chance to get closer to my own flesh and blood and prove to him that I cared. It was a selfish thing to do, *especially at Christmas* when we were celebrating the unselfish thing that Jesus did for us.

One summer, my wife and I decided to take a vacation at Estes Park, Colorado, and relax for a week, do some reading, walk the trails, and enjoy the beautiful scenery.

"Let's try to slip in anonymously," I said as we drove to our lodgings. But while we were in the office signing in, one of the women from our home church walked in and welcomed us warmly! At worship the next morning, four different people in the congregation spotted us and came over to greet us! So much for being anonymous.

Later, as I pondered what happened, I realized why I'd wanted to be anonymous: somebody might want to bend my ear and burden me with her problems. Or somebody might have a book manuscript and want me to read it. (That did happen.) But after all, wasn't I on vacation? Didn't I deserve a week without professional duties? But once again, I was the loser. How could I honestly enjoy all that God would give me that week if I was unwilling to give of myself to others? Granted, it's harder when you're on vacation, and you wish it wouldn't happen; but it happens, so we "count it all joy."

While it's true we need time alone with our family, and such times aren't selfish, we still must avoid the tendency to become selfish even while doing our best for ourselves and our family. It's walking a knife's edge, I know, and being successful at it isn't easy. That's the problem with selfishness: if we aren't careful, it will gradually dry up the springs of life within us so that we're in danger of losing the ability to enjoy both the Giver and His gifts. When I close the doors to others, I also close the doors to the Lord because He has taken His place with the suffering others: "Inasmuch as you did it to one of the least of these My brethren, you did it to Me" (Matt. 25:40).

We make the mistake of thinking that service to others has to involve some stupendous deed or dramatic sacrifice. Jesus clearly taught us otherwise: "And whoever gives one of these little ones only a cup of cold water in the name of a disciple, assuredly, I say to you, he shall by no means lose his reward" (Matt. 10:42). Once or twice in a lifetime, we may have an opportunity to perform the extraordinary deed; but opportunities to do ordinary deeds in extraordinary ways come to us almost daily. "Great services reveal our possibilities," said George H. Morrison, "but small services reveal our consecration.'"[10]

THE RESOURCES OF GOD'S GRACE

Grace living requires faith as well as love. We all have plenty of work to do, and there are only so many available hours in the day. If I spend too much time giving myself to others, who will prepare the sermons, write the books, earn the income to pay the bills, or answer the mail that stacks up on the desk and silently aggravates me? While I'm doing other people's work for them, who is doing my work for me?[11]

But if people are more important than things, then grace living will help me adjust my priorities so that I'll make the most of the time God gives me each day. Furthermore, compassionate contact with people is one of the best ways for me to prepare my heart to study the Bible, organize sermons, and write books. I've often told ministerial students in seminary classes, "Remember, people will forget your sermons, but they'll remember your kindnesses."

I recall a Saturday morning years ago when I was in deep trouble because my Sunday morning message wasn't really prepared. (I'm the kind of preacher who likes to have my Sunday message prepared by Friday noon.) It had been one of those weeks when my study time had evaporated like an ice cube in the Sahara. As I sat in my study at the church, desperately trying to give birth to a sermon, I recalled that there was a funeral service at the mortuary across the street, and that the deceased was connected distantly with one of our church families. I doubt that anybody in the family expected me to attend the service, but the Lord seemed to say in my heart, "Go and show that you care. I'll take care of the sermon."

I left my study, walked across the street, and entered the chapel. I sat among the mourners and prayed for God to comfort them. The longer I sat there, without my even thinking about it, the clearer my message became in my mind! It was like mixed-up tiles falling into place and forming a beautiful mosaic. When I got back to my study, I took time to thank God for His mercy; and then I quickly prepared the message. Once again the Lord had reminded me, "Give, and it will be given to you" (Luke 6:38).

Grace living makes all the resources of God's grace available to us. He promises, "And God is able to make all grace abound toward you, that you, always having all sufficiency in all things, may have an abundance for every good work" (2 Cor. 9:8). The universals in that promise are staggering: all grace, always, all sufficiency, all things, every good work.[12] But this promise is fulfilled only for those who qualify, and they're described in the previous verse: "So let each one give as he purposes in his heart, not grudgingly or of necessity; for God loves a cheerful giver" (2 Cor. 9:7).

GRACE GIVING

The calculating saint will be neither holy nor happy. It's the hilarious giver, the extravagant giver, who gets the blessing. When we start to calculate how much we can afford to do or to give, we stop living by faith and depending on grace. Of course, we should not be careless and wasteful, although my idea of wastefulness might be God's idea of generosity. Mary of Bethany is a case in point:

> Then, six days before the Passover, Jesus came to Bethany, where Lazarus was who had been dead, whom He had raised from the dead. There they made Him a supper; and Martha served, but Lazarus was one of those who sat at the table with Him. Then Mary took a pound of very costly oil of spikenard, anointed the feet of Jesus, and wiped His feet with her hair. And the house was filled with the fragrance of the oil. But one of His disciples, Judas Iscariot, Simon's son, who would betray Him, said, "Why was this fragrant oil not sold for three hundred denarii and given to the poor?" This he said, not that he cared

for the poor, but because he was a thief, and had the money box; and he used to take what was put in it. But Jesus said, "Let her alone; she has kept this for the day of My burial. For the poor you have with you always, but Me you do not have always" (John 12:1–8).

Mark adds a noteworthy statement from Jesus: "Assuredly, I say to you, wherever this gospel is preached in the whole world, what this woman has done will also be told as a memorial to her" (Mark 14:9).

Mary gives us an example of what's involved in grace giving and grace living. When your giving is an act of worship to the Lord Jesus, motivated by grace, you don't count the cost. The value of her gift amounted to a year's income for an average worker, which is probably more than most of us have ever given the Lord at one time. In Mary's time, bottles of precious ointment were actually used as retirement investments, the equivalent of our modern pension funds, because the ointment always increased in value. Judas and the disciples thought what she did was extravagant; Jesus said that what she did was eternal; it would be written in His Word and forever associated with His gospel.

Moses didn't count the cost when he turned his back on Egypt and identified with the suffering people of God (Heb. 11:24–26). The four fishermen didn't count the cost when they left everything to follow Jesus (Luke 5:1–11). David didn't count the cost when he offered his sacrifice to the Lord, but said, "I will not take what is yours for the LORD, nor offer burnt offerings with that which costs me nothing" (1 Chron. 21:24). Calculating Christians save their lives only to lose them.

When your giving is motivated by grace, not only do you not count the cost, but you don't care about the criticism. People who live by grace are constantly misunderstood, even by those who follow the Lord. All of the disciples joined Judas in criticizing Mary, so it was a unanimous opinion (Matt. 26:8–9).

Mary of Bethany was accustomed to being misunderstood. She was misunderstood by her own sister Martha who felt that Mary was neglecting her work by sitting and listening to Jesus teach (Luke 10:38–42). When Mary left the house to go to meet Jesus, her friends thought she was going to her brother's tomb to weep (John 11:28–31). Our Lord's own disciples misunderstood her act of love and accused her of ignoring the needs of the poor. What they said sounded very spiritual, but it was very worldly.

In my lifelong reading of Christian biography, I have yet to find a godly believer who wasn't misunderstood and criticized. Both Jesus and Paul were considered crazy (Mark 3:21; Acts 26:24), and evangelist D. L. Moody was called Crazy Moody by some of the people in Chicago. Today, we call Charles Haddon Spurgeon the Prince of Preachers; but in his own day, critics called him "a clerical poltroon" and "an actor," and his sermons were dismissed as "trash."[3] When William Whiting Borden gave away his personal fortune and headed for the mission field, only to die in Egypt, his critics said he'd acted the fool; and a similar accusation was made about the five missionaries who were martyred by the Aucas in Ecuador.

I'm told that there is an invisible but very real line a certain distance above sea level, beyond which you won't find any snakes. Hikers on mountain trails are always glad when they get beyond the snake line; and people who buy mountain property frequently ask, "Is it above the snake line?" People who practice grace living and grace giving have to live above the snake line, and they ignore the malicious criticism aimed at them. If you don't count the cost, why care about the criticism?

Mary teaches us another truth about grace giving: you can't begin to comprehend the consequences. Here's a Jewish woman, in a small Jewish village, at a dinner of perhaps seventeen people,[14] who did something that was eventually recorded in Scripture and talked about around the world. Her beautiful act of worship became like a series of widening circles, like what happens when you toss a stone into a quiet pond.

To begin with, what Mary did was a blessing to Jesus; and that's the most important thing. If Jesus isn't pleased with what we do, then we're better off not doing it. Her act of worship was also a blessing to the house of Simon, for the fragrance of her gift filled the whole house. But the blessing didn't stay there: what she did brought blessing to Bethany, the little village in which she lived, and carried its name around the world.

Even more, what she did has blessed the church around the world. First, the story was passed from congregation to congregation by word of mouth, and then it was written in the Scriptures. For twenty centuries, wherever the Gospels have gone, believers have been encouraged and helped by Mary's act of worship. When she knelt at Jesus' feet that evening, she had no idea that would happen; but when you practice grace giving to the glory of Jesus, you can't begin to comprehend the consequences.

In one way or another, people who practice grace giving and grace living touch a whole world by what they do; and the fragrance of their lives and their witness spreads from person to person, from year to year, to the glory of God. When I think of people I've never met, some of whom lived centuries ago, who have touched my life and shared the fragrance of Christ, it overwhelms me; and it makes me want to be like them.

Mary wasn't an apostle, a prophetess, a worker of miracles, or an influential woman in society; but she gave her best to Jesus, and He has kept that blessing going!

That's what grace living and grace giving are all about.

Chapter 20

DELIGHT: FINDING PLEASURE IN GOD

O n Sunday morning, June 15, 1862, Charles Haddon Spurgeon preached from the text, "Delight yourself also in the LORD, and He shall give you the desires of your heart" (Ps. 37:4). Among other things, he said to his large London congregation:

> Our religion is our recreation, our hope is our happiness, our duty is our delight. . . . Delight and true religion are as allied as root and flower, as indivisible as truth and certainty; they are, in fact, two precious jewels set side-by-side in the same socket of gold.[1]

This kind of talk is sheer foolishness to unconverted people, the ones Jesus called "the sons of this world" (Luke 16:8). They usually equate anything religious with boredom and bondage, not recreation and happiness. It's interesting to note that on June 15, 1950, eighty-eight years after Spurgeon preached his sermon, missionary martyr Jim Elliot wrote this in his journal:

> Ephesians 2:2—the walk of the unregenerate is according to the age of this world—meaning partially, I think, that a man without Christ has his roots only in his own times, and his fruits as well. He has nothing to tie him to eternity.[2]

That explains why "the sons of this world" see no delight in cultivating the Christian life and learning to enjoy God.

THE GOD WE WORSHIP

Is the God you worship a happy God?

Confronted with that question, many believers hesitate and then cautiously reply, "Well, I guess so. At least, I hope so."

But apparently some of God's people don't believe that the God they worship is indeed a happy God. I made the statement at a summer Bible conference that Jesus Christ was a happy person and certainly must have smiled and laughed, even though Isaiah called Him "a Man of sorrows and acquainted with grief" (Isa. 53:3). I can't conceive of *anybody*, especially Jesus, taking a child in His arms and not smiling.

Between sessions, a pugnacious woman accosted me and proceeded to scold me as if I had denied the virgin birth or the blood atonement. According to her, Jesus was *only* a sad and sorrowful person; and there was no more to be said, world without end.

When she stopped chattering, I opened my Bible and showed her John 15:11: "These things have I spoken to you, that My joy may remain in you, and that your joy may be full." Then I turned to John 17:13: "But now I come to You, and these things I speak in the world, that they may have My joy fulfilled in themselves."

"If Jesus had talked about giving joy to His disciples," I asked, *"but they had never seen Him express that joy,* do you think they would have believed Him? And how could He give them something that He didn't have Himself?" Then I showed her Luke 10:21: "In that hour Jesus rejoiced in the Spirit." Without saying a word, but with her jaw set, the woman spun around and left the tabernacle.

I wonder what she would have done if the speaker that morning had been Alexander Maclaren and he had preached his sermon "The Gospel of the Glory of the Happy God," based on 1 Timothy 1:11. "If the word *happy* seems too trivial," Maclaren says, "suggesting ideas of levity, of turbulence, of possible change, then I do not know that we can find any better word than that which is already employed in my text, if only we remember that it means the solemn, calm, restful, perpetual gladness that fills the heart of God."[3]

Yes, in spite of the way some of His people act and look, our God is a happy God.

DELIGHT AND THE CREATION

Let s begin with the fact that *God delights in His creation and His creation delights in Him:* "Then God saw everything that He had made, and indeed it was very good" (Gen. 1:31). Even the angels entered into the joy of the occasion "when the morning stars sang together, and all the sons of God shouted for joy" (Job 38:7). I can't read Psalm 104 without getting excited about the way God rejoices in His creation and cares for it. He even created some creatures just to play in the waters (Ps. 104:26)! I think of that verse when I watch the whales breach and the porpoises frolic. What beautiful creatures they are!

Nature unashamedly expresses its joy to the Lord:

Let the field be joyful, and all that is in it.
Then all the trees of the woods will rejoice before the LORD
(Ps. 96:12).

Let the rivers clap their hands;
Let the hills be joyful before the LORD (Ps. 98:8).

The mountains and the hills
Shall break forth into singing before you,
And all the trees of the field shall clap their hands (Isa. 55:12).

Since the fall of humankind, creation has been in bondage and travail, but creation is eagerly expecting the return of Christ and the joyful liberty that His return will bring for His creation and His children (Rom. 8:18–22). Satan may be "the god of this age" (2 Cor. 4:4), but "This is my Father's world!"

Three practical applications come from the truth that God enjoys His creation and His creation rejoices in Him.

1. To destroy or waste God's creation is sinful. Ecology isn't only a matter of economics and survival; it's a matter of theology and worship. Wanton destruction of trees and pollution of water are morally equivalent to stabbing or poisoning a choir while they're joyfully praising God. If that happened in one of our churches, the nation would recoil in horror; but it happens every day to nature, and we compliment ourselves on the growth of the gross national product.

2. *We must worship the God of nature, not the nature God created.* My wife and I once sat through half a concert (we left during the intermission) during which one of the two performers extolled nature but said nothing about the God who created it all. His verbose commentary and weird music would have been more suitable in a druid winter solstice celebration at Stonehenge than in the lovely church auditorium where the concert was held. To give thanks for the gifts but to ignore the Giver is the essence of idolatry. Paul spoke of it in this way: "Who exchanged the truth of God for the lie,[4] and worshiped and served the creature rather than the Creator, who is blessed forever" (Rom. 1:25).

3. *God's people should rejoice at God's creation, study it carefully, and praise God for it.* After contemplating God's great works in creation, the musician who wrote Psalm 104 confessed,

> I will sing to the LORD as long as I live;
> I will sing praise to my God while I have my being.
> May my meditation be sweet to Him;
> I will be glad in the LORD (vv. 33–34).

Another singer wrote, "The works of the LORD are great, studied by all who have pleasure in them" (Ps. 111:2). When we study science, history, or any other subject, we're only thinking God's thoughts after Him; and if our hearts are right, we're engaging in worship:

> The fear of the LORD is the beginning of wisdom;
> A good understanding have all those who do His commandments.
> His praise endures forever (Ps. 111:10).

Secularists study science and refuse to see God. But Paul commented, "For since the creation of the world His invisible attributes are clearly seen, being understood by the things that are made, even

His eternal power and Godhead, so that they are without excuse" (Rom. 1:20). Of all blindness, willful blindness is the worst.

Methodist Bishop Ralph Spaulding Cushman expressed the joy of worshiping the Creator in these words:[5]

Oh the sheer joy of it!
  Living with Thee,
God of the universe,
  Lord of a tree,
Maker of mountains,
  Lover of me!

Oh the sheer joy of it!
  Breathing Thy air;
Morning is dawning,
  Gone every care,
All the world's singing,
  "God's everywhere."

Oh the sheer joy of it!
  Walking with Thee,
Out on the hilltop,
  Down by the sea,
Life is so wonderful,
  Life is so free.

Oh the sheer joy of it!
  Working with God,
Running His errands,
  Waiting His nod,
Building His heaven
  On common sod.

Oh the sheer joy of it!
  Ever to be
Living in glory,

Living with Thee,
Lord of Tomorrow,
Lover of me![6]

Isaac Watts agreed with Bishop Cushman:

I sing the mighty power of God that made the mountains rise,
That spread the flowing seas abroad and built the lofty skies.
I sing the wisdom that ordained the sun to rule the day;
The moon shines full at His command, and all the stars obey.

I sing the goodness of the Lord that filled the earth with food,
He formed the creatures with His word and then pronounced
    them good.
Lord, how Thy wonders are displayed where'er I tum my eye;
If I survey the ground I tread or gaze upon the sky.

There's not a plant or flow'r below but makes Thy glories
    known;
And clouds arise and tempests blow by order from Thy throne;
While all that borrows life from Thee is ever in Thy care,
And everywhere that man can be, Thou, God, art present there.

DELIGHT AND GOD'S PEOPLE

God delights in His people:

He does not delight in the strength of the horse;
He takes no pleasure in the legs of a man.
The LORD takes pleasure in those who fear Him,
In those who hope in His mercy (Ps. 147:1–11).

God delights in those who are blameless in their ways (Prov. 11:20) and who deal truthfully (Prov. 12:22). Another proverb states, "The sacrifice of the wicked is an abomination to the LORD, but the prayer of the upright is His delight" (15:8). Zephaniah 3:17 pictures God as a loving parent, rejoicing over a child:

The LORD your God in your midst,
The Mighty One, will save;
He will rejoice over you with gladness,
He will quiet you with His love,
He will rejoice over you with singing.

The phrase "rejoice over you" (or "take pleasure in you") uses a Hebrew word that, according to Ronald B. Allen, "describes playful abandon of exuberant joy.'" It's difficult for me to understand how God can look at me, with all my failures and sins, hold me close to His heart, and love me with exuberant joy; but He does. He can joyfully delight in His people because we're in His Son; and when the Father looks at His Son, He says, "This is My beloved Son, in whom I am well pleased" (Matt. 3:17). Paul calls this "accepted in the Beloved" (Eph. 1:6).

In his song of praise celebrating God's deliverance, David dared to sing, "He delivered me because He delighted in me" (Ps. 18:19; 2 Sam. 22:20). During David's difficult years of exile, when he was hiding from Saul, he was careful to please the Lord and keep the commandments. He declared,

For I have kept the ways of the LORD,
And have not wickedly departed from my God (Ps. 18:21).

The steps of a good man are ordered by the LORD,
And He delights in his way (Ps. 37:23).

"He who has My commandments and keeps them," said Jesus, "it is he who loves Me. And he who loves Me will be loved by My Father, and I will love him and manifest Myself to him" (John 14:21). It delights God when we obey Him, pray to Him, and seek to do His will. It grieves God when we substitute sacrifices for obedience (1 Sam. 15:22; Ps. 51:16) and mere outward religious ceremony for the sincere devotion of the heart (Isa. 1:11).

OUR DELIGHT IN HIM

God delights in His creation and His creation delights in Him.

God also delights in His people, *and His people should delight in Him*. For the child of God not to delight in the Lord is to remain immature and miss the highest privilege and greatest pleasure possible to a Christian believer. The Lord said,

> Let not the wise man glory in his wisdom,
> Let not the mighty man glory in his might,
> Nor let the rich man glory in his riches;
> But let him who glories glory in this,
> That he understands and knows Me,
> That I am the LORD, exercising lovingkindness, judgment,
>   and righteousness in the earth.
> For in these I delight (Jer. 9:23–24).

At the beginning of this chapter, I quoted Psalm 37:4; and now it's time to explain and apply it: "Delight yourself also in the LORD, and He shall give you the desires of your heart." This promise is not carte blanche to get what we want from God just because we belong to His family. David is saying that, if we truly delight in the Lord, we will want to know Him better; and the better we know Him, the more we will become like Him. *His* desires will become *our* desires, and our greatest desire will be to know Him even more and enjoy Him in an ever-deepening way.

"God Himself is the heart's desire of those who delight in Him," said Alexander Maclaren in a sermon on this text, "and the blessedness of longing fixed on Him is that it ever fulfills itself."[8] The Westminster Catechism tells us that "the chief end of man is to glorify God and to enjoy Him forever." Psalm 37:4 says that *now* is the time to start glorifying God and enjoying Him.

But what does it mean to enjoy God? Let me remind you of William Temple's description of worship that I quoted in Chapter 8:

> For worship is the submission of all our nature to God. It is the quickening of conscience by His holiness; the nourishment of mind with His truth; the purifying of imagination by His beauty; the opening of the heart to His love; the surrender of will

to His purpose—and all of this gathered up in adoration, the most selfless emotion of which our nature is capable and therefore the chief remedy for that self-centeredness which is our original sin and the source of all actual sin.

Using this excellent definition as our guide, let's take inventory of our relationship with God and discover how much we really enjoy Him.

GOD'S HOLINESS, TRUTH, AND BEAUTY

Do I delight in His holiness? "A true love to God must begin with a delight in his holiness," wrote Jonathan Edwards,

> and not with a delight in any other attribute; for no other attribute is truly lovely without this. . . . Therefore, it is impossible that other attributes should appear lovely, in their true loveliness, until this is seen; and it is impossible that any perfection of the divine nature should be loved with true love until this is loved.[9]

That's a lot of meat all in one helping, and it's worth reading again.

From decade to decade, different attributes of God receive emphasis, depending, I suppose, on the spiritual perceptions of preachers and the needs of their people. One time it will be the transcendence of God, and this will be followed by an emphasis on the immanence of God. The emphasis today seems to be on the love of God, almost to the exclusion of His holiness. The God some people worship today smiles at sin, automatically forgives disobedience, and never chastens anybody. This explains why songs about the blood atonement are being excised from hymnals, for a God who condones sin would never allow His own Son to die for the sins of the world.

If you listen to the worship presented in heaven, you will hear voices extolling the holiness of God. Isaiah heard the seraphim crying, "Holy, holy, holy is the LORD of hosts; the whole earth is full of His glory!" (Isa. 6:3). The apostle John heard a similar song of praise from the four living creatures:

Holy, holy, holy,
Lord God Almighty,
Who was and is and is to come! (Rev. 4:8).

David proclaimed, "Give unto the LORD the glory due to His name; worship the LORD in the beauty of holiness" (Ps. 29:2).[10] To the unregenerate heart and mind, there is nothing beautiful or splendid about holiness; but to God's children who have the divine nature within, God's holiness is awesome, captivating, and magnificent. The righteousness of the scribes and Pharisees was artificial and brittle, but the holiness of the Son of God whom they opposed was genuine and living. Seeking sinners saw in Jesus the beauty of holiness, and they came to Him.

Do I delight in His truth? "But his delight is in the law of the LORD, and in His law he meditates day and night" (Ps. 1:2). We know the voices of people who delight us, and we rejoice to hear them. We enjoy spending time with them and listening to what they have to say. One of the marks of Christ's sheep is that they recognize His voice and follow Him, but they won't respond to the voices of strangers (John 10:1–5). When professed believers follow false teachers and even cultists, you wonder if they have ever heard the voice of the Shepherd and trusted Him.

We delight in God's truth because it reveals God's heart and mind, not because the Bible is a fascinating book to read, study, and teach. We come to the Scriptures not as critical scholars, analyzing a book, but as prostrate worshipers, hearing the voice of the living God.

At least nine times in Psalm 119, the writer says that he delights in the Word of God (vv. 16, 24, 35, 47, 70, 77, 92, 143, 174). And Psalm 112 states, "Blessed is the man who fears the LORD, who delights greatly in His commandments" (v. 1). To delight in God's truth means we take time daily to read the Word and meditate on it, and to rejoice when He speaks to us from the sacred page, teaching us a new truth or giving us a new application of a familiar truth.

But the important thing is that we see God and hear His voice as we read His Word. It isn't enough merely to know the truth of God in a doctrinal way; we must also know the God of truth in a personal way.

DELIGHT

Do I delight in His beauty? David said,

> One thing I have desired of the LORD,
> That will I seek:
> That I may dwell in the house of the LORD
> All the days of my life,
> To behold the beauty of the LORD,
> And to inquire in His temple (Ps. 27:4).

David was a successful warrior, poet, musician, and king; but his deepest desire was to devote himself to the contemplation of the beauty of God. He envied the priests and Levites who lived in God's house and were daily in contact with holy and beautiful things.

In his *Confessions,* Augustine dares to call God "my Father, supremely good, beauty of all things beautiful."[11] In one of his mystical poems, Frederick Faber says,

> How beautiful, how beautiful
>   The sight of Thee must be,
> Thou endless wisdom, boundless power,
>   And awful purity![12]

That God is characterized by wisdom, power, and purity, most people would not debate; but in what sense is God beautiful? God is spirit, so the reference is obviously not to physical features. The beauty of God describes His moral character. God is holy, pure, just, loving, wise, longsuffering, merciful, gracious, and so much more; and these attributes exist in perfect harmony and are manifested in perfectly balanced ways. God's beauty is the beauty of perfection, a beauty that borrows from nothing and no one and to which nothing or no one may be compared.

Beautiful music, beautiful words, beautiful buildings, beautiful actions, and beautiful scenes in nature are all only inadequate glimpses of the beauty of God. But inadequate as they may be, our worship of Him ought to be beautiful and make use of these gifts, whether we're surrounded by the stately beauty of a majestic cathedral or the quiet beauty of a simple colonial chapel. Our tastes in worship may differ, but one thing must be true of all worship: it must focus on the beauty of God and encourage us to allow that beauty to become a part of our character.

GOD'S LOVE AND PURPOSES

Do I delight in His love?

As the deer pants for the water brooks,
So pants my soul for You, O God.
My soul thirsts for God, for the living God (Ps. 42:1–2).

O God, You are my God;
Early will I seek You;
My soul thirsts for You;
My flesh longs for You
In a dry and thirsty land
Where there is no water (Ps. 63:1).

My soul longs, yes, even faints
For the courts of the LORD;
My heart and my flesh cry out for the living God (Ps. 84:2).

Can I make these statements and really mean them, or is spending time with God just one of many options in my life and perhaps not the most exciting? Several times in these pages, I've discussed God's love for us and our love for Him so I need not elaborate further. But if God is the greatest person, and if the greatest commandment is to love God with all our being, then not to love Him is to commit the greatest sin.

Do I delight to fulfill His purposes? David declared, "I delight to do Your will, O my God, and Your law is within my heart" (Ps. 40:8). When I discover from the Scriptures what God wants to do in this world, do I make myself available to Him to do it? Paul wrote, "Now to Him who is able to do exceedingly abundantly above all that we ask or think, *according to the power that works in us*" (Eph. 3:20, italics mine). The almighty power of God works "in us"; therefore, we must be available to God for whatever purposes He wants to fulfill.

Dag Hammarskjold wrote in *Markings*, "In our era, the road to holiness necessarily passes through the world of action."[13] I may be wrong, but I think what he's saying is that spiritual growth must not be divorced from practical service. Holiness ought to lead to helpfulness, sanctity to service. If my delight in the Lord isolates me from a real world that's bleeding from its wounds, and I do nothing to help, then what I think is delight is really deception. Isaiah's response to his vision of Christ was, "Here am I! Send me" (Isa. 6:8). Delighting in God shouldn't lead to selfish enjoyment; it should lead to selfless employment.

Do I sincerely adore Him? Am I occasionally speechless as I wait before the Lord? Do I sometimes wait before Him in mingled brokenness and joy, trembling and delight? Do I lose track of time as I worship Him? William Temple calls adoration "the most selfless emotion of which our nature is capable," but it's an emotion that only God's Spirit can generate in our hearts.

Listen to the language of delight:

Nevertheless I am continually with You;
You hold me by my right hand.
You will guide me with Your counsel,
And afterward receive me to glory.
Whom have I in heaven but You?
And there is none upon earth that I desire besides You.
My flesh and my heart fail;
But God is the strength of my heart and my portion forever (Ps. 73:23–26).

THE ONGOING PROCESS

The purpose of life is to glorify God and enjoy Him forever.

We can't glorify Him unless we enjoy Him, but we can't enjoy Him if we don't really know Him.

The only way to get to know Him is to delight in Him and worship Him, taught by the Word, led by the Spirit.

But we can't worship Him as we should unless we come to Him, and that means having priorities and exercising discipline.

We aren't likely to come to Him unless we have a longing in the heart to be with Him and to know Him better.

Jesus said, "Blessed are those who hunger and thirst for righteousness, for they shall be filled" (Matt. 5:6).

These words of Martin Luther hang in my study and encourage me:

> This life, therefore, is not righteousness
> > but growth in righteousness;
> not health but healing;
> not being but becoming;
> not rest but exercise.
> We are not yet what we shall be,
> > but we are growing toward it;
> the process is not yet finished
> > but it is going on;
> this is not the end,
> > but it is the road.
> All does not yet gleam in glory,
> > but all is being purified.

"Let everything that has breath praise the LORD. Praise the LORD!" (Ps. 150:6).

NOTES

Chapter 1

1. The Greek word translated "again" (*anothen*) also means "from above," and in most versions it is translated that way in John 3:31 and 19:11. The theological term for the new birth is *regeneration*.

2. "Born of water" refers to physical birth because every baby is cradled in a sac of water that breaks before birth occurs. Nicodemus told Jesus it was impossible to enter "a second time into his mother's womb" (John 3:4), which Jesus called being "born of water." To make water in this text stand for baptism is to change the meaning of baptism, for baptism in Scripture is identified with *death*, not *birth*. "Born of water" is physical birth; "born of the Spirit" is spiritual birth. In the New Testament, people confessed Christ as Savior by being baptized; but they were not baptized in order to be saved. Note the sequence in Acts 10: the people heard the word of the gospel, believed, and received the Holy Spirit; and then they were baptized (vv. 42–48).

3. There is a difference between escaping the world's *corruption* because you have a new nature within and merely escaping the world's *pollution* because you've changed your ways outwardly. You can take a pig out of the mud, wash it, perfume it, and help it escape pollution; but the first chance it gets, the pig will return to the mire because that's its nature. In 2 Peter 2:18–22, Peter uses this illustration to show the difference between false professors of the faith and true possessors of salvation. The pig looked better after being washed, and the dog felt better after throwing up; *but neither of them had become a sheep!* The nature of the beast makes the difference.

4. Charles Haddon Spurgeon, *Metropolitan Tabernacle Pulpit* (Pasadena, Tex.: Pilgrim Publications, 1984), 17:501.

Chapter 2

1. I quoted from the New International Version because the translation brings out the tenses of the verbs. John isn't teaching sinless perfection, because that would contradict what he wrote in 1 John 1:5–10. The present tense of the verbs indicates that John has the settled habit of sin in mind and not the occasional act of sin. "In this whole section," writes John Stott, "John is arguing rather the incongruity than the impossibility of sin in the Christian." For an excellent discussion of this verse, see volume 19 of the "Tyndale Bible Commentaries," *The Epistles of John* by John Stott (Grand Rapids: Eerdmans, 1964), pp.124–36.

243

2. Peter H. Davids, *New International Commentary on the New Testament: The First Epistle of Peter* (Grand Rapids: Eerdmans, 1990), p. 193.

Chapter 3

1. Romans 9:4 uses "adoption" to describe God's choice of the Jewish people to become His own "firstborn son" (Ex. 4:22; Jer. 31:9; Hos. 11:1). With this adoption came many privileges, but national adoption isn't the same as personal adoption because not everybody in Israel had put saving faith in the Lord.

2. In the Book of Acts, the coming of the Holy Spirit was sometimes announced by people speaking in tongues; but this is not necessarily the norm for today. "Do all speak with tongues?" Paul asked (1 Cor. 12:30), and the construction of the sentence in the original Greek indicates that he expected a negative answer. The New American Standard Bible reads, "All do not speak with tongues, do they?" The *Jewish* believers spoke in tongues at Pentecost (Acts 2:1–13); the *Samaritans*, who were part Jew and part Gentile, spoke in tongues when Peter and John laid hands on them (Acts 8:17); and the *Gentile* believers spoke in tongues when they believed on Christ as Peter preached the gospel (Acts 10:43–48). Thus the plan outlined in Acts 1:8 was fulfilled: "in Jerusalem, and in all Judea and Samaria, and to the end of the earth."

3. "But the natural man does not receive the things of the Spirit of God, for they are foolishness to him; nor can he know them, because they are spiritually discerned" (1 Cor. 2:14).

4. Especially note Isaiah 41:10, 13–14; 43:1; 44:2, 8; 51:7; and 54:4. I've heard it said that there are 365 "fear not" statements in the Bible, one for every day of the year; but, alas, this isn't true. However, there are enough affirmations to cover all the problems of life that might bring fear to our hearts.

5. Whether to call God "Daddy" or "Papa" in public praying is something each believer must decide in his or her own heart, but I prefer not to use it. Jesus taught us to pray, "Our Father in heaven" (Matt. 6:9); and "Father" is the address He used in His prayers (Matt. 11:25–26; 26:39, 42; Luke 23:34, 46; John 12:27, 28; 17:1, 5, 11, 21, 24, 25). I don't find the great saints of the church publicly addressing God as "Daddy," and they are far more worthy to use the word than I am! I would hate to have any worshiper in the congregation accuse me of publicly showing off my supposed intimacy with God. Luke 18:9–14 comes to mind.

6. If you need to brush up on Old Testament history, you'll find the story in Genesis 16; 17; and 21. In Galatians 4:21-31, Paul uses the same cast of characters to argue for the freedom of the believer from the Law of Moses.

7. Peter learned his lesson. In his first epistle, he frequently joined suffering and glory. (See 1:7–8, 11, 18–21; 4:12–16; 5:1, 10.)

Notes

Chapter 4

1. Norman P. Grubb, C. T. Studd, Athlete and Pioneer (Grand Rapids: Zondervan, 1946), p. 129.

Chapter 5

1. The prophet Jeremiah compared backsliding to sickness when he wrote, "Return, you backsliding children, and I will heal your backslidings" (3:22). Jeremiah lamented the fact that the false prophets had "healed the hurt of My people slightly, saying, 'Peace, peace!' when there is no peace" (6:14).

2. Our Lord's denunciation of the Pharisees must not be interpreted to mean that all of them were hypocrites, because some of them no doubt were sincere in their desire to please God. Nicodemus was a Pharisee, and he eventually identified himself as a believer in Jesus Christ (John 3; 7:45–52; 19:38–42). No doubt our Lord's heart was broken as He spoke the words recorded in Matthew 23 and exposed the shallowness and deception of their religious faith.

Chapter 6

1. To be sure, His enemies and even His family accused Him of being either "beside Himself" or demonized (Mark 3:20–22); but that's the fate of anybody who exposes the follies and sins of the world and who lives by the power of God. Paul received the same kind of treatment (Acts 26:24). When Paul was persecuting the church and hurting people, nobody said he was crazy; but when he became a Christian and started helping people, his enemies said he was mad.

2. For a practical, biblical, and time-tested book on this subject, see Balancing the Christian Life by Charles C. Ryrie (Chicago: Moody Press, 1969).

3. "Ministry takes place when divine resources meet human needs through loving channels to the glory of God." See my book On Being a Servant of God (Nashville: Oliver-Nelson, 1993) for a discussion of this approach to ministry.

4. The references in John's Gospel to His appointed "hour" are 2:4; 7:6–8, 30; 8:20; 12:23; 13:1; 16:32; 17:1.

5. In using the words heart and mind, I'm not suggesting that human beings are compartmentalized. Certainly, what I think affects how I feel because mind and body definitely affect each other. However, the functions of thinking and feeling are distinct enough to make this difference, even though they are not independent of each other.

6. Spurgeon's Morning By Morning and Evening By Evening, Sept. 5 P.M.

7. There is a basic "faith which was once for all delivered to the saints" (Jude 3), and on these fundamental doctrines all true Christians agree. But there are other matters about which even the most godly teachers don't agree, and that's where we exercise patience and love. I think it was Augustine who said, "In essen-

tials, unity; in non-essentials, liberty; in all things, charity." Paul wrote, "But avoid foolish and ignorant disputes, knowing that they generate strife. And a servant of the Lord must not quarrel but be gentle to all, able to teach, patient, in humility correcting those who are in opposition, if God perhaps will grant them repentance, so that they may know the truth" (2 Tim. 2:23–25). A humble, teachable spirit is a mark of godliness, but a proud spirit is an invitation for the devil to create trouble. Unfortunately, the pride and dogmatism of some preachers and teachers encourage such disputes; and their disciples become troublemakers instead of peacemakers.

Chapter 7

1. When the Holy Spirit came on the day of Pentecost, "there came a sound from heaven, as of a rushing mighty wind" (Acts 2:2). The image of the Spirit as breath is found in the beautiful hymn "O Breath of Life" composed by Bessie P. Head.

2. When Jesus spoke about eating His flesh and drinking His blood, He wasn't referring to the Lord's Supper (Communion, Eucharist), because the Lord's Supper hadn't even been established yet. Why would He discuss a special celebration like the Communion with a group of unconverted people who finally deserted Him? If participating in the Lord's Supper is essential to salvation, then nobody in the Old Testament was saved, and the disciples weren't saved until the evening of the Last Supper. It seems clear that our Lord was speaking in symbolic language: just as we receive food into the body to sustain life, so we must receive Christ, the Living Bread, into our inner being to have eternal life.

3. It's worth noting that many of the titles and attributes given to Jesus Christ are also given to the Word of God. Jesus is holy (Luke 1:35) and the Word is holy (2 Tim. 3:15). Both are bread (John 6:48; Matt. 4:4) and light (John 8:12; Ps. 119:105), and both are truth (John 14:6; 17:17). Both have life (John 5:26; Heb. 4:12), both impart life (John 5:21; Ps. 119:93), and both are involved in the miracle of the new birth (1 John 5:18; 1 Peter 1:23).

4. You find the same image in Hebrews 5:12–14. Babies obviously don't have the physical equipment needed to chew on solid food; but as they develop, they get what they need. In Hebrews, the "milk" of the Word refers to the truths about what Jesus did on earth; while the "solid food" (meat of the Word) refers to what Jesus Christ is now doing in heaven, His high priestly ministry. The writer wanted to share the "solid food" with his readers, but they weren't mature enough to receive it. We never outgrow our need for the kind of nourishment milk gives; but milk is predigested food, and we should learn to "chew" God's truth ourselves. New Christians need spiritual mothers to nurse them (1 Thess. 2:7–8), but there comes a time when the children need to be weaned and start feeding themselves.

5. As we mature in the Lord, we discover that the Word that is sweet to us can sometimes bring bitterness because of what it says about the judgments of God and the trials of God's people. The prophet Ezekiel ate the scroll of the Word, and it was sweet in his mouth; but before long, he was experiencing bitterness within (Ezek. 3:1–3, 14). When the apostle John ate the little book, it was sweet in his mouth but bitter in his stomach (Rev. 10:8–11). Maturing Christians experience heights of joy and depths of sorrow, but the Lord knows how to balance them for our good and His glory. Our Savior was "a Man of sorrows and acquainted with grief" (Isa. 53:3), but He possessed a joy within that He shared with His own (John 15:11; 17:13; see Luke 10:21). Philippians has joy as one of its major themes; yet in that letter, you find Paul mentioning sorrow (2:27) and even weeping (3:18). Paul also wrote, "As sorrowful, yet always rejoicing" (2 Cor. 6:10).

6. The Greek word *parakletos* can be translated "counselor, helper, encourager, comforter," and even "advocate," in the legal sense. The word means "called to one's side" with the idea of giving help. The Holy Spirit doesn't work *in spite of* us or *instead of* us; He works *with* us to lead us into an understanding of the truth. Note that the Holy Spirit is a person, not simply an influence, and that He should always be referred to and addressed as a person. The Holy Spirit doesn't enjoy being called "it."

7. Inspiration is the divine process by which the Holy Spirit influenced "holy men of God" (2 Peter 1:21) so that what they wrote was the living, inerrant, trustworthy, and authoritative Word of God. Revelation has to do with the content of the Word, what the Scriptures say; inspiration has to do with how this revelation was recorded. To say that Moses and David were inspired in the same sense as Shakespeare and Beethoven is to miss the point completely. The Bible is a special book, and no other book is like it. The Bible is the only book about which we can confidently say, "Therefore I esteem right all Thy precepts concerning everything" (Ps. 119:128 NASB).

8. Having said that, I want to affirm that I think the Bible is on the side of the early risers: Jesus (Mark 1:35); Abraham (Gen. 19:27; 21:14; 22:3); Moses (Ex. 24:4; 34:4); Joshua (Josh. 3:1; 6:12; 7:16; 8:10); and Samuel (1 Sam. 15:12). "My voice You shall hear in the morning, O LORD; in the morning I will direct it to You, and I will look up" (Ps. 5:3). (See also Ps. 119:147–48.) For that matter, why not do both? "But his delight is in the law of the LORD, and in His law he meditates *day* and *night*" (Ps. 1:2, italics mine).

9. Some people are upset when they read that John was "the disciple whom Jesus loved" (John 13:23; 19:26; 20:2; 21:7, 20), thinking that this kind of relationship is either effeminate or perverted. They're also upset because John leaned on Jesus' bosom (John 13:23), and they don't want to sing hymns like "Jesus, lover of my soul/Let me to Thy bosom fly." Nobody has to defend the purity of John's

friendship with Jesus or the reality *and necessity* of this close relationship with the Lord on the part of believers today. John was every inch a man's man, a rugged fisherman who suffered for his faith. His nearness to Jesus was an evidence of strength, not weakness.

10. Mature believers who are experienced in the devotional life probably don't need the counsel in this section, but new Christians should find it helpful. If you're a mature believer, I suggest you read this section anyway, if only to get ideas for counseling younger Christians who need help with their personal devotions.

11. Many believers read the Bible through in one year as a supplement to their daily devotional reading; and this is a helpful practice. There are several Bible reading calendars available, the most popular being the one arranged by Robert Murray M'Cheyne. Your pastor, denominational headquarters, or local Christian bookstore should be able to help you find a schedule that best meets your needs.

12. I hesitate to tell you what schedule to follow in reading your Bible. As a young believer, just getting started in my devotional life, I first read straight through the New Testament. Then I added a psalm a day. Now I like to start with Genesis 1, Psalm 1, Isaiah 1, and Matthew 1, and just keep reading until I've completed the whole Bible. I finish reading the New Testament first, so l go back to Matthew 1 and begin again. Some days I don't read all four chapters because I get so engrossed in one chapter that I spend all my time there. No problem; the other chapters will wait until tomorrow, and I don't feel guilty in postponing them. Devotional reading must be leisurely and meditative, not driven and careless. You're walking with the Lord through the garden of His Word; you're not running a marathon race. The Father knows what He wants to say to you each day, so let Him direct you; and "take time to be holy."

13. Baker Book House has published *The Bumps Are What You Climb On, Turning Mountains into Molehills,* and *Devotional Thoughts for People Who Do God's Business.* The latter book I wrote with our son David Wiersbe. *Thoughts for Men on the Move* is published by Moody Press, and *With the Word,* a devotional commentary on the entire Bible, by Thomas Nelson.

Chapter 8

1. In Philippians 4:3, Paul used this verb (with the prefix *sun-,* "together with") when he wrote that Euodia and Syntyche had "labored with [him] in the gospel." Literally, he was saying, "We were playing on the same team!"

2. This isn't to suggest that Christians who are physically challenged or chronically ill are not spiritually mature or pleasing to God. Some of the greatest saints have had to endure bodily afflictions, including the apostle Paul (2 Cor. 12). If we depend on the grace of God, suffering can be a tool to build us up and bring

glory to God (1 Peter 5:10). But too many Christians ignore the care of the body while they major on the care of the soul. It's good to pray without ceasing but not to eat without ceasing. According to Romans 12:1, what I do with my body is as important as what I do with the inner person.

3. Romans 5:21 makes it clear that grace reigns through righteousness, not through selfish indulgence or undisciplined conduct. Grace and law don't compete with each other; they complement each other. Law convinces me that I need grace, and grace enables me to fulfill the righteous demands of the law (Rom. 8:1–4). Law without grace would be slavery, but grace without law would be anarchy. One fruit of the Spirit is self-control (Gal. 5:23), which means a disciplined life. Nobody preached the grace of God with more clarity and power than Charles Haddon Spurgeon, and yet he had this to say about the law of God: "I find it sometimes profitable to myself to read the ten commandments, and to think over my sins against each one of them. What a list it is, and how it humbles you in the dust to read it over" (Metropolitan Tabernacle Pulpit [Pasadena, Tex.: Pilgrim Publications, 1984], 23:431).

4. These are fictitious titles based on actual book titles that I've seen. If there are such titles, it is purely coincidental.

5. For a more detailed study of biblical worship see my book Real Worship: It Will Transform Your Life (Nashville: Oliver-Nelson, 1986); O Come Let Us Worship by Robert G. Rayburn (Grand Rapids: Baker Book House, 1980); and Ralph P. Martin's The Worship of God (Grand Rapids: Eerdmans, 1982) and Worship in the Early Church (Grand Rapids: Eerdmans, 1974).

6. William Temple, Readings in St. John's Gospel, 1st ser. (London: Macmillan, 1939), p. 57.

7. We're commanded to praise the Lord with "psalms and hymns and spiritual songs" (Eph. 5:19). Churches or individuals who ignore the psalms and hymns and use only "praise choruses" need to develop balance in their worship. All three are important. The psalms are inspired Scripture, written to be sung; hymns are songs based on biblical history and theology; spiritual songs come spontaneously from the believer's heart and bear witness to what the Lord is doing in the person's life today. Blessed are the balanced!

8. The same word is used in Romans 12:2 to describe the "renewing of [the] mind." As we surrender the whole being to the Lord each day, worship Him, and meditate on His Word, the Spirit of God does this gracious work of transformation. Paul calls this "[putting] on the new man which was created according to God, in true righteousness and holiness" (Eph. 4:24). According to Romans 12:2, we are going to be conformed to the world or transformed by the Spirit. We make the choice.

9. Samuel Johnson told James Boswell that "to reason philosophically on the

nature of prayer is very unprofitable." *Life of Samuel Johnson,* Everyman's Library ed. (London: James Dent, 1973), 1:429. It reminds me of the fable of the ant and the centipede. The ant asked the centipede how he knew which legs to move next as he walked, and the centipede replied, "I've never really thought about it." But the more he thought about it, the more perplexed he became; he soon found himself unable to walk at all! The best way to learn to pray is to read the Bible—and pray! I would rather experience answers to prayer personally than be able to explain prayer philosophically.

10. We call it the Lord's Prayer because the Lord Jesus taught it, but He could not pray it since He had no sins to confess. Perhaps the Disciples' Prayer is a better title, since it's the kind of prayer we all need to pray.

11. The tense of the verb *come* indicates a crisis experience in history and not a gradual process. It refers to the return of Jesus Christ to establish His reign on earth. Peter says that, by their "holy conduct and godliness," God's people prove that they are "looking for *and hastening* the coming of the day of God" (2 Peter 3:11-12, italics mine). It seems incredible that we should have a part in "hastening" anything that God has already determined will happen; but the more we obey the Word, the more people we witness to and win to Christ, the more we support world evangelism, and the more we pray, the sooner His church will be completed and the Lord return for His bride. As Dr. D. Martyn Lloyd-Jones said, "This again is a great mystery. If these things are determined, how can we hasten them?" (*Expository Sermons on Second Peter* [Edinburgh: Banner of Truth Trust, 1983], p. 206). But Peter says we can!

12. It's worth noting that daily bread, a physical need, comes before forgiveness, a spiritual need. But consider: if God provides the necessities of life for people who are *not* His children (Matt. 5:45; Acts 14:15–17; 17:24–28), surely He will see to it that His own children, even if disobedient, will be cared for and not perish. Furthermore, it is God's goodness, not our badness, that leads us to repentance (Rom. 2:4). The prodigal son remembered how generous his father was, repented, and went home (Luke 15:17–19). The Lord fed the prophet Elijah before dealing with his disobedience (1 Kings 19), and Jesus fed Peter breakfast before He dealt with his sin and then restored him to ministry (John 21:9–19). Fortunately, God's ways are not our ways.

13. God doesn't tempt us, although He will test us (James 1:12–18; 1 Cor. 10:13). "Lead us not into temptation" means, "Don't let me tempt myself by playing with sin and putting myself in danger. Don't let me tempt others by being a bad example and encouraging them to disobey. And don't let me tempt You, Lord, by deliberately getting into a difficult situation from which only You can rescue me." By going into the high priest's courtyard, Peter, though warned by Jesus, tempted himself. By criticizing Mary, Judas tempted the other disciples to do the same, and they did (John 12:1–8). And by repeatedly complaining, the nation of

Israel tempted God in the wilderness and "dared" Him to act (Pss. 78:18, 41, 56; 95:9; 106:14; Heb. 3:9–11). "He who has been born of God keeps himself, and the wicked one does not touch him" (1 John 5:18).

14. Spurgeon, *Metropolitan Tabernacle Pulpit*, 7:451. Later in the message, he said, "When it is well with you, then think of me. I pray that you use it [intercessory prayer] on the behalf of the poor, the sick, the afflicted, the tempted, the tried, the desponding, the despairing; when thou hast the King's ear, speak to him for us" (p. 452).

15. I find it profitable to use prayer calendars from various Christian ministries. They help me pray systematically and intelligently for people and needs that I might otherwise forget.

16. The Christian doctrine of election states that though the gospel is for all the world, and we are to preach it to the whole world, God has from eternity chosen some to be saved. See Matthew 25:34; Acts 18:9–10; Romans 8:29; 9:11; and Ephesians 1:4–5, 11. Election is the sovereign act of God and isn't based on human merit or on what God foresees we will do. Not all Christian theologians agree on their interpretation of this profound doctrine, but all would agree that "salvation is of the Lord" (Jonah 2:9) and that nobody deserves to be saved (Eph. 2:8–10). It is all by the grace of God.

17. I am concerned that some people teach that it's not biblical to pray for the lost. In 1 Timothy 2:1–7, Paul commands us to pray for "all men," which certainly includes the lost; and he connects this ministry of prayer with God's concern to save "all men" and Christ's sacrificial death for "all men." If Paul prayed for lost Jews (Rom. 10:1), it's reasonable to expect that the Apostle to the Gentiles would pray for lost Gentiles as well. When King Solomon dedicated the temple in Jerusalem, he prayed that unsaved Gentiles would hear about God's glory and trust Him (1 Kings 8:41–43); and the psalmist prayed that "all the peoples" might come to know God and praise Him (Ps. 67). Listen again to Spurgeon: "Until the gate of hell is shut upon a man we must not cease to pray for him. And if we see him hugging the very doorposts of damnation, we must go to the mercy seat and beseech the arm of grace to pluck him from his dangerous position" (*Metropolitan Tabernacle Pulpit*, 14:53).

18. See Leviticus 16. "You shall afflict your souls" (Lev. 16:29, 31; 23:27, 32; Num. 29:7) is interpreted to mean fasting. The word translated "humbled" in Psalm 35:13 ("I humbled myself with fasting") is translated "afflict" in Leviticus 16. (The NIV translates it "deny.") See also Zechariah 7:5; 8:19.

19. Fasting usually means voluntarily going without food and water, but it could also include giving up marital relations (1 Cor. 7:1–6) and sleep (Luke 6:12; Ps. 119:147–48).

20. There are many editions readily available of *The Practice of the Presence of God* by Brother Lawrence (Nicholas Herman). The original book, though pub-

lished in 1692, is easy to read and is quite contemporary. For an excellent modem adaptation, see the edition edited by Donald E. Demaray and published in 1975 by Baker Book House. *The Practice of the Presence of God is* one of those devotional classics that believers need to read at least once a year.

21. After his longer prayer in chapter 1, eight of Nehemiah's "telegraph prayers" are recorded in the book: 2:4; 4:4; 5:19; 6:9, 14; 13:14, 22, 31.

Chapter 9

1. All Jews under the old covenant had to leam what was "clean" and what was "unclean" if they wanted to be acceptable to the Lord. Following the instructions given in the Book of Leviticus, the priests taught the people about clean and unclean foods, clean and unclean practices, and how they could get clean if they had been defiled. Until they were cleansed, unclean people were separated from the covenant community because they had the ability to defile others and make them unclean. For a practical exposition of Leviticus and its application to believers today, see my book *Be Holy* (Wheaton, Ill.: Victor Books, 1994).

2. As our High Priest, the Lord Jesus Christ gives us grace to resist temptation and not sin. But if we do sin, He is our Advocate to represent us at the throne, hear our confession, and cleanse us. When the prodigal son (Luke 15) came home, the father welcomed him, and he was accepted. But then the father dressed him in clean clothes to make him acceptable.

3. This section is an amplification of an outline found on pages 443–44 of my *Expository Outlines on the Old Testament*, published by Victor Books (1993), and used by permission.

4. A young man, whom I doubt was a Christian, asked me, "What's wrong with sinning? I can always come to God and ask for forgiveness." Apart from his shallow view of both sin and forgiveness, this young man forgot that *sin can bring its own consequences even after we are forgiven.* God in His grace will forgive His children when we sincerely confess sins (1 John 1:9), but God in His govemment allows sin to work out its tragic results in our lives. Even after he was forgiven and restored, David paid dearly for his sins by what his sons and some of his servants did to him. I can still hear the late president of the Moody Bible Institute in Chicago, Dr. William Culbertson, praying, "And, Lord, from the tragic consequences of forgiven sins, please deliver us."

5. God took the Holy Spirit away from King Saul, David's predecessor on the throne, because of Saul's willful disobedience (1 Sam. 16:14; 2 Sam. 7:15). Jesus promised that the Holy Spirit would always abide with believers (John 14:16), and Paul wrote that the Spirit has sealed believers to the day of redemption (Eph. 1:13–14). If Christians sin and refuse to confess it to the Lord, they will grieve the Spirit (Eph. 4:30) and possibly quench the Spirit's working in their lives (1 Thess. 5:19); but the Spirit will not abandon a believer.

6. Clearly, Jesus is speaking figuratively and not telling us to have actual surgery because surgery wouldn't end the problem. A blind friend told me that his blindness didn't prevent him from "seeing" lustful images in his mind because, of course, the problem is in the heart. In using such strong language, Jesus is reminding us of the awfulness of sin and of the importance of dealing with it drastically.

7. *Morning and Evening*, Oct. 13.

8. For a contrast, consider the way David treated his sons Absalom and Amnon and never confronted them with their sins. (See 2 Sam. 13—15.)

9. In Psalm 51:1–2, David used three different words for sin and three different words to describe forgiveness, revealing himself to be a capable theologian. *Transgression* means "to cross over a line"; *iniquity* refers to something twisted and perverse; *sin* means "missing the mark." The request "blot out" pictures sin as a debt and forgiveness as God wiping out the debt. "Wash me" pictures sin as defilement and forgiveness as cleansing, including clean clothes. "Cleanse me" pictures the ceremonially unclean person, such as a healed leper (Lev. 14), being restored and received back into the fellowship of God's people. Forgiveness, then, is the wiping out of a debt, the washing away of filth, and the restoring of fellowship.

10. *Morning and Evening*, Oct. 13.

11. The Greek verbs for "washed," "sanctified," and "justified" are aorist passive, meaning decisive actions done for us by the Lord, actions that are final. The word for "washed" means "to wash thoroughly."

12. As the Jewish priests served in the tabernacle and the temple, they became defiled and had to frequently wash their hands and feet at the laver. If they didn't, they were in danger of death. See Exodus 30:17–21 and note the repeated phrase "lest they die." If our personal cleansing were a matter of life or death, we would keep short accounts with God!

13. When we look at the believers' relationships in the local church, we'll examine some of the many "one another" statements found in the New Testament.

Chapter 10

1. The word *fellowship* in Acts 2:42 means "to have in common" and probably refers to the sharing of their material goods (vv. 44–45). Paul thanked the Philippian saints for their "fellowship in the gospel" (Phil. 1:5), which refers to their financial support of his ministry (Phil. 4:15). Paul called the gifts of the Gentile Christians to the church in Judea "the fellowship of the ministering to the saints" (2 Cor. 8:4). "Contribution" in Romans 15:26 is the Greek *koinonia*—fellowship—and refers to the same offering.

2. See John 13:34–35; 15:12, 17; Romans 13:8; 1 Thessalonians 3:12; 4:9; 1 Peter 1:22; 1 John 3:11, 23; 4:7, 11–12; 2 John 5.

3. Among the twelve disciples, Peter, James, and John comprised an "inner

circle" (Matt. 17:1–13; Luke 8:51; Matt. 26:36–46); and John was "the disciple whom Jesus loved," who leaned on Jesus' breast (John 13:23; 19:26; 20:2; 21:7, 20, 24). In his excellent book *Enjoying Intimacy with God,* J. Oswald Sanders reminds us that each believer is as near to God as he or she chooses to be. It's a sobering thought.

4. The other two "body life" passages also deal with the same three topics: *unity* (Rom. 12:1–5; 1 Cor. 12:1–13), *diversity* (Rom. 12:6–8; 1 Cor. 12:14–31), and *maturity* (Rom. 12:9–21; 1 Cor. 13—14). For a brief discussion of these topics and of the image of the church as a body, see my book *Preaching and Teaching with Imagination: The Quest for Biblical Ministry* (Wheaton, Ill: Victor Books, 1994), pp. 184–85.

5. I realize that there are more than 400,000 Christian congregations in America alone, so that nobody can authoritatively say what the condition of "the church" really is. Only God knows how His people are behaving. But when you read in the *World Christian Encyclopedia* that there are 20,000 Christian denominations around the world, it stuns you. Jesus felt that the unity of the church was one of the best evidences to the world of the love of God (John 17:20–21), and He prayed that His people might be one. He was praying, of course, for a spiritual unity and not for some kind of organizational uniformity; but the spiritual does have to manifest itself in the saints working together. Otherwise, how would the world see it?

6. Quoted in *Freedom for Ministry* by Richard John Neuhaus (Grand Rapids: Eerdmans, 1992), p. 119.

7. See "Churches on the Fringe" by Ronald Enroth, in *Eternity,* October 1986, pp. 17–22. Also *Churches That Abuse* by Ronald Enroth (Grand Rapids: Zondervan, 1992); *Damaged Disciples* by Ron and Vicki Burks (Grand Rapids: Zondervan, 1992); and *Faith That Hurts, Faith That Heals: Understanding the Fine Line Between Healthy Faith and Spiritual Abuse* by Stephen Arterburn and Jack Felton (Nashville: Thomas Nelson, 1992).

8. See *Sharpening the Focus of the Church* by Gene Goetz (Chicago: Moody Press, 1974), pp. 112–17.

9. I'm speaking here not about matters of Christian doctrine but of Christian practice. While the whole church has not yet come to "the unity of the faith" (Eph. 4:13), and we still disagree on some matters, there is general agreement among believers as to the basics of Christian doctrine. It's when we start to explain what God hasn't explained that we find ourselves disagreeing and sometimes disputing. I'm grateful for the help that the theologians give us, and I read what they write; but fortunately, the simplest Christians who can't define *supralapsarianism* can still love God, get answers to prayer, witness, and do good to their neighbors.

10. Some people seem to be genetically resistant to change, but there's no reason why they can't learn to love and appreciate people they disagree with. After all, we have a wonderful new spiritual genetic structure when the Holy Spirit moves in; and He helps us to experience joyful oneness in Christ.

Chapter 11

1. Being made in the image of God has nothing to do with physical resemblance, for God is Spirit (John 4:24), and spirits don't have bodies. When the Bible speaks about "the eyes of the Lord," "the hand of the Lord," or "the mouth of the Lord," the inspired writers are only using human analogies to reveal divine truths. Though God is spoken of in masculine terms in Scripture, He has no gender since He has no body. The "fatherhood of God" may be emphasized in Scripture, but the "motherhood of God" is not absent. (See Ps. 131; Isa. 49:14–16; 66:13; Zeph. 3:16–17; Matt. 23:37–39.)

2. The Bible uses words like *soul, spirit,* and *heart* to describe the inner person. Mark 12:30 commands us to love God with all the heart, soul, mind, and strength, that is, with the whole being. Paul prayed that the "whole spirit, soul, and body" of each believer in Thessalonica would be kept blameless until Jesus returned (1 Thess. 5:23). Materialists and behaviorists tell us that we are only bodies and that our behavior can be understood with reference to the physical drives within us and the environment around us. There is no such thing as "the spiritual." Therefore, we are fundamentally animals, not masterpieces created in the image of God.

3. The immediate reference in Isaiah 14 is to the fallen king of Babylon (vv. 16–17), but the ultimate reference is to Lucifer ("Day Star"), one of God's special angels who rebelled against God and was cast out of heaven. The pride that the king of Babylon manifested was first seen in Lucifer.

4. This doesn't mean we should be "so heavenly minded we're no earthly good." (Those are D. L. Moody's words.) Colossians 3:2 isn't describing an impractical mystical visionary, but a Christian who has the mind of Christ and thinks biblically. He or she looks at earth from heaven's point of view and makes decisions on the basis of heaven's values and priorities. But some professed believers look at heaven from earth's point of view and choose the things of this world instead of the blessings of God. This is illustrated in Genesis 13, the contrast between Abraham and Lot.

Chapter 12

1. Consider these verses: "The sight of the glory of the LORD was like a consuming fire on the top of the mountain in the eyes of the children of Israel" (Ex. 24:17); "For our God is a consuming fire" (Heb. 12:29).

2. Dennis J. Hester, ed., *The Vance Havner Quote Book* (Grand Rapids: Baker Book House, 1986), p. 233.

Chapter 13

1. Paul wrote, "Not that I have already attained, or am already perfected; but I press on, that I may lay hold of that for which Christ Jesus has also laid hold of me" (Phil. 3:12). Bishop J. C. Ryle defined *Christian perfection* as "an all-around consistency, and a careful attention to all the graces which make up the Christian character." See J. C. Ryle's *Holiness* (London: James Clarke, 1956), p. 12.

2. The epistle to the Hebrews was addressed to believers who were in their "second childhood" spiritually and had to be taught again the ABCs of the Christian life (Heb. 5:12). If we don't go forward in the Christian life, we go backward; and one of the first symptoms of this regression is a loss of appetite for solid spiritual food from the Word. Like children, we want to be entertained, not enlightened and edified.

3. Robert Payne, *The Life and Death of Adolph Hitler* (New York: Praeger, 1973), p. 461.

4. If you want a blow-by-blow account of this experience, see my autobiography *Be Myself* published by Victor Books (1994). If the Lord hadn't saved me, I probably would have gone through life hating myself and envying others instead of becoming the person I was born to be.

5. It's unfortunate that so much Christian ministry focuses attention only on "the days of His flesh" and ignores our Lord's present glorious ministry in heaven. The Babe in the manger, the gentle Teacher of Nazareth, the crucified Savior, and the resurrected Lord are all basic to the gospel story; and knowing only these truths, believing sinners can be saved. But if these are the only truths they know, they won't grow very much. The New Testament doesn't stop with John 21. Jesus Christ is not in the manger or on the cross. He is reigning from the throne, and He invites us to "reign in life" through Him (Rom. 5:17). J. B. Phillips (1958) translates it "that . . . men . . . live all their lives like kings." No wonder Paul prays that our eyes might be opened to see where He is and what He is doing from the throne (Eph. 1:15–23)!

6. The word translated "reckon" has financial overtones and means "to calculate, count, impute, put to one's account." If you tell me you've deposited a thousand dollars in my bank account and I immediately start writing checks, I'm "reckoning" on what you've done and said. If I thank you but continue to complain about all the bills I have to pay, I'm not reckoning at all. The New Testament epistles in particular tell us what the work of Christ means to us *today* as we reckon on His faithfulness.

NOTES

7. The word *carnal* means "fleshly." Some believers are immature because they haven't had time to grow, and some have had time to grow but haven't taken advantage of it (Heb. 5:12). They live for the things of the flesh and not the things of the Spirit (Col. 3:1–11): "For those who live according to the flesh set their minds on the things of the flesh, but those who live according to the Spirit, the things of the Spirit" (Rom. 8:5). Because we're "born of God," we're God's "little children"; but we should grow to become "young men" and "fathers" in the family (1 John 2:12–14), "kings' daughters" and "mothers in Israel" (Ps. 45:9; Judg. 5:7).

8. The Greek word *sunathleo* means "to struggle together with, to contend in the games together."

9. See Nehemiah 1; 9; Daniel 9; Ephesians 1:15–23; 3:14–21; Philippians 1:9–11; Colossians 1:9–12; 1 Thessalonians 3:11–13; 2 Peter 1:5–11. Many of the psalms can be turned into prayers simply by making them personal. See *Answering God: The Psalms as Tools for Prayer* by Eugene H. Peterson (San Francisco: Harper and Row, 1989).

10. John Calvin, *Institutes of the Christian Religion* (Philadelphia: Westminster Press, 1960), 2:1023, 1025.

11. Max Lerner, *The Unfinished Country* (New York: Simon and Schuster, 1959), pp. 538–39.

12. George H. Morrison, *The Wings of the Morning* (London: Hodder and Stoughton), p. 203.

13. Jesus said, "Peace I leave with you, My peace I give to you; not as the world gives do I give to you" (John 14:27); "These things I have spoken to you, that My joy may remain in you, and that your joy may be full" (John 15:11); "In the world you will have tribulation; but be of good cheer, I have overcome the world" (John 16:33).

Chapter 14

1. How anyone who has carefully studied the Bible can call it a sexist book is difficult for me to understand. God the Father is Spirit (John 4:24) and therefore has no body and no gender. Because the Bible came out of an ancient Hebrew culture, which was strongly masculine, the images used for God are primarily masculine: father, warrior, shepherd, king, and so on. We refer to God as "He" rather than "It" because God is a person, not a thing. God the Spirit is sexless and inhabits the bodies of both male and female believers. Jesus died to create a church in which "there is neither Jew nor Greek, there is neither slave nor free, there is neither male nor female; for you are all one in Christ Jesus" (Gal. 3:28).

2. See Deuteronomy 1:30–31; 32:6; Psalms 68:5; 89:26; 103:13; Isaiah 63:16; 64:8; Jeremiah 3:4, 19; Malachi 1:6; 2:10. The New Testament references are

numerous and familiar. Jesus used "Father" fifty-three times in His Upper Room Discourse and high priestly prayer (John 13—17).

3. Isaiah 40—66 is "the book of consolations" and majors on the comforts God gives to His needy children. (See 40:1–2; 51:3, 12; 57:18; 61:1–3.)

4. In this passage, God the Father sings. God the Son sang at the Passover feast in the Upper Room (Matt. 26:30; Mark 14:26) and on the day of His resurrection (Ps. 22:22; Heb. 2:12). God the Spirit sings through the church as God's people worship Him (Eph. 5:18–20).

5. The image of being under God's wings sometimes refers to the wings of the hen, but it can also refer to the wings of the cherubim in the Holy of Holies in the tabernacle or temple. To be "under His wings" means to be in the sacred place of protection and communion with God. (See Ruth 2:12; Pss. 36:7–8; 61:3–4.)

6. George MacDonald, *Creation in Christ* (Wheaton, Ill.: Harold Shaw Publishers, 1976), p. 10.

7. See Robert Payne, *The Life and Death of Adolph Hitler* (New York: Praeger, 1973), p. 167.

8. When some people read church history, they get upset because of the debates, conflicts, and councils. But they forget that the faith of the church is worth defending, and many defended it with their lives. Over the centuries, the church has had to contend with all sorts of heresy; and the only way to protect the faith and define doctrine accurately was to do battle against the enemy. Were it not for the courageous witness of Christian theologians in centuries past, "the faith which was once for all delivered to the saints" (Jude 3) would be in shambles. Let's give thanks for brave believers who hammered out the basic creeds that help us express the Christian faith today.

9. For a practical exposition of Galatians, see my book *Be Free*.

10. To "fall from grace" doesn't mean to "lose one's salvation." It means to stop living in the sphere of divine provision and to move into the sphere of self-effort. If we live in the sphere of law, then we have to try to please God in our own strength; and the result is frustration and failure. If we live in the sphere of grace, God works in and through us by His grace; and the result is freedom and spiritual growth.

11. The question answered in Romans 6 is, "How can I stop doing bad things?" The answer is our identification with Christ in His death, burial, and resurrection. The old life has been buried, and we've been raised to walk in newness of life. The question answered in Romans 7 is, "I still have a nature that's prone to sin. How, then, can I ever do good things?" The answer is the ministry of the Holy Spirit in the life of the believer who walks in the Spirit and who minds the things of the Spirit. Romans 7 describes Paul's experience as a converted man, confronted by God's holy law and his own sinful nature. In this chapter, God warns the

believer not to depend on self-determination for growth in holiness. The law of sin and death says that whenever I determine in my own strength to do a good thing, I won't do it; and whenever I determine in my own strength not to do a bad thing, I'll do it. The only way to counteract the law of sin and death is to submit to "the law of the Spirit of life in Christ Jesus." God didn't repeal the law of sin and death, for the wages of sin is still death; He simply put a new law into effect, based on the death and resurrection of Jesus Christ. Just as the laws of aerodynamics counteract the law of gravity, so the law of the Spirit of life overcomes the law of sin and death.

12. Obviously, I'm not referring to doctrinal changes that weaken the church's witness, but generational changes that come to all individuals and groups. Some things about contemporary worship bother me, but I don't make them a test of fellowship or orthodoxy.

13. Will Durant, *The Age of Faith* (New York: Simon and Schuster, 1950), pp. 282–83.

14. John Newton, *Voice of the Heart* (Chicago: Moody Press, 1950), p. 288.

Chapter 15

1. Benjamin Spock, *Dr. Benjamin Spock's Baby and Child Care* (New York: Pocket Books, 1959), p. 147.

2. The Greek text of Matthew 26:49 literally reads, "And affectionately kissed Him again and again."

3. Consider these verses: "You have assigned me my portion and my cup" (Ps. 16:5 NIV); "Are you able to drink the cup that I am about to drink?" (Matt. 20:22). In his famous poem on old age "Rabbi Ben Ezra," Robert Browning writes, "My times be in Thy hand!/Perfect the cup as planned!"

4. I'm disturbed by those who teach that believers are supposed to "forgive God" for the things He has permitted to happen in their lives. I find no biblical basis or example for such a practice, and I think the teaching is pernicious. God cannot sin, and He doesn't make mistakes. For what should I forgive Him7

5. In Jeremiah 19, the prophet gave a public object lesson using a *finished* vessel. After preaching a sermon, he broke the vessel, symbolizing the judgment that was coming to Judah (Babylonian captivity). The nation had spumed God's appeals, tried His long-suffering, hardened in its sins, and therefore found no place for repentance.

6. Obviously, this doesn't suggest that we passively accept everything everybody does to us. Some people are evil and want to do evil things that we must oppose. But in painful situations beyond our control, by faith we can accept the hurtful hands of people as the holy hands of God and trust Him to accomplish His will.

Chapter 16

1. Personally, I don't believe that. If it were true, the population of the world would be up to its eyeballs in flowers, and every florist would be out of business. Yet I've heard this song sung at so-called Christian weddings, apparently with church approval. Theologians call "faith in faith" *fideism,* from the Latin word for faith *(fides).* They point out that "faith in faith" is purely subjective, based on feelings, and has no objective basis in fact. Singers exhort me to "walk on, walk on, with faith in your heart"; and I want to shout to them, "Faith in what?" The Bible knows nothing of blind faith. God has demonstrated His power and faithfulness enough for His people to have confidence that He will do what He promises. The essence of faith isn't that we believe in spite of evidence, which is superstition, but that we obey in spite of consequence.

2. If these stories are unfamiliar to you, I suggest you stop now and read Genesis 16; 2 Samuel 7; and Acts 27.

3. Some Bible students think that these leaders were dead, perhaps martyred. If so, their memory would bring encouragement to the saints who sat under their ministry and watched their lives.

Chapter 17

1. The wisdom discussed so fully in the Book of Proverbs is the kind of spiritual radar that I'm referring to. Spiritual wisdom is the practical skill we learn from God for guiding our lives so that we avoid the pitfalls of sin and make the most of the many opportunities God gives us along the way. That's why I called my exposition of the Book of Proverbs *Be Skillful* (Victor Books, 1995). When we yield ourselves to God, meditate on His Word, and obey what we read, He renews our minds so that we start to think God's thoughts and gradually incorporate God's ways. This gives the Holy Spirit something to use in our hearts and minds when we turn to God for guidance.

2. Leon Morris, *The Epistle to the Romans* (Grand Rapids: Eerdmans, 1988), p. 436.

Chapter 18

1. C. S. Lewis, *Christian Behavior* (New York: Macmillan, 1946), p. 55.

2. Dr. and Mrs. Howard Taylor, *Biography of James Hudson Taylor* (London: China Inland Mission, 1965), p. 140.

3. Since Moses is the author of Psalm 90, and its message about life and death is so solemn, some Bible scholars connect the psalm with Israel's disobedience at Kadesh-Barnea (Num. 14). Because the people refused to believe God and enter the land, the nation was condemned to march in the wilderness for forty years until the older generation died. That would make "Teach us to number our days"

a most meaningful prayer. Read Psalm 90 in the light of Numbers 14 and see if you think they may go together.

4. Henry David Thoreau, *Walden*, ed. J. Lyndon Shanley (Princeton, N.J.: Princeton University Press, 1971), p. 90.

5. While ministering in Scotland some years ago, I had the privilege of preaching at the Harper Memorial Church in Glasgow. While chatting with the people as they were arriving, I happened to see a lad about twelve years old who seemed to be lonely, so I walked over to greet him. During the course of our conversation, I asked him, "And what would you like to do when you get out of school?" "Please, sir," he replied, "I'm just trying to get through next week!" "Teach us to number our days."

6. See 2 Peter 1:14: "Knowing that shortly I must put off my tent, just as our Lord Jesus Christ showed me." Peter was referring to John 21:20–25.

7. The word bar in this setting refers, of course, to the shallow part of a body of water where the sand is just below the surface and poses a hazard for the pilot.

8. J. C. Ryle, *Holiness* (London: James Clarke, 1956), p. 23.

Chapter 19

1. The Sermon on the Mount (Matt. 5—7) is for today and not for some future kingdom. I can't believe that in Christ's future kingdom, believers will be persecuted (5:10–12), tempted to commit murder or adultery (5:21–30), get divorced (or even be married [5:31–32]), and have enemies whom they must love (5:43–48). Will believers worry during the future kingdom (6:25–34) or be deceived by false teachers (7:15–20)? Since Satan is imprisoned during the kingdom age (Rev. 20:1–3), why would believers pray, "Deliver us from the evil one" (Matt. 6:13)? The conditions and challenges described in the Sermon on the Mount fit our present age but not some perfect future age.

2. Carl Sagan, "Life," in *Encyclopedia Britannica*, 15th ed.

3. These quotations are taken from the section entitled "Life" in *The Dictionary of Quotable Definitions*, ed. Eugene E. Brussell (Englewood Cliffs, N.J.: Prentice-Hall, 1970).

4. Dag Hammarskjold, *Markings*, trans. Leif Sjoberg and W. H. Auden (New York: Knopf, 1965), p. 55.

5. He was also willing to go to hell if it would have saved the lost Jewish people who so burdened his heart: "I have great sorrow and continual grief in my heart. For I could wish that I myself were accursed from Christ for my brethren, my countrymen according to the flesh" (Rom. 9:2–3). In this, he was following the example of Moses when Israel made the golden calf: "Yet now, if You will forgive their sin—but if not, I pray, blot me out of Your book which You have written" (Ex. 32:32).

6. Dietrich Bonhoeffer wrote from prison, "As time is the most valuable thing that we have, because it is the most irrevocable, the thought of any lost time troubles us whenever we look back." *Letters and Papers from Prison*, ed. Eberhard Bethge (New York: Macmillan, 1972), p. 3.

7. Neither Jesus nor Paul taught that it was wrong to receive as the result of our giving. Jesus promised, "Give, and it will be given to you" (Luke 6:38); and Paul warned, "He who sows sparingly will also reap sparingly, and he who sows bountifully will also reap bountifully" (2 Cor. 9:6). But receiving must not be the main motive for our giving. Christian industrialist R. G. LeTourneau used to say, "If you give because it pays, it won't pay."

8. I recommend you read 2 Corinthians 8—9 before you continue your reading of this chapter, and mark the word *grace* wherever you find it.

9. This incredible message of our Lord's taking the worst from us and giving the best to us is beautifully illustrated in the story "Ragman" by Walter Wangerin, Jr., found in his book *Ragman and Other Cries of Faith* (San Francisco: Harper and Row, 1984).

10. George H. Morrison, *The Return of the Angels* (London: Hodder and Stoughton, 1909), p. 113.

11. I realize that activities like answering the mail, writing books, preparing sermons, and paying bills are also ministries to others; but they're not as personal as when we weep with those who weep. I also realize that all of us must be careful not to be so available that we cater to people who devour our time seeking attention but not spiritual help, people who wouldn't know how to live if their problems *were* solved. We can waste a lot of time counseling when all they want is consoling. It takes discernment, faith, and courage to plan a productive schedule.

12. The "always" verses in 2 Corinthians are worth noting: always triumphant (2:14–17); always dying and living (4:11); always confident (5:6); always rejoicing (6:10); always suffficient (9:7).

13. C. H. Spurgeon, *Autobiography: The Early Years*, compiled by his wife and private secretary (London: Banner of Truth Trust, 1962), pp. 303ff.

14. The number included Jesus, the twelve disciples, Lazarus, Mary, Martha, and Simon the leper (Mark 14:3). If Simon had a family, there could have been more people at the banquet.

Chapter 20

1. C. H. Spurgeon, *Metropolitan Tabernacle Pulpit* (Pasadena, Tex.: Pilgrim Publications, 1985), 8:326.

2. Elisabeth Elliot, ed., *The Journal of Jim Elliot* (Old Tappan, N.J.: Revell, 1978), p. 258.

3. Alexander Maclaren, *Christ in the Heart and Other Sermons* (New York: Funk and Wagnalls, 1902), p. 272.

4. "The lie" is Satan's promise to Eve, "You will be like God" (Gen. 3:5). Eve focused on the creation, not the Creator; and the results were sin and death.

5. It's significant that the first heavenly worship scene recorded in the Book of Revelation focuses on God the Creator (Rev. 4). The next scene (chap. 5) magnifies Christ the Redeemer.

6. Ralph Spaulding Cushman, *Hilltop Verses and Prayers* (Nashville: Abingdon-Cokesbury Press, 1945), p. 17. Used by permission. In stanza four, I would prefer "Bringing His heaven" to "Building His heaven," lest we give the impression that we're able to bring in the kingdom by our own efforts.

7. Ronald B. Allen, *A Shelter in the Fury* (Portland, Ore.: Multnomah Press, 1986), p. 120.

8. Alexander Maclaren, *Expositions of Holy Scripture* (Grand Rapids: Baker Book House, 1974), 4:256.

9. Jonathan Edwards, *The Works of Jonathan Edwards,* revised and corrected by Edward Hickman (Edinburgh: Banner of Truth Trust, 1976), 1:279.

10. The Hebrew word translated "beauty" means "ornament, splendor, honor." It's translated "majesty" in Psalm 29:4. The phrase "beauty of holiness" is also found in 1 Chronicles 16:29, 2 Chronicles 20:21, and Psalm 96:9 in the King James Version and New King James Version. The Revised Standard Version translates it "in holy array." "The splendor of holiness" is a good translation; but keep in mind that God's holiness is splendid and beautiful, and that's why we worship Him. "In holy array" gives the impression that we come to God dressed in holy beauty, and that's not what David is saying.

11. Philip Schaff, ed., *A Select Library of the Nicene and Post-Nicene Fathers of the Christian Church* (Grand Rapids: Eerdmans, 1979), 1:63. Since there are numerous editions of Augustine's *Confessions*, let me add that this quotation is from chapter 6.

12. Quoted in A. W. Tozer, *The Knowledge of the Holy* (New York: Harper & Brothers, 1961), p. 114.

13. Dag Hammarskjold, *Markings*, trans. Leif Sjoberg and W. H. Auden (New York: Knopf, 1965), p. xxi.